HISTORY OF
LEATHERHEAD

A TOWN AT THE CROSSROADS

To dear Shirley r Alan with love, of course Edwina V. 1989

£10

EDITED BY
EDWINA VARDEY

LEATHERHEAD AND DISTRICT LOCAL HISTORY SOCIETY

History of Leatherhead – a Town at the Crossroads
ISBN 0 9506009 1 1

Cover design and photograph by Lewis Vardey

Published by De Valery Company Limited

Produced by P.P.C. Ltd, Leatherhead, Surrey
Printed by L. R. Printing Services Ltd plc, Crawley, Sussex

For my five children and all who grew up in Leatherhead

Preface

WHEN I WAS asked as a writer to produce this book for the Leatherhead and District Local History Society I had little idea where to begin. But with the discovery of the *Proceedings,* the Society's annual collection of members' researches since 1947, there was gold to be mined and the right foundation on which to build this book.

Members and friends volunteered to research further and I was fortunate that Dr John Blair of The Queen's College, Oxford, who wrote the Medieval and Church chapters, generously acted as historic adviser throughout. Dr Derek Renn, a Vice-President of the Society, wrote the Introduction and the Prehistory to the Middle Ages chapter and set the style for the researchers. Alphabetically, they are: Doris Burchell, Roderick Clubbe, Eileen Crellin, Pamela Day, Jane Elders, Stephen Fortescue, Geoffrey Hayward, Linda Heath, Jean Herriott, Ralph Hume, R. A. Lever, Gina and Gilbert MacKenzie. Teresa Vanneck-Murray, Mary Rice-Oxley, Steve Poulter, Jack Studdard, Norman West and Roma White.

I thank them all very sincerely especially Geoffrey Hayward's team, Doris Burchell, Gina and Gilbert Mackenzie and Roma White, who took nearly three years to read and catalogue every issue of the *Leatherhead Advertiser* from 1898 onwards, and Linda Heath who researched and wrote on Schools and schooling while producing her own book on the subject. Betty Eldridge volunteered and enhanced the Buildings Past and Present chapter with her drawings and Beryl Higgins drew a number of the maps. Mr and Mrs E. W. Crawforth willingly put their knowledge of the town, transport and their picture collection at my disposal and Joan MacAlpine of the Thorndike Theatre generously shared her Second World War researches with me. Alison Wright very kindly provided photographs, and took some specially for the Then and Now feature.

I cannot thank Rosemary Ellison enough for undertaking the arduous task of typing all the manuscripts which the President, John Lewarne, then commented upon with his usual wisdom and good humour. The Society's Chairman, Laurie Smith, has been courteously helpful, making the archives available to us and showing exemplary patience throughout the whole project.

All the teams have worked hard in this labour of love but none harder than Jack Studdard. Not only has he compiled the Index on page 344 but he has been invaluable as a scholarly assistant to me over the years we have spent putting the researches together. I shall always be grateful to him.

Finally, I must thank the freelance artist who as my partner in most things, has devoted so much of his time to designing a book which can only add pleasure to the reading of it – to my husband Lewis, my heartfelt thanks.

Edwina Vardey

FETCHAM 1988

Contents

Foreword

WHEN some years ago, the Leatherhead and District Local History Society considered producing a history of Leatherhead, their first thought was that it must be adequately researched and, second, it must be well written and well put together.

It will be agreed, I think, that these objectives have been fully met and for this we have to thank Edwina Vardey, who undertook the onerous job of Editor; Lewis Vardey, who designed the book and the host of willing helpers who undertook much painstaking research over a period of some seven years. Without them the book would never have appeared. Their names are listed on pp. 4 & 5 and, on behalf of the Society, I would like to record here my most grateful thanks and to congratulate them on the excellent outcome of their years of effort.

I know that every possible step has been taken to search out all relevant information but in an enterprise of this kind, it is inevitable that someone somewhere knows something which could have been of interest if only we had known about it. Such omissions are unfortunate but cannot be avoided if a date for publication is to be met.

It will be clear from the following pages that Leatherhead might have become an important town from very early times, with its weekly market and its courts for the administration of justice but, for some reason, it failed to live up to its medieval promise. On a crossroads serving important towns to the north, south, east and west, Leatherhead was well placed to become the County town of Surrey. Instead, over the centuries it sank into obscurity until the railway came.

Today, it is still small, destined by strict planning constraints to develop within itself but trying hard to make up the ground lost between the 16th and 19th centuries. Unfortunately, the kind of redevelopment taking place in the town does nothing to enhance the small country town image of former years. Leatherhead is fast becoming a commercial centre for businesses unconnected with the surrounding countryside and villages and, in this sense, it has passed the crossroads. The town will never be the same again and for many, this is a matter of regret.

This Society has played in the past, and will continue to play in the future, its part in trying to ensure that development proposals in Conservation Areas and those relating to Listed Buildings are in keeping with the existing environment but pressure is very great. One can only hope that when the current spate of redevelopment has run its course, the town will be able to settle down and the inhabitants will be able to acclimatise themselves to the new look. Hopefully, the chairman's foreword to a reissue of this history in say 25 years' time will sound rather less pessimistic and, on looking back to this edition, people may well wonder what all the fuss was about. *Plus ça change, plus ça la même chose.*

L. A. Smith

CHAIRMAN, LEATHERHEAD AND DISTRICT LOCAL HISTORY SOCIETY

Introduction

LEATHERHEAD is a very 'middle' sort of place, somewhere between a village and a town. It is halfway along the course of the River Mole and almost exactly in the centre of the old county of Surrey (before so much of it disappeared into Greater London). In transport terms, it is midway between Gatwick and Heathrow airports and is the mid-point of the railway line from Horsham to London.

The layout of Leatherhead has changed again and again. It is often compared with Guildford, another old town sited at the major ford of a river which has cut its way through the North Downs. At Leatherhead, the old townscape is on a smaller scale than Guildford and needs more searching-out. Few people, arriving by rail at Leatherhead, notice the imposing station building of 1866, little altered over the years. Even fewer travellers on the M25 realise that 2000 years ago the fields alongside were cleared for farming from the ancient woodland; or that their motorway now crosses its Roman predecessor, built for fast traffic between Londinium, the capital, and Regnum (Chichester), the naval base. Even today's gipsy site on the Leatherhead bypass is close to the spot where travellers first camped in the district several thousand years ago.

Although at times called the county town (at least as far as the administration of justice was concerned),[1] Leatherhead never rose above being a small town and local market centre. Like so many other Surrey towns, it was concerned with the cloth trade during the middle ages. Later, its connections with the large neighbouring agricultural

[1] Anon., 'Leatherhead, the county town in 1515', *Proc. LDLHS*, **2** (3), 1959, p. 68. Manning and Bray, *A History of Surrey*, II, p. 665. *Victoria County History of Surrey*, I, p. 349, II, p. 294

estates saw it through economically until the beginning of this century, when cheap rail travel and an expansion of light engineering and research laboratories pointed local employment in new directions.

The name of Leatherhead

Although leather-working and tanning were trades in the town as recently as 1905,[1] Leatherhead does not get its name from leather. In Victorian times the spelling was usually Letherhead, going back to the medieval Latin version *Lered*. The earliest known version is *Leodridan*, an estate bequeathed by King Alfred about AD 880.[2] Place-name experts have translated this as the public ford, from the Old English word *leode* and *ride*, but an alternative derivation and meaning have recently been put forward: grey (or brown – *llwyd*) ford, from the Celtic *letorito*.[3] The River Mole is and was fordable in many places, although today crossings are usually by a bridge. The ford – wherever it was originally – gave its name to the settlement nearby.

History and topography can support either meaning. The fords directly upstream and downstream from Leatherhead itself gave access to private estates before the Norman Conquest, so a public ford between them might be so distinguished. Equally, the colour of the river at Leatherhead can be markedly different from that elsewhere, either because of the permanent springs at Thorncroft and Watersmeet nearby, or because of drainage through the Tertiary sands and clays here. Similarly Guildford – the golden ford – may get its name from the yellow sands or the kingcups at the crossing-place near St Nicolas' church.[4]

The landscape of Leatherhead

The parish of Leatherhead lies mainly on the east or right bank of the River Mole after it emerges from the gap it has cut through the North Downs at Mickleham.[5] A small part of the parish south-west of the town lies on the other side of the river. The northern half of Leatherhead lies on London Clay, a dark brown or greyish clay which weathers on exposure to a yellow colour. Further south is the Upper Chalk, with a narrow band of well-drained clays and gravels between the two on which human settlements grew up along the dip-slope of the North Downs, partly sheltered from the wind and rain.

In the terms of geological time, these strata are quite young. The

[1] F. B. Benger, 'The Ragge, Lloyd and Walker families', *Proc. LDLHS*, **2** (5), 1961, pp. 144–54.

[2] F. E. Harmer, *Select English Historical Documents of the Ninth and Tenth Centuries* (Cambridge, 1915), p. 15.

[3] E. Ekwall, *Dictionary of English Place-Names* (Oxford, 1931).
A. Mawer and F. M. Stenton, *The Place-Names of Surrey* (Cambridge, 1934), p. 79.
R. Coales, 'Methodological reflexions on Leatherhead', *Journal of the English Place-Name Society*, **12**, 1979–80, p. 70.

[4] *The Place Names of Surrey*, p. 10.

[5] 'A cartographical survey of the area; introductory note', *Proc. LDLHS*, **1** (9), 1955, p. 18.

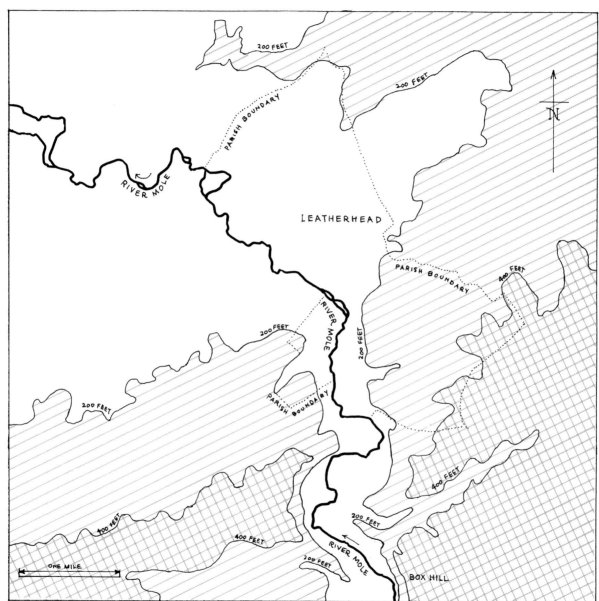

Contour map showing the River Mole winding through the gap in the North Downs.

Birds

In the Mole's wooded valley and on its banks are many species of birds. Visiting migrants such as Redpoll and Siskin winter in the riverside alders. Waders like the common Sandpiper appear in the shallows in spring and autumn while Heron can be seen throughout the year. Breeding birds like Mute Swan, Mallard, Little Grebe, Kingfisher and Grey Wagtail have recently been joined by the Mandarin Duck. Since its springs have been capped by the Water Company, Fetcham mill pond has lost its rarer species of breeding and migrant birds. There is an established population of feral birds like the ring-necked Parakeet who seem to be able to survive the winters in spite of a southern origin. The woods and commons also support many species although the Wrynecks and red-backed Shrikes seem to have disappeared. Conversely the birds of prey like Sparrowhawks and Kestrels are recovering from 19th-century persecution and 20th-century pesticides. Nightingales are much less numerous but can still be heard on Bookham Common.

– JEFFREY WHEATLEY

[1] A. W. G. Lowther, 'A note on the geology of the Leatherhead district of Surrey', *Proc. LDLHS*, **1** (10), 1956, pp. 11–12.
R. G. Sherlock, *British Regional Geology; London and the Thames Basin* (London, 1947).
[2] C. C. Fagg, 'Swallow holes in the Mole Gap', *South-eastern Naturalist and Antiquary*, **LXII**, 1958, p. 1.
[3] A. T. Ruby, 'The Leatherhead river', *Proc. LDLHS*, **2** (8), 1964, pp. 228–47.

chalk was originally deposited in a shallow area, overlying the coarser clays and greensand. Earth movements caused these strata to bulge upward as a giant dome, which was eroded by ice to produce the broken Wealden landscape inside the crater-rim of the North and South Downs. The Upper Chalk stratum near Leatherhead is divided into two, the lower formation containing heart-shaped fossils of the sea urchin Micraster and the upper, the six-sided plates of sea lilies, Marsupites. On top of the chalk lay the Reading beds of mottled clay and the Thanet beds of sand, covered in their turn by the London Clay which still blankets most of the Thames basin.[1]

The Weald is drained by several rivers which broke through the surrounding chalk ridge in different places and directions. In Surrey, both the Rivers Mole and Wey turn northward to run through the gaps they have cut, flowing onward to the Thames and the sea. The Mole created the Mickleham Gap, and the Leatherhead–Dorking road still follows the flood plain through it. Changes in the climate resulted in several gravel terraces being laid down beside the river, and fissures in the chalk were dissolved to produce the 'swallow holes' which are such a feature of the river bed in times of drought when the water flows down these fissures as if down a plug hole of an enormous bathtub.[2] Only one swallow hole lies within the parish of Leatherhead, but there are a score or more a little further upstream near Burford Bridge in the parish of Mickleham. This underground river reappears at Leatherhead where there are permanent springs at Thorncroft and Watersmeet.

Except at flood-time, the Mole is a very sluggish stream through Leatherhead, varying considerably in width (especially at the islands near Leatherhead Bridge). Some man-made alterations to its course can be seen: Capability Brown's ornamental canal at Thorncroft; the railway embankment crossing a meander at Cannon Court, Fetcham, and straightening at the site of the former bridge at Young Street.[3]

The old name for the river was Emele and later Emlyn; 'Mole' only appears in the 16th century, as in Spenser's *Faerie Queene*

> 'And Mole, that like a nousling mole doth make
> His way still under ground till Thames he o'ertake'

The explanation of the name being due to the 'swallow hole' phenomenon has been challenged and suggested alternatives are of a back-formation from Molesey (Mul's island) or from the Latin for mill (*mol*), of which there were plenty on the river.

The ice sheet covering what is now Southern England retreated northward about 10,000 years ago, leaving behind a wetter but warmer climate than that of today. As vegetation returned, alder bushes predominated on the marshy ground which was far more extensive than now. Birch and hazel dominated the lighter soils, with beech and lime on the chalk downland and oak with hornbeam on the lower clay-lands. Other tree species took over from time to time, and the full sequence remains to be worked out in detail.[1] So much clearance has taken place probably none of the original wildwood remains around Leatherhead. But the yew and box groves clinging to the near-vertical sides of Box Hill (places where man is unlikely ever to have cleared or planted extensively) give some idea of what the early landscape of Leatherhead may have been like, at least in the chalky part of the parish. The relict patches of woodland by the old open fields east of the town need to be botanically examined.[2] Nevertheless, with so many varied habitats in the area, it is not surprising that 500 species of wild plants, including shrubs and trees, have been recorded.[3]

An overview of Leatherhead

The parish is shaped like an hour-glass, but with a rather wilder 'neck' along the line of the High Street and its extensions Bridge Street and Epsom Road. A fold in the ground northwards conceals the fact that the north part of Leatherhead on the floor of the river valley is very flat. Southward the ground rises steadily away from the river flats to the downs.

Leatherhead's layout has been altered many times, its plan scribbled over by different ages. Sixty years ago it was a simple cross-road settlement, with two-storey houses and shops packed together around the road junction, an old Surrey traffic bottleneck. Beyond the railway station northward, the houses thinned out and became larger, but in the other direction, they extended no further south than the parish church. This settlement was surrounded by large farms or estates, one or two between each pair of roads radiating to Kingston, Ashtead, Headley, Mickleham, Fetcham and Cobham.

Since then there has been extensive development, particularly near Kingston Road and the railway line. Near the station, warehouses

Wildlife

Most of the rarer animals in the area are nocturnal; even so, the roe and fallow deer can often be seen browsing in woodland in early evening. Where Stane Street crosses the M25, the motorway contractors built a tunnel for badgers as a small attempt to stem the decline in their population. There are no such worries about the fox who wanders fearlessly both day and night, often making its lair in gardens. The otter disappeared from Surrey about 10 years ago and among the smaller mammals, the dormouse is now an endangered species. Rare butterflies and moths seen on Box Hill and Fetcham Downs include the Marbled White, Dark Green and Pearl-bordered Fritillary, Common Blue, Silver-spotted Skipper and Purple and Green Hairstreak.

– SURREY WILDLIFE TRUST

[1] M. P. Topping, 'The vegetation of the Leatherhead district in prehistoric times', *Proc. LDLHS*, **1** (10), 1956, pp. 13–14.
[2] O. Rackham, *Trees and Woodland in the British landscape* (London, 1976).
O. Rackham, *Ancient Woodland: its History, Vegetation and Uses in England* (London, 1980).
[3] John Sankey, *Juniper Hall Field Studies.*

and small factories have increased but the great names of Ronson and Goblin (further away at Green Lane) are no more. Trade research laboratories flank Randalls Road and are backed by groups of terraced or semi-detached houses as far as Woodbridge. Beyond, both north and south of the town, the large estates have been cut up into large building plots for detached properties. The low ground west of the river has been laid out for every kind of leisure pursuit. To the east, St John's School and the Royal School for the Blind have had a considerable effect on the life of Leatherhead. More recently, the centre of the town has acquired a shopping mall and an inner relief road, but there are still many alleyways and old buildings to be found. Leatherhead does not display its treasures openly, but even in the main shopping streets, a glance upwards often reveals an interesting façade above the uniform plate glass and fascia.

Prehistory to the Middle Ages
c. 4000 BC–600 AD

ALTHOUGH crude flint handaxes have been found on the open heaths farther east,[1] the earliest traces of human occupation at Leatherhead so far discovered are better-worked flints dating from the Mesolithic period around 4000 BC, about the time that Britain became an island. The people of that time were fishermen and hunters, eating fruit, plants and nuts in season. They may have cleared some open forest but as they were not farmers and settlers, they tended to move on. Three Mesolithic hearths of burnt birch-wood, covered in worked flints, were found about 5 ft down when a new channel for the river was cut at Young Street in 1952. The hearths were based on a layer of chalky marl covering a peaty layer of compressed sedges and grasses and even tree trunks. This would have been rather unstable, and the hearths may originally have been higher up the valley side and subsequently washed down by heavy rains like a number of similar later finds hereabouts. A selection of the flints mainly cores and scrapers, the residue of a factory perhaps, are shown on page 19. The fine complete tranchet axe came from rather deeper down than the rest, and was found some way away from them. The general quality of the workmanship was not as high as that on finds made in south-west Surrey.[2] Today's travelling people still camp nearby, but such anthropological parallels can be misleading.

After about 3000 BC, the climate became colder and drier, and the forest cover became thinner, particularly on the chalk uplands where both elm and lime declined in importance. By 2000 BC, most of the

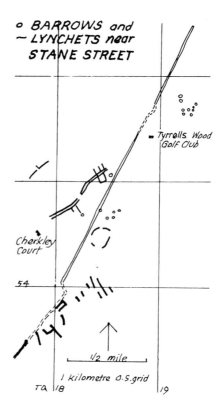

° BARROWS and
~ LYNCHETS near
STANE STREET

Tyrrells Wood
Golf Club

Cherkley
Court

54

½ mile

1 kilometre O.S.grid

TQ 18

19

Page 17

[1] L. W. Carpenter, 'The paleoliths of Walton and Banstead Heaths', *Proc. LDLHS*, **1** (10), 1956, pp. 6–10. 'A paleolithic floor from Lower Kingswood', *Proc. LDLHS*, **2** (4), 1960, pp. 99–101. 'More paleoliths from Walton Heath', *Proc. LDLHS*, **2** (7), 1963, p. 202.

[2] L. W. Carpenter, 'A mesolithic site near Leatherhead', *Proc. LDLHS*, **1** (6), 1952, pp. 5–11.

Page 18

[1] Leatherhead Museum collection.

[2] S. R. C. Poulter, 'Neolithic find', *Proc. LDLHS*, **3** (7), 1973, p. 185.

[3] W. F. Rankine collection (colophon to *Proc. LDLHS*, **1** (5), 1951).

[4] 'A cartographic survey of the area, III: The Bronze and Iron Ages', *Proc. LDLHS*, **2** (1), 1957, pp. 4–6; see also **1** (4), 1950, p. 4, and *SAC*, **75**, 1984, pp. 288–92.

[5] L. W. Carpenter, 'An early Bronze Age discoidal knife of polished flint found at Leatherhead', *Proc. LDLHS*, **2** (1), 1957, p. 4.

[6] F. A. Hastings, 'Excavation of an Iron Age farmstead at Hawks Hill, Leatherhead', *SAC*, **62**, 1965, pp. 1–43.

[7] S. S. Frere, 'An Iron Age and Roman site on Mickleham Downs', *SAC*, **49**, 1944–5, pp. 104–5.

Page 21

[1] Noted in *Proc. LDLHS*, **1** (1), 1947, p. 6, and copied on to OS map owned by the Society.

[2] 'Celtic and Roman coins found in the district', *Proc. LDLHS*, **3** (5), 1971, p. 128.

[3] F. G. Aldsworth, 'Occasional note', *Proc. LDLHS*, **2** (10), 1966, pp. 279–80. Ernest Crossland.

[4] A. W. G. Lowther, 'An enamelled bronze roundel of the Romano-British period', *Proc. LDLHS*, **2** (7), 1963, pp. 202–3.

upland had been cleared of forest. Stone tools of this Neolithic period range from the crude flint axe found in a garden in Highlands Avenue recently[1] to a fragment of a fine polished one dredged from the river near Young Street[2] and a macehead made of quartzite pebble found 'in Leatherhead'.[3] The battered end and worn hole for the wooden handle, point to the mace's use for hammering.

About 1800 BC, a new wave of immigrants, able to work metals, and in particular bronze, arrived. Bronze was rather scarce and a trading system had to be set up to maintain supplies of ore and to sell the products. A trackway, now known as the Harroway, came into use, following the sheltered slope of the downs, where water could be found issuing on the springline between the impervious chalk and the sands and clays. The trackway extended from what we now call Kent as far as Hampshire and Wiltshire. In Surrey, it roughly followed the line of present-day towns and villages between Croydon and Farnham. The Harroway probably entered Leatherhead from the east along the general alignment of Green Lane, turning south-west along the Epsom road to cross the river about where the Leisure Centre is now, to climb Hawks Hill through the waterworks grounds.

Many burial mounds (barrows or tumuli) can be seen from the air above Leatherhead Downs, in particular near the easternmost corner of the parish near Thirty Acres Barn. One barrow near Cherkley Court was excavated and burial urns were found but not dated.[4] All these barrows probably date from the Bronze or Iron Age. The only true Bronze Age finds again come from the floodplain near Young Street, some flint arrowheads and a disc-knife: scratches in the flint contained iron pyrites, probably from a Wealden iron stone pebble used to smooth it.[5]

About 500 BC the climate became warmer and wetter and beech trees spread on the chalk, as did oak and alder on the clay. Celtic tribes, displaced by the Roman invasions of what we call France, moved into Britain, bringing with them the ability to till heavy soils with an improved plough which had a mould-board to turn over the earth. Constant ploughing in one direction causes the soil to creep downhill to the edge of the field, and the consequent banks (lynchets) can be traced on the ground or from the air. There are many such banks and enclosures surrounding the Iron Age farm at the top of Hawks Hill, Fetcham,[6] and traces of fields on Leatherhead and Mickleham Downs.[7]

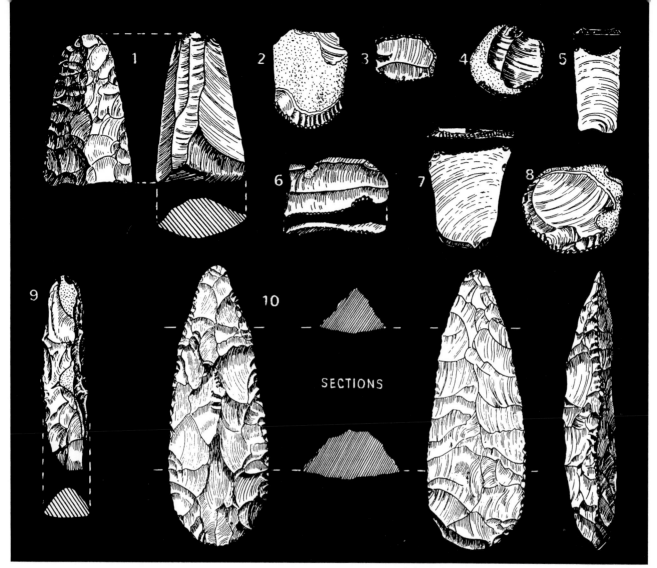

SECTIONS

Some of the many flints found in 1952 when a new channel for the river was cut at Young Street. Although mesolithic sites existed in and along the Mole Valley, there is no evidence these were from any particular site.

Above (1) a greyish-brown flint with one striking platform; (2) and (3) are probably roughened and side scrapers made from cores with two striking platforms. Striking platforms are the flat surfaces that provide a point to strike off the flint flake in order to make a tool. (4) has been used both as an end (conclave) scraper and a side scraper and is highly glossy. (5) Blue-grey flint with hard core has also been worked as a scraper at the striking platform end. (6) Dark grey flint with high gloss. (7) is thickly patinated and not the usual mesolithic type of flint. (8) is pale grey with high gloss and (9) is a cylindrical core of grey flint with two striking platforms. The most valuable find is (10), the tranchet axe. Found in 7 ft of yellow clay silt close to the bridge, it is honey-coloured with patches of cream and has a bluish-white patina. Called tranchet because of the method of sharpening and resharpening by means of a transverse blow to detach a flake along the cutting edge at right angles to the flint, it was probably used as a digging tool.

19

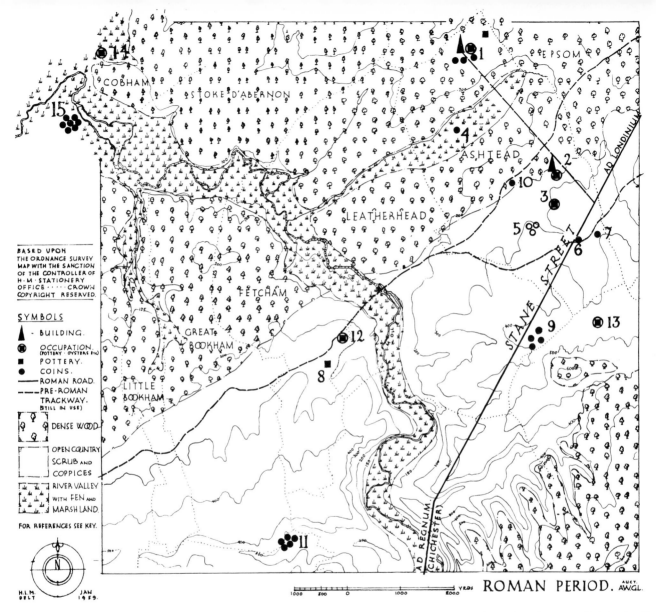

Map of Roman Leatherhead showing the sites of finds. (1) Abandoned about AD 200, a brickworks and villa. (2) Building near Ashtead Parish Church. (3) Site with corn-storage pits and pottery in Park Lane, Ashtead. (4) and (5) Coins, the latter when High Warren Ashtead was built. (6) Iron linch-pin from large wagon found at Stane Street. (7) Coin 400 yards from Stane Street. (8) Pottery at Young Street. (9) Coins found at Tyrrells Wood golf course. (10) Bronze key ring found in Ashtead village. (11) Hoard of coins found in 1715 at Bagden Farm, Great Bookham. (12) Site with corn-pits, drying ovens, burnt grain, pottery and brooches at Hawks Hill, Fetcham. (13) Site at Headley Court. (14) and (16) Sites at Cobham. (15) Copper coins found in 1883 and in 1772.

Several 'Celtic' fields flank a double-ditched trackway just north-east of Cherkley Court;[1] a large oval enclosure nearby may be the site of the settlement itself. Belgic coins have been found in two Leatherhead gardens. One is clearly a copy of a stater of Philip of Macedon, current in Gaul after the plunder of Greece in 278 BC.[2] Iron Age pottery has been found on the extreme north and south edges of the parish, at Woodlands Park and at Givons Grove.[3]

At Woodlands Park, the occupation of the hilltop seems to have gone on throughout the Roman period, but exactly what form the activities took is not clear. A flint-paved and drained area produced pottery fragments dating as late as the 4th century AD, together with an enamelled roundel with a trumpet-like pattern. Scattered Roman pottery and coins have turned up elsewhere, particularly when the golf course at Tyrrells Wood was being laid out.[4]

Roman Leatherhead

The Roman development of Leatherhead was strongly agricultural, using the woodlands for building as well as for fuel. Excavation of the Romano-British farmstead on the top of Hawks Hill, Fetcham, revealed burnt grains, storage pits and drying ovens as well as the post-holes of the farm buildings themselves. On the other side of Leatherhead, the heavy clays north of Ashtead were exploited in a large brickworks, whose products were often re-used elsewhere.[5] There are Roman bricks in Leatherhead and Fetcham parish churches and a quantity of Roman glass, tiles and pottery were found on the site of the medieval manor house of Pachenesham.[6]

Part of the parish boundary, Stane Street, is the Roman road running in a straight line from London to Chichester, with 'service areas' at Ewell and Dorking. From Dorking to Burford the exact line of the road is uncertain, but beyond Juniper Hill it can be followed as a footpath (Pebble Lane) north-eastward over Mickleham Downs and beyond to Epsom. Aerial photographs indicate that, including side ditches, it was about 55 ft wide, although the one section cut across Stane Street showed only a 15 ft width of metalling[7] with flints set in sand in the manner of the 18th century turnpikes.

Leatherhead and the Anglo-Saxon settlement

After the withdrawal of the Roman army and administration in 410

Found in Rowhurst, Oxshott Road, in 1960, this pre-Roman coin, a stater is gold, weighs 5.850 g and is shown actual size.

This Celtic bronze roundel is patterned and the enamel whirl preserved is in deep red. The central hole may have housed a miniature portrait or a stud for fixing the roundel to another object. Such roundels have been found on Romano-Celtic temple sites and were perhaps votive offerings. Found on a clay hill opposite Dorincourt, this is reproduced actual size.

[5] J. N. Hampton, 'Roman Ashtead' in *Ashtead: a Village Transformed* (LDLHS, 1977), p. 26.
[6] D. F. Renn (ed.), 'Pachenesham, Leatherhead . . .', *SAC*, 74, 1983, p. 26.
[7] J. Fox, 'Stane Street', *SAC*, 51, 1949, pp. 147–51.

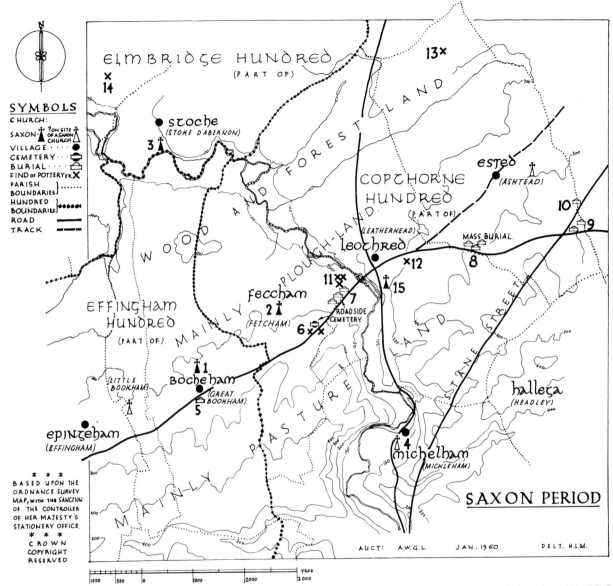

SAXON PERIOD

AUCT: A.W.G.L.   JAN. 1960   DELT. H.L.M.

(1) Great Bookham Church. (2) Fetcham Church. (3) Stoke d'Abernon Church. (4) Mickleham Church. (5) Skeletons found in 1953 in Bookham Grove. (6) Saxon cemetery extending up Hawks Hill, Fetcham. (7) Burials forming part of the above cemetery lower down the hill nearer Leatherhead. (8) Mass burial of dismembered bodies found in pit in 1927 beside Green Lane trackway. (9) Burials south of Ashtead Park beside Headley crossroads found in 1910. (10) Burial found in 1932 along the line of Stane Street. (11) Collection of Saxon objects found in 1929 and 1930 at Watersmeet, near Fetcham mill pond. (12) Late Saxon pin and hand-made pottery found in garden of Leatherhead Hospital. (14) Saxon spearhead found in 1926 at Leigh Hill, Cobham. (15) Leatherhead Church.

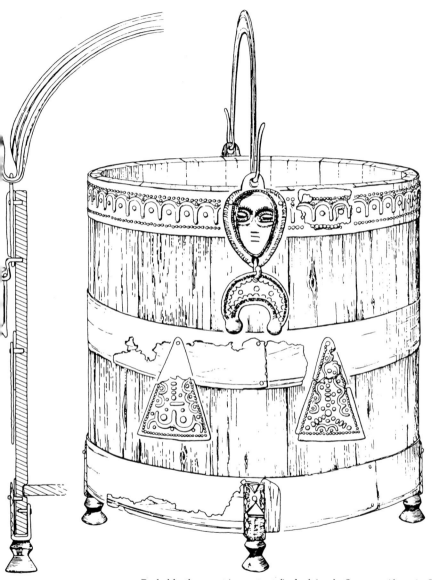

Close-up of bronze plaque from the bucket.

Detail of bronze attachment to plaque.

Probably the most important find of Anglo-Saxon artifacts in Surrey, a wooden bucket with bronze attachments found on Mizen land at Fetcham mill pond in 1929.
Reconstructed here in a drawing by David Williams reproduced with permission of SAC.

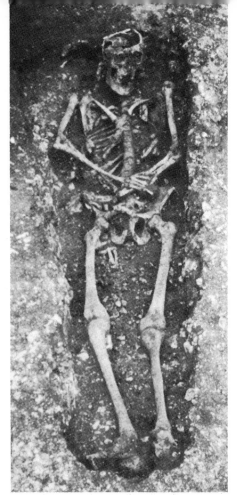

Skeleton, one of 30 unearthed in Ermyn Way in 1985. All had well-preserved teeth with no caries but were worn down due to grit in stoneground flour in their diet.

[1] D. F. Renn 'The Hawks Hill cemetery' (forthcoming).

[2] 'A cartographic survey of the area V: The Saxon period c. A.D. 410–1066', *Proc. LDLHS*, **2** (3), 1959, pp. 69–72.

[3] D. J. Turner.

[4] 'Occasional note', *Proc. LDLHS*, **1** (4), 1950, pp. 4–5.

[5] R. Poulton, 'Saxons and Sinners', *The London Archaeologist*, Autumn 1987.

AD, the Saxon settlement began in the southern coastal regions. By the late 6th century there were pagan Saxon cemeteries in north-east Surrey. Place-names suggest that the colonisation of central Surrey took place by way of the Weald, the pioneers pushing up the side valley from the rivers. Over the last 200 years a very extensive Saxon cemetery has been discovered piecemeal on both sides (and under) the modern road running up Hawks Hill, just over the Fetcham boundary.[1] A mass grave-pit, cut 6–8 ft deep in the chalk alongside Green Lane in Ermyn Way was found in 1927[2] and a Saxon spearhead was found nearby 50 years later.[3] Nearer Leatherhead itself, a faceted pin and potsherds dated 800 AD came from a garden near the hospital which was once part of the Common Field.[4] Swords, spearheads and parts of a decorated bucket, perhaps swept down in a flood, were found on the site of the present Fire Station.[2]

In 1985 the Goblin Works in Ermyn Way was demolished and the contractors uncovered several graves cut into the solid chalk immediately below the shallow top soil. Esso, who owned the site, generously funded a full excavation of this undisturbed area. Nearly 30 skeletons of men, women and children were found. Seventeen graves were all aligned with the heads to the west. In some, the bodies were laid on their backs, in others, they were crouched on their sides. Most graves carried artifacts. Two of the men were buried with their spears and most had iron knives. One spearhead was exceptionally long. The graves of the women contained a bone comb, beads and a panther shell, probably a fertility symbol, and a necklace of similar shells from the Red Sea. One male had been decapitated and the head was buried between his ankles. The artifacts showed that these were pagans of around the 6th or 7th century AD.

The other skeletons, all male, were in ill-formed rough holes, not clearly defined as the other graves and with no artifacts. Several of them showed signs of having been beheaded and the position of the bones of the hands, some in front and some behind, indicated they had been tied together suggesting they had been executed. Late 12th century pottery found in a large hole suggested a gibbet had been erected there. In all probability, judging by the close proximity to the regular graves, these were criminals buried at a later time by Christians in a place known to them to have been a pagan cemetery.[5]

Stane Street today at Tyrrells Wood

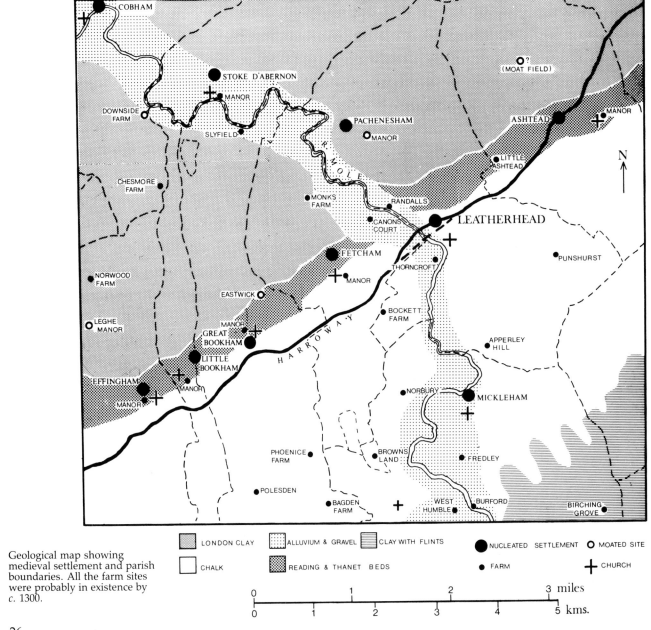

Geological map showing medieval settlement and parish boundaries. All the farm sites were probably in existence by *c.* 1300.

LONDON CLAY ALLUVIUM & GRAVEL CLAY WITH FLINTS ● NUCLEATED SETTLEMENT ○ MOATED SITE

CHALK READING & THANET BEDS • FARM ✝ CHURCH

0   1   2   3 miles

0   1   2   3   4   5 kms.

The Early Middle Ages
c. 600–1250

By the 13th century, Leatherhead had assumed the form of a roughly hourglass-shaped parish with the town at its centre. South-eastwards, on fertile land following the dip-slope of the Downs, lay the intensively farmed Common Field. West of this, crossing the river and sweeping up towards Fetcham, was a block of old enclosures, and around the southern edge of the cultivated land lay the high, open Downs. The north half of the parish consisted entirely of enclosed fields, ascending to the heavy, wooded London Clay. The town is one of a series of settlements strung out along an old west–east trackway which follows the dip-slope. Geography explains the strip-like form of parishes in this area: each was an economic unit, its main settlement lying near good arable land between Downland pasture for sheep and woodland pasture for cattle.[1]

Once it was assumed that this pattern of settlement and economy was stamped on the landscape by the earliest Anglo-Saxons. But now it is known that villages and common fields are the end-product of a long evolution, the crucial stages of which probably lie in the 10th and 11th centuries.[2] To rediscover Anglo-Saxon Leatherhead the picture of the integrated village and parish community must be set aside, and a search made among the farms and field-boundaries for traces of a lost, older world. In that world, Leatherhead was a place of more than local importance. It was important not as a town but as a key place in the startlingly systematic 'local government' of mid-Saxon England: a centre of royal authority and the site of a minster church.

[1] *EMS*, Ch. I.
[2] C. Taylor, *Village and Farmstead* (London, 1983); T. Rowley (ed.), *The Origins of Open-Field Agriculture* (London, 1981).

The royal vill

Great advances have lately been made in understanding how kings exercised power within the early kingdoms.[1] It seems that hundreds, the basic units of local government from the 10th century onwards, are merely subdivisions of larger, earlier territories which had taken shape at least by the late 7th century. At the heart of each territory lay a king's manor-house or royal vill (*regia villa* in Latin, *cyninges tūn* in English) from which law was administered on the king's behalf. The governmental centre was also the economic centre: the territory was assessed according to a regular, structured system of taxes which its inhabitants owed to the royal vill.

This system, which survives most clearly in the early Kentish divisions called 'lathes', also underlay the Hundreds of Surrey. For instance, Chertsey and Woking Hundreds represent an early territory based on Woking, from which Chertsey Hundred (the original Chertsey Abbey estate) was split away as early as the 670s.[2] Reconstructing the early boundaries must be speculative, but there are grounds for thinking that Copthorne, Effingham and Wotton Hundreds may represent an early territory running in a broad strip from the London Clay, across the Downs and through the Weald to the Sussex border. Copthorne and Effingham Hundreds shared one meeting-place, and a large tract of Downland which crossed the two Hundreds but was known by the single name of 'Polesden' suggests an early unity.[3] One aspect of the early economy – the seasonal driving of pigs from the more open lands to fatten in the Wealden woods – has left clues in the form of Wealden land attached to manors several miles northwards. An especially clear case is Newdigate parish, on the Sussex border, much of which belonged to manors in Leatherhead, Ashtead and Ewell. Two peasant holdings there can be traced in the records of Thorncroft manor, Leatherhead, from the 1270s onwards, recalling the days when, every year, Leatherhead pigs were driven 10 miles to root among the acorns of Newdigate.[4]

Leatherhead can be identified as a royal vill on the best possible evidence: it is one of five in Surrey listed in King Alfred's will (879–888).[5] In Domesday Book (1086, with data for 1066) such ancient centres often still appear as royal manors, and in Surrey some are immediately obvious: Godalming, Woking, Wallington, Stoke-by-Guildford and of course, Kingston. By 1066 the two manors of

[1] E.g. J. Campbell (ed.), *The Anglo-Saxons* (Oxford, 1982), pp. 41, 61.

[2] *EMS*, Ch. I.

[3] J. H. Harvey, 'The hundred of Copthorne and Effingham', *SAC*, **1**, 1946–7, pp. 157–61; Idem, 'Polesden: the name and the place', Ibid., pp. 161–4.

[4] *EMS*, Ch. II. The Thorncroft holdings in Newdigate were: (a) Held by rector of Newdigate for 3*s*. p.a. in 1275 (MM 5777c); acquired by Walter at Gosebrugge in 1332 (MM 5788ᵛ); in a rental dated 1333 (but apparently in fact an updated copy of several years later), 'one virgate . . . once of Walter Gossebrigge in Newdegate', and the 3*s*. rent, are split between two tenants (MM 5778). (b) Held by Herbert de Sumerberie for 3*s*. p.a. in 1275 (MM 5777c); after 1333, Robert Cudforde pays 3*s*. for 'a messuage and virgate of land . . . in Newdegate which Henry [*sic*] de Somerberi formerly held' (MM 5778).

[5] F. E. Harmer, *Select English Historical Documents of the Ninth and Tenth Centuries* (Cambridge, 1914), pp. 15–19.

Leatherhead were both in private hands, but there are good grounds for identifying the lost royal centre with Pachenesham, on the London Clay in the north-west of the parish (see p. 34). It has the oldest place-name in the parish: 'Pæccin's *hām*' (homestead) was probably established in the first stages of English settlement. In the 13th century this manor was held for services associated with royal justice; finding a prison, a pound for beasts distrained for the king's debt, and a bench for the county court where it was normally held.[1] This is supported by a statement of the county jurors in 1259 that the county court, recently moved to Guildford, had 'always' been held at Leatherhead.[2] So it seems that Leatherhead was remembered as a place which had once had important judicial functions, and that these were linked in some way to Pachenesham.

The minster

Leatherhead also had an ancient and important church, one of those churches, in fact, which were known by the 10th century as the 'old minsters'.[3] Mostly founded in the early days of English Christianity, they were collegiate churches supporting 'team ministries': groups of priests who served large territories equivalent in size to several later parishes. Between royal vill and minster there was often a close link. Many minsters were founded by kings at their vills; the minster parish might be identical with the vill's territory, and church finance might be based directly on existing secular taxation. But as thousands of local churches were founded in the 10th and 11th centuries, the minsters lost most of their pastoral role and much of their wealth and status. In Domesday Book their endowments are often annexed to support royal clerks or other absentees.

In the light of this should be seen an enigmatic note in the Domesday entry for Ewell, a royal manor: 'To this manor is attached the church of Leatherhead with 40 acres of land. It is worth 20s. Osbern de Ow holds it.'[4] This entry shows two characteristic marks of an ex-minster; a separately assessed endowment and valuation, and separate tenure by a named cleric (in this case a noted pluralist who held other Surrey minsters and a prebend at St Paul's Cathedral).[5] Slightly later sources provide another strong hint of minster status; in 1107–1129 Ashtead church was founded as a chapel of Leatherhead mother church.[6] The sequence of events must have been something like this:

C1100   C1250

The origins of the town, showing the development between *c.* 1110 and *c.* 1250.

[1] *Proc. LDLHS*, **1** (1), p. 10; cf. *VCH Surrey*, **iii**, p. 295.

[2] P.R.O. Just, 1/873 m.4 and m.5.

[3] J. Blair, 'Secular minster churches in Domesday Book', in P. H. Sawyer (ed.), *Domesday Book: a Reassessment* (London, 1985), pp. 104–42.

[4] *VCH Surrey*, **I**, p. 297.

[5] Blair, 'Secular minster churches in Domesday Book', pp. 106–12, 127.

[6] *Proc. LDLHS*, **3** (10), pp. 328–9.

Copthorne Hundred had once contained a large block of royal land stretching from Leatherhead, with the main centre and the minster church, across to Ewell. Before 1066 this was broken up and mostly given away, leaving only Ewell in royal hands with the now isolated minster, 11 miles away, linked to it for administrative purposes. This helps to explain why Leatherhead, unlike so many other royal vills, lost its early secular importance.

What happened to the old minster?[1] The answer to this question is apparently not the obvious one – that it became the parish church – since this seems to have been founded separately to serve the Domesday manor of Thorncroft (see p. 34). But an enclave of land in the north of the parish, near the medieval centre of Pachenesham (and so probably near the lost royal vill) is first recorded in the 13th century as held of Ewell manor for 20s. rent. This suggests an intriguing possibility that the minster church simply disappeared, its Domesday valuation of 20s. remaining fossilised as a rent from the former glebeland, and somewhere in the Pachenesham area an Anglo-Saxon church may still await the archaeologist. The minster's parochial rights must have been transferred to the estate church of Thorncroft, more conveniently sited near the river-crossing, which thus emerges with jurisdiction over Leatherhead parish and Ashtead chapelry. With evidence growing for such drastic reorganisation elsewhere, this is less unlikely than it would once have seemed. It can be shown, for instance, that almost exactly the same thing happened at Godalming, again leaving a deserted minster site.[2] Both cases illustrate what seems to be a general pattern: major changes in settlement between the 10th and 13th centuries which left ancient centres redundant.

Early land-units and boundaries

One of the strongest forces for change in late Anglo-Saxon England was the swift advance of manorialisation: the break-up of great, complex territories, each containing numerous settlements but run from one royal or monastic centre, to provide thousands of smaller, private lordships. What we now think of as 'normal' or 'parish-sized' manors seem to have been proliferating in the 10th and 11th centuries, and with them came manor-houses and manorial churches. Also established well before the Conquest was the distinction between 'demesne' (farmed directly by the lord) and smallholdings (in the

[1] W. J. Blair, 'The origins of Leatherhead Parish Church', *Proc. LDLHS*, **3** (10), pp. 323–9.
[2] *EMS*, Ch. IV.

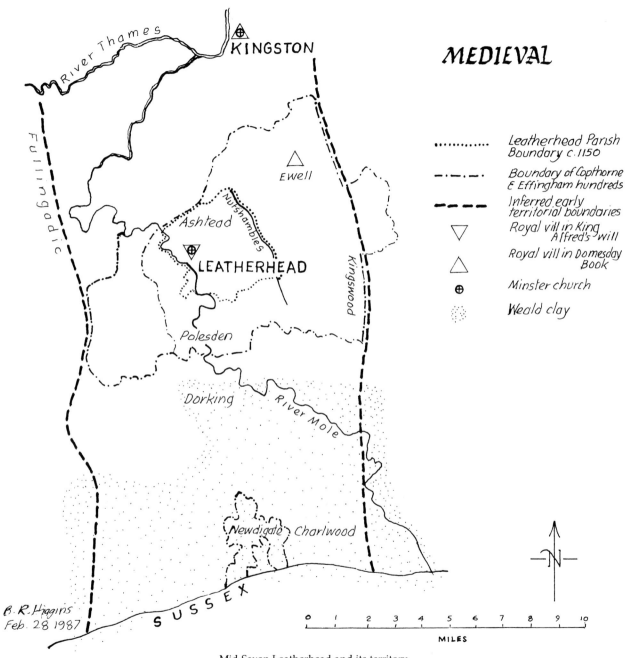

MEDIEVAL

River Thames

⊕ KINGSTON

Fullingadic

Ewell △

Ashtead

Nutshambles

⊕ LEATHERHEAD

Kingswood

Polesden

Dorking

River Mole

Newdigate Charlwood

S U S S E X

B. R. Higgins
Feb. 28 1987

Legend:
- ·············· Leatherhead Parish Boundary c.1150
- ·–·–·–· Boundary of Copthorne & Effingham hundreds
- – – – – Inferred early territorial boundaries
- ▽ Royal vill in King Alfred's will
- △ Royal vill in Domesday Book
- ⊕ Minster church
- ⣿ Weald clay

N

| 0 | 1 | 2 | 3 | 4 | 5 | 6 | 7 | 8 | 9 | 10 |

MILES

Mid-Saxon Leatherhead and its territory.

hands of tenants) which was to be basic to all manorial history. Great changes in rural settlement and economy were linked, directly or indirectly, to the needs of a broad, relatively new class of minor gentry.

The territory once ruled from Leatherhead royal vill had fragmented by 1066 into a series of strip-like manors divided across the geographical zones: Effingham, Great and Little Bookham, Fetcham and Ashtead. Between the last two lay what is now known as Leatherhead, but in Domesday Book it is not (apart from the church reference in the Ewell entry) described as such. Instead there are entries for two manors, Pachenesham and Thorncroft, which between them comprised the area of the later parish. Perhaps the name 'Leatherhead' (*Leodridan* in Alfred's will, *Leret* in Domesday Book) had once denoted the whole territory of the royal vill; hence the Domesday clerks used it for the minster, but not for the two private manors which were to assume it later.

Whether Pachenesham and Thorncroft were already halves of a coherent whole in 1066 – in other words, whether 'Leatherhead' as we know it meant anything – is by no means clear. Certainly they were separate tenurially. In Edward the Confessor's time 'Aelmer' (Æthelmaer or Ælfmaer) held the main part of Pachenesham (four hides), apparently from royal demesne; Earl Harold held another 2¼ hides, with Leofric and 'Aelmer' (presumably the same man) holding under him.[1] Thorncroft was in the hands of Cola, a Surrey thegn who also held Betchworth and Coombe; with some extra lands (1¼ hides held by Merwin, one hide held by Ælfric and 'Aelmer' and one hide held by Coleman the hunter) it supported the very large assessment of 25½ hides.[2]

The topography of these manors, as it can be reconstructed from the late 13th century onwards, is described in the next chapter. The demesne lands of Pachenesham were essentially the north-west part of the parish, while those of Thorncroft lay in the south-west though with some fields on the east parish boundary towards Ashtead. At first sight the Common Field seems to prove an economic unity between the two manors, for in it their tenants' strips lay intermixed. But close analysis (see p. 47) suggests that in the late middle ages only about 10 per cent of these strips were held of Pachenesham, the remainder belonging to Thorncroft or its offshoots. It looks very much as though the Common Field is of Thorncroft origin, and that the two manors

[1] *VCH Surrey*, **I**, p. 303.
[2] *VCH Surrey*, **I**, pp. 319–20.

had once lain as separate blocks: Thorncroft was the south half of the parish plus some land along its north-east boundary, and Pachenesham was the remainder.

How, then, did 'Leatherhead' come into being? The explanation may be partly parochial, partly topographical. Following a common pattern, it is the 'rump' of the old minster parish left by the carving-out of local parishes. Fetcham, Mickleham and the Bookhams had independent churches before records start, while Ashtead church, originally a chapel of Leatherhead, was free by c. 1200; Thorncroft and Pachenesham were simply what remained. At the same time, the growth of a small town on the boundary between the two manors (see p. 29) created a physical and commercial focus. Developments in agriculture, and in the land-market, gradually brought about an inter-mixture of holdings and a sharing of resources which forged Pachenesham and Thorncroft into one economic unit. It is symptomatic that Thorncroft church assumed the attributes of the abandoned minster and a new status as Leatherhead church. So medieval Leatherhead is perhaps best visualised as two fragments of the old royal territory, split tenurially but then re-combined around a new centre.

Manor and parish boundaries often preserve landmarks from a pre-manorial age. One such is the linear bank called 'Nutshambles' which divides Ashtead and Headley on the west from Epsom and Walton on the east. The name appears in 1496 as *Motschameles* and seems likely to mean *mot scaemol*, 'the seat of the moot'. The convergence of many roads at a high point on the line of the earthwork suggests an important meeting-place.[1] Possibly this preserves memories of a primitive folk-moot in the territory of Leatherhead vill.

Another case is still more intriguing. The block of Thorncroft demesne fields along the north-east boundary of the parish is almost rectilinear, defined by lanes and boundaries as two rough squares. Eastwards lay the major of Little Ashtead and Ashtead common field,[2] bounded by the intersecting alignments of Barnett Wood Lane, Ottways Lane, Woodfield Lane, Skinners Lane and Harriots Lane to form two more rough squares of almost identical size. Viewed as a whole, the area looks as though it has been deliberately laid out on an irregular grid-plan – and one which is respected by manor and parish boundaries. Close at hand lies the Ashtead Roman villa and tile-works, with a

[1] D. Nail, 'The Meeting-Place of Copthorne Hundred', *SAC*, **lxii**, 1965, pp. 44–53.
[2] *VCH Surrey*, **iii**, pp 249–50; *Proc. LDLHS*, **I** (7), pp. 18–19; map reproduced *Proc. LDLHS*, **I** (10), opp. p. 21. For plan of suggested Roman land-division see *SAC*, **lxxii**, 1980, p. 235.

possible road link to Stane Street on the alignment of the grid. All this, in the light of a similar system in Essex of undoubted Roman date,[1] suggests a remarkable conclusion that boundaries connected with the villa survived to define land-units throughout the Anglo-Saxon period.

Manors and landlords after the Conquest

Pachenesham, like so many manors, was held in 1086 by the king's rapacious half-brother, Odo of Bayeux. Two tenants, Ranulf and Baynard, had the portions held under Earl Harold in Edward the Confessor's day. When Odo fell two years later, it reverted to royal demesne, which may have been its status until shortly before the Conquest. Pachenesham should probably be identified with the 100s. rent in Leatherhead which Hugh de St Omer held of the crown from before 1155 until 1161.[2] In 1198 Richard I granted 10s. rent there to William de Eys, whose descendants held it until 1233 when it passed to Matthew Bezille. King John granted the larger portion of Pachenesham to Brian de Therfeld ('the usher') in 1203, when it was valued at 70s. 2d., to be held at the yearly rent of a Norwegian falcon. It descended to Brian's son-in-law, Philip de Thorp of Essex; his heir Walter was overlord in c. 1300, when it was still being called 'the King's fee'.[3]

In 1086 Thorncroft was a demesne manor of another great Norman lord: Richard fitz Gilbert, founder of the honour of Clare. The church is not mentioned in Domesday Book, but independent evidence suggests that it existed by the 1080s and passed as a dowry to Richard's son-in-law Eudes the Sewer. Soon after 1100 he gave it to Colchester Abbey as 'in Thorncroft the church of that vill and one hide of land'.[4] On topographical grounds, the main block of glebeland seems to have been formed out of the Thorncroft demesne. A generation later, the rest of the manor formed the dowry of Richard's granddaughter, Margaret, on her marriage to an Essex knight named William de Montfichet. In c. 1190 Richard de Montfichet, grandson of William and Margaret, sold Thorncroft to John de Cherbrugh, a Wiltshire knight who lived to a great age and held the manor until c. 1260.[5]

The Eys, Therfeld, Thorp and Montfichet families were all nonresident, drawing revenues from Leatherhead but having little to do with local concerns. John de Cherburgh was more active in Copthorne

[1] P. J. Drury and W. J. Rodwell, 'Investigations at Asheldham, Essex', *Antiquaries Journal*, **lviii**, 1978, pp. 134–7.
[2] *Pipe Rolls 2–7 Henry II; Red Book of Exchequer*, II, p. 666.
[3] *VCH Surrey*, **III**, p. 295; *1235 Eyre*, **II**, p. 549; *Proc. LDLHS*, **I** (1), pp. 9–11; *Proc. LDLHS*, **3** (8), p. 230; *SAC*, **lxxiv**, 1983, p. 6.
[4] *Proc. LDLHS*, **3** (10), pp. 323–9.
[5] *Proc. LDLHS*, **4** (1), pp. 3–4.

Hundred affairs and maintained a household at Thorncroft, but it was still only one of his manors.[1] In the 12th century, however, a gentry family was established who long remained the principal local residents, and who took, as befitted their status, the surname 'de Leatherhead'. By c. 1300 they lived on a small manor in the north of Leatherhead parish known as 'Little Pachenesham', later Randalls, where a mansion existed until replaced by the Randalls Park Crematorium (see p. 36). The origins of this property are obscure. It seems to have been held under the d'Abernons, tenants of Clare and Warenne in nearby Fetcham and Stoke,[2] so it may derive from a manor on the Fetcham bank of the river rather than from Domesday Pachenesham.

The key to this family's origins is a charter, issued by Margaret de Montfichet in c. 1170, establishing title to land in the south of the parish which they held of Thorncroft manor. Margaret recounts how her husband William on his deathbed had asked her to restore to the heirs of Fulk son of Amfrid of Thorncroft, slain in his service, the land which Fulk had held. Accordingly, she confirms to Amfrid son of Fulk his father's lands, comprising half a hide in Thorncroft and a mill, and further grants him 'the hide which Ailwin and Hugh de Punesherst and Fulk de Punesherst and Ailmer hold', and a virgate in Aperlderle (Aperdele, see p. 37) which he already holds in demesne.[3]

By remarkable good luck, a correlation of the rents specified in this charter with a rental of c. 1300 makes possible an almost complete identification of the lands. What Margaret confirmed and granted to Amfrid was: the farm and fields south-west of Thorncroft later called Bockett Farm (probably the original half-hide); a holding (probably the de Punesherts' hide) of about 127 acres, a quarter in a field called Joyesfield on the Headley boundary and the rest dispersed in the Common Field; and fields along the east bank of the Mole to the south of Thorncroft manor (the virgate in 'Aperderle'). In doing this, she cut a big slice out of the Thorncroft demesne lands as well as alienating lordship over several common-field holdings.

The endowment of knights with portions of demesne land was common in Anglo-Norman England,[4] and Fulk son of Amfrid's original half-hide was evidently in this category. Much larger than the average peasant farm, it was none the less small by the standard of Domesday military holdings and represented only a fraction of the

[1] *1235 Eyre*, **i**, p. 180.
[2] *Proc. LDLHS*, **4** (1), p. 6.
[3] This and the next two paragraphs are based on W. J. Blair, 'A military holding in twelfth-century Leatherhead: Bockett Farm and the origins of Pachenesham Parva', *Proc. LDLHS*, **4** (1), pp. 3–12.
[4] S. Harvey, 'The knight and knight's fee in England', *Past and Present*, **xlix,** 1970, pp. 22–4.

knight's fee for which the whole manor of Thorncroft was held. The family presumably originated as soldiers in the Montfichet entourage; the names Amfrid and Fulk are both Norman rather than English. Fulk was slain in William de Montfichet's service, and since William himself was dead by the early 1150s, it seems likely that this happened during the civil war of Stephen's reign. We see here with unusual clarity the modest holding of a man-at-arms who held his land for actual military service, as his death graphically demonstrates. By contrast, after *c.* 1170 Fulk's son Amfrid was to hold the land by hereditary succession and at sizeable rents: he was more a resident proprietor than an armed retainer. The family appear regularly thereafter, and were calling themselves 'de Ledrede' (Leatherhead) by the 1220s. By *c.* 1300 John de Leatherhead was holding the Montfichet land jointly with 'Little Pachenesham', and on his death in 1326 the inheritance passed to his daughter's son John. This man was probably identical with John Randolf, head of a family which held the joint manor for at least three generations and from which it was to be called 'Randalls'. Thus the descendants of a man-at-arms maintained on one of his lord's demesnes were transformed into minor gentry of the later middle ages.[1]

The farming community

In Midland England the pressures of an intensive grain-producing economy necessitated, at least by the 12th century, communal and highly organised farming systems.[2] Surrey, by contrast, belongs to the 'wood–pasture' zone, in which an abundance of wastes and commons allowed the agricultural community to remain relatively free and unstructured. Leatherhead is no exception; there were still large commons on the clay northwards and the Downs southwards, and less than half the arable lay in scattered intermixed strips in the Common Field. So it comes as no surprise to find a community of prosperous farmers, most of whom held by free tenure.

While the de Leatherheads were the main local family, several others appear when records become fuller after 1200 and are then mentioned regularly in deeds and lawsuits. Foremost among these were the de Aperdeles, the de Punshursts (already mentioned in Margaret de Montfichet's charter), the de Bradmeres, the del Broks, the de Oxencrofts, the le Hores and the Pinchuns.[3] These people

[1] This pedigree is based on *Proc. LDLHS*, **4** (1), pp. 4–5; *1235 Eyre* **ii**, p. 550; P.R.O., KB26/130 m. 4*d*; *Proc. LDLHS*, **3** (8), pp. 218–23; MDLD 223.

[2] See general discussion in H. S. A. Fox in Rowley (ed.), op. cit., note 2.

[3] The following are examples of numerous references: William de Appedurlee v. William de Oxecroft in 1240–1 (P.R.O. JUST 1/867) m.11ᵛ); Robert de Hameledon v. William de Brademer in 1207 (P.R.O., CP25(i)/225/3 (79)); Nicholas son of John de Brademere in *c.* 1240–50 (MDLD 92); grant by Ranulf del Brok to Gilbert le Hore of a virgate in Leatherhead in 1235–7 (cited P.R.O. KB26/133 m.7d); William Viel of Oxenecrofte in *c.* 1250–60 (MDLD 93); Thomas Pinchun v. Gilbert de Oxenecroft in 1229 (P.R.O. CP25(i)/225/6 (105)); Simon de Ponte and Gilbert le Hore v. John de Cherburgh in 1235 (*1235 Eyre*, **ii**, nos. 160, 230–1). For William de Brademere see also *1235 Eyre*, i, pp. 170–1, and for other families see *Proc. LDLHS*, **I** (4), pp. 14–16.

cannot be called peasants: they were substantial freeholders, frequently occupied in the affairs of Copthorne Hundred and in private litigation. Such independent, well-established farming families are characteristic of 12th and 13th century Surrey, making it more like the free society of Kent than the servile peasant communities of the Midlands.

Lesser families are rarely mentioned, though stray references show that some familiar Leatherhead names of the 14th century were already known in the 13th. Usually the humble only appear in assize rolls which record their crimes or violent deaths. Thus it is known that Bernard the miller of Pachenesham was crushed to death by a cart in 1235,[1] and that Levina daughter of William Baynguard was raped at Leatherhead by William Balemund in 1241;[2] while a roll for 1224–1225 provides the delightful names of two Leatherhead sheep-stealers, William Bullfinch and Henry Chop.[3]

It may be an important distinction between the greater and lesser families that the former usually lived in farmsteads which stood apart on the enclosed fields of their farms. Thirteenth-century Leatherhead, like the adjoining parishes, had a pattern of dispersed settlement which was in all likelihood older than the villages.[4] The manor-houses of Pachenesham, 'Little Pachenesham' and Thorncroft all stood alone (unless the first already had a satellite village) – p. 40. The main families took their names from locations within the parish (Aperdele, Punshurst, Bradmere and Oxencroft appear later as field-names on the Gwilt map) – p. 120,[5] and there they must have lived. The old Aperdele homestead can be traced through the Thorncroft records from c. 1275 to a map of 1629, where it is shown as a deserted enclosure called 'Apperley Hill'.[6] Later abandonment of these sites disguises the strongly individual character of agrarian life in much of the 13th century parish.

The Common Field

In the Common Field, matters were very different. Originally there may have been compact farms here too, some memory of which is preserved in furlong and landmark names suggesting ancient proprietorship: Buntanlond, Dondene, Edolvesdone, Godhivedene, Katebardene, Kenchescrofte, Lomleshegg, Lyndene, Swyndolvestorne, Tibeliesdene, Tonnerscroft.[7] Partible inheritance, and a growing

[1] *1235 Eyre*, **ii**, No. 493.
[2] P.R.O., JUST 1/867 m. 19.
[3] P.R.O., JUST 1/863 m. 5.
[4] For an argument along these lines see *EMS*, Ch. II.
[5] For Punshurst see MDLD 216–24, 227–40, 260–85.
[6] Adam de Apelderele pays 5s. p.a. in c. 1275 (MM 5777c). In the first 1333 rental 'John de Aperdele [son of Adam, see MDLD 100] holds one virgate of land of his inheritance' for 5s. p.a. (MM 5779). In the updated 1333 rental 'Roger de Aperdely [son of John] holds a messuage and one virgate of land ['in Aperleyhill' written in] where he now lives' for 5s. p.a. (MM 5778). The 1629 survey includes 'one parcell of land in *Letherhed* called *Apperley* hill estimated at 20tie acres' held for 5s. p.a. (MM 5.28 f. 16).
[7] *EMS*, Ch. III.

demand for land on the fertile strip during the late Anglo-Saxon period, would have caused progressive fragmentation of holdings into scattered strips. Manorial records show (more clearly, in fact, than for any other Surrey parish) that by 1270 these strips were apportioned between tenants in regular 13-acre shares. Rentals of both Thorncroft and 'Little Pachenesham' show this feature; since the common-field holdings of these manors were separated in *c.* 1170, the apportionment must have occurred at some earlier date.[1] There is probably a glimpse here of a deliberate act of planning, by some late Anglo-Saxon or Norman lord of Thorncroft, which involved reorganising the Common Field into uniform subdivided holdings, probably with uniform rents and services to match.

The Common Field is, in fact, a smaller and simpler version of a 'classic' Midland system; organised, integrated and regular. The tenants may have lived side-by-side in some nucleated 'Thorncroft village' (on and around Church Road is a likely area) which was later obscured by the growth of the town.[2] This little community first evolved, and was then planned and organised, within the old haphazard landscape of dispersed farms. But it never obliterated it completely, for Leatherhead shares the distinctive Surrey character of combining the 'primitive' mid-Saxon with the 'developed' Saxo-Norman pattern of organisation.[3]

The origins of the town

As suggested above, the town must lie near the early boundary between Thorncroft and Pachenesham. The church, Thorncroft's in origin, is not far away, and near it may have been a Thorncroft peasant settlement. On the other hand, Pachenesham had a bigger Domesday population than Thorncroft. Later evidence seems to show the bulk of town centre tenements attached to Pachenesham, while the market rights belonged to its lord.[4] By the late 11th century, tenants from Pachenesham may already have established a permanent settlement near the river-crossing. Perhaps some act of reorganisation should be envisaged, initiated from the Pachenesham side, which had the effect of subsuming existing settlements around the road–river intersection into a single larger one.

An important piece of topographical evidence is the town street pattern,[5] which seems to be based on an earlier layout. Elm Road, now

---

[1] *EMS*, Ch. III.

[2] Giles atte Boxe's 13-acre virgate, described in a Thorncroft court roll of 1307 (MM 5781 m.23ᵛ), included a messuage at 'Cherlane' (i.e. Church Lane, modern Church Road) between tenements of Gilbert le Glover and William Glover.

[3] *EMS*, Ch. III.

[4] A Pachenesham rental of 1418 (*Proc. LDLHS*, **3** (10), pp. 330–6) shows the large number of town properties belonging to that manor.

[5] This was first noticed by Dr J. H. Harvey. For a fuller discussion of the road pattern, with maps, see J. Blair, *Discovering Early Leatherhead*, LDLHS Occasional Paper I, 1976. An interesting parallel is Godstone, a settlement on the line of a Roman road from which the modern road diverges where it passes through the village (L. Ketteringham, 'The Roman road, Godstone', *SAC*, **lxx**, 1974, pp. 13–17).

merely a small lane behind the High Street, can be projected west-wards along a straight tenement boundary and the parish boundary to join the main road on Hawks Hill, continuing the course of the old trackway with less deviation than the line of Bridge Street and High Street. Near the Thorndike Theatre car park, Elm Road turns a right-angle into Church Walk, which joins Worple Road to form a trackway running south towards Dorking. Worple Road divided the Common Field eastwards from the main Thorncroft demesne westwards, and common-field strips were aligned on it.

Almost certainly at the junction of Elm Road and Church Walk, there was an early crossing of the main west–east route by a north–south trackway. Thorncroft manor lay south of the main road, with the trackway dividing its enclosed demesne from its open field. Subse-quently a different alignment was superimposed on this crossroads , obliterating its northern and western arms. It is at least a reasonable hypothesis that some lord of Pachenesham required a street pattern from which tenement plots could be laid out on all sides over his own territory, without impinging on Thorncroft land.

Throughout England, the 12th and early 13th centuries saw urban growth and rapid expansion of internal trade. Landowners were quick to see the advantages of founding and fostering market towns on their manors, from which they could expect returns in the form of rent and market tolls. Thus many small towns, often under seigneurial control and without corporate privileges, appear in these years; others, based on existing market centres, were enlarged or replanned.[1] In Surrey there are the examples of Farnham, Haslemere, Reigate and Bletchingley,[2] the latter an especially relevant parallel in that it seems to have been replanned around an existing boundary crossroads shortly before appearing as a town in the 1220s.[3] It seems very likely that Leatherhead as we now know it appeared in similar circumstances and at a similar date. A royal grant in 1248 of a weekly market and annual fair at Leatherhead (confirmed to the lord of Pachenesham Magna in 1331) may have been connected with its foundation.[4] However founded, the town and its market were henceforth to pro-vide a focus for Leatherhead and to dominate the lives of its people.

[1] M. Beresford, *New Towns in the Middle Ages* (1967).

[2] M. O'Connell, *Historic Towns in Surrey* (Surrey Archaeol. Soc. research vol. 5, 1977).

[3] J. Blair, 'The Surrey Endowments of Lewes Priory before 1200', *SAC*, **lxxii**, 1980, p. 109.

[4] *Cal. Close Rolls 1247–51*, 40; *Cal. Charter Rolls* iv, p. 226.

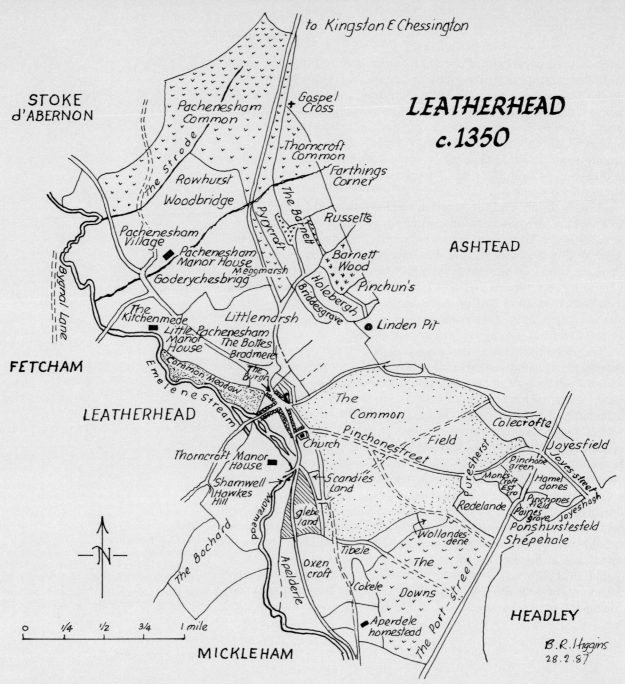

LEATHERHEAD
c.1350

STOKE
d'ABERNON

to Kingston & Chessington

Pachenesham Common

Gospel Cross

Thorncroft Common

Farthings Corner

The Strode

Rowhurst Woodbridge

Pydcroft

The Barnet

Russetts

ASHTEAD

Pachenesham Village

Pachenesham Manor House

Meggmarsh

Goderychesbrigg

Barnett Wood

Holebergh

Bradesgrave

Pinchun's

Bygnal Lane

The Kitchenmede

Little Pachenesham Manor House

Littlemarsh

The Bottes

Bradmere

Linden Pit

FETCHAM

Common Meadow

The Burgh

Emelene Stream

LEATHERHEAD

The Common Field

Pinchonestreet

Colecrofte

Joyesfield

Joyesstreet

Pinchone green

Monks Croft Est Esto

Hamel dones

Purehurst

Redelande

Pinchones Field

Paines grove

Joyeshagh

Ponshurstesfield

Shépehale

Church

Thorncroft Manor House

Sharnwell Hawkes Hill

Scandies Land

glebe land

Wollandesdene

Tibele

The Downs

The Bochard

Apelderle

Oxen croft

Cokele

The Port-street

HEADLEY

Aperdele homestead

MICKLEHAM

0   ¼   ½   ¾   1 mile

N

B.R.Higgins
28.2.87

The intersection of roads from Kingston to Dorking and from Epsom to Guildford was already established in the middle ages

The Late Middle Ages
1250–1558

Iɴ 13th century England the population rose, markets grew and the economy flourished. Inflation from 1180 to 1220 began more than a century of high prices, happy years for all who could send surplus crops to market.

Great landlords, previously content to draw fixed rents from their demesne estates, now took them under direct control. This was the age of 'high farming' in which the wealthy and powerful concerned themselves with agriculture and estate management, and spent lavishly on manor-houses, barns and equipment.[1]

The manors and their lands 1250–1350

Through the records of this activity more is known about some aspects of English rural life between 1250 and 1350 than for any other pre-industrial period. The account rolls, court rolls and private deeds show a world in which life was becoming more varied and material prosperity was growing for all but the poorest classes. They also provide the field-names and topographical data from which the first detailed view of the Leatherhead landscape can be reconstructed.

By 1250 Leatherhead was a united community to the extent that it had one main settlement and one common field, but manorially it remained divided. Pachenesham was still in some sense distinct from Thorncroft or Leatherhead: thus a petition of *c.* 1330 is in the name of 'the poor people of Leatherhead and of Pachenesham', and refers to 'the same vills'.[2]

[1] For the general background, E. Miller and J. Hatcher, *Medieval England: Rural Society and Economic Change 1086–1348* (London, 1978); Colin Platt, *Medieval England* (London, 1978), Ch. 2.

[2] P.R.O. SC8/165/8204.

Pachenesham

Pachenesham, the old royal manor, remained material for royal patronage. Between 1286 and 1343 its lords were civil servants, their lives based more on the court than on Leatherhead. In 1286 the manor passed to Sir Eustace de Hacche, a busy administrator whose duties included building works at Edward I's castles.[1] Little of his time can have been spent at Pachenesham, but he did maintain a household there where his grandson was born in 1291.[2] Hacche died in 1306; two years later Edward II granted the manor to his favourite Gaveston, who sold it in 1309 to Robert Darcy. Darcy, like Hacche before him, followed a career in the King's service but lived intermittently at Leatherhead.[3]

His attitude to his tenants and neighbours there seems to have been somewhat rapacious and aggressive, especially during the three years after Edward II's murder in 1327 when he was favoured by the Mortimer government. He consistently refused the old 20s. rent to Ewell manor, and made use of his influence at court when the lord of Ewell (by then Merton Priory) finally distrained on his cattle in 1327.[4] In 1328 Darcy himself distrained on the vicar of Leatherhead for failing to find a chaplain to serve St Margaret's chapel in Pachenesham manor; in 1330 the local inhabitants complained of oppressions which he and his bailiffs had inflicted on them since obtaining judicial rights through Mortimer's favour, and Sir John d'Abernon protested that Darcy had demolished his pillory at Leatherhead.[5]

Hacche and Darcy had enough interest in Pachenesham to follow current fashion and improve the manor-house. Today a deserted, tree-grown moat, it was excavated by the Leatherhead and District Local History Society between 1946 and 1953.[6] The site seems to have been occupied well before 1200, but in the 13th century the moat was dug and provided with a cluster of buildings dominated by a large hall. Unfortunately the sequence and dating of the excavated buildings remains imprecise, but it is a fair presumption that some of them were the work of Hacche or Darcy, and perhaps of both. In 1293 Hacche was accused of having taken horses and carts from strangers at Kingston market to carry timber to his manor of Pachenesham,[7] and this may well have been for building the hall.

The Pachenesham demesne surrounded the manor-house in the north-west of the parish. Northwards they extended to the Stoke

---

[1] For Hacche see *Proc. LDLHS*, **I** (2), p. 8; A. Lowther *et al.*, 'Pachenesham, Leatherhead', *SyAC*, **lxxiv**, 1983, pp. 6–7.

[2] *Complete Peerage* **vi**, p. 390.

[3] For Darcy see *Proc. LDLHS*, **I** (6), pp. 15–16.

[4] MDLD 66.

[5] *Proc. LDLHS*, **I** (6), p. 16, and **I** (5); P.R.O. SC8/165/8204; *V.C.H. Surrey*, **iii**, p. 296. The right complained of was view of frankpledge, granted in 1328: *Cal. Charter R.* **iv**, 94.

[6] Lowther *et al.*, 'Pachenesham, Leatherhead'.

[7] *Proc. LDLHS*, **I** (1), p. 10.

D'Abernon, Fetcham and Chessington boundaries, southwards to the damp soil north of the town called Meggmarsh and Littlemarsh.[1] This was heavy, unsympathetic land,[2] its northern half covered with the woodland and scrub termed *bruera* in Latin documents. Land here, held of Ewell manor, should perhaps be identified as the glebe of the old minster church (see p. 30); if so, it had long since reverted to scrub, and it seems unlikely that there was much cultivation north of the Rye Brook in the early 13th century.

Here Sir Eustace de Hacche made a permanent mark on the landscape by enclosing new arable from the waste. In 1287/1288 he made an agreement with his neighbour, Sir John d'Abernon, allowing him to enclose 16 acres in Leatherhead parish towards Kingston over which John and his tenants had common rights.[3]

This episode must be connected with a complaint in 1293 that Hacche had enclosed 18 acres of *bruera* there and diverted the roads to Oxshott, Stoke and Kingston. Evidently this diversion produced the layout north of Gutters Bridge (the crossing of the Rye Brook by the Leatherhead–Stoke road), where the roads branched to encircle a block of land, indeed of some 18 acres, immediately west of the moated site.[4]

As a part of these operations Hacche seems to have created, or at least enlarged, a small village.

The inquiry made at Robert Darcy's death in 1343 lists 10 bondmen at Pachenesham, and in *c.* 1380 eight villein tenements, six of 10 acres each and the rest smaller, are recorded north of 'Goderychesbrygg' (Gutters Bridge).[5] These must have been partly on land enclosed by Hacche in the late 1280s, and the regularity of the 10-acre holdings suggests a degree of planning.

So it seems that the open land between the bridge and Patsom Green once contained a 13th century 'marginal' settlement. It was on poor soil, servile in status, and quickly depopulated after the Black Death.

Rentals of 1418 and 1474/1475[6] are the earliest record of Pachenesham land in the south of the parish. In so far as these reflect earlier conditions they suggest that most town-centre properties were held of this manor, as were the fields called Oxencroft, Cokele and Tibele. But in 1418 Pachenesham seems to have had only some 90 acres of tenant land in the Common Field; the fact that in 1545 the land at Pachenesham itself was reckoned as three-quarters of the manor[7] emphasises the relative unimportance of the rest.

[1] An extent of 1545 (P.R.O. Cl42/72 (89), summarised *VCH Surrey*, **iii,** p. 295) shows that Pachenesham then included all land in the parish north of the Rye Brook except Thorncroft common; the south boundary, between 'Woodbridge' and 'Bygnallane', is vaguely described. For Littlemarsh see e.g. MDLD 207; for Meggmarsh see e.g. MM 5791 and 5779c, *Proc. LDLHS*, **ii** (5), pp. 147–8. In 1327 Darcy's cattle were pastured in 'la Mershe' (MDLD 66).

[2] Darcy's inquisition *post mortem* of 1343 (*Proc. LDLHS*, **iii** (9), pp. 292–3) places little value on the Pachenesham arable 'because it is waterlogged ground'.

[3] MDLD 25.

[4] *Proc. LDLHS*, **I** (2), pp. 8–10.

[5] *Proc. LDLHS*, **3** (9), pp. 292–3, 296–7.

[6] *Proc. LDLHS*, **3** (10), pp. 330–40.

[7] P.R.O. Cl42/72 (89).

Reconstruction by A. G. W. Lowther of Pachesnesham manor house, 'The Mounts', at the time of Sir Eustace Hacche.

Thorncroft

Thorncroft experienced lordship of a very different kind. John de Cherburgh sold the manor to a noble family, who in turn sold it to Walter de Merton, Henry III's chancellor, in 1266.[1] Walter used it to endow his 'house of Merton's scholars' at Maldon, soon to become Merton College, Oxford.[2] The scholars of Merton were in the forefront of 13th century estate management, and they remained lords of Thorncroft until 1904. Hence through the later middle ages the manorial administration was both stable and efficient, producing a splendid series of court rolls and accounts still preserved at Oxford.

Thorncroft manor-house lay on or near the site of its 18th century succcessor, south of the town near the river: the accounts contain numerous references to the house, barns, granaries and byres.[3] Beside it were the demesne meadows Mermede and Kuchenmede, and stretching westwards up to Hawks Hill the arable enclosures called la Bochard.[4] The detached block on the Ashtead boundary contained the other demesne enclosures: Barnett, Russette, Pyrycroft, Briddesgrave and Holebergh, and Barnett Wood of which remnants survive today.[5] Thorncroft demesne in the Common Field is harder to quantify, but from the amounts of grain sown there annually, and the frequent 'sales of pasture' at named common-field locations (as at Brokley, la Limost, la Linche and Longfurllang in 1278/1279),[6] it was clearly extensive. In 1629 the Common Field seems to have contained about 600 acres of Thorncroft desmesne,[7] and although this must include former tenant holdings which had reverted to the lord, there can scarcely have been much less than some 300 acres in the middle ages.

The accounts provide much information about Merton's farming practice, the crops sown, and even such details as the names of two Thorncroft plough-horses: Balle ('Patch') in 1314/1315 and Traunches ('Plodder') in 1328/1329.[8] Because so much of the demesne lay in separate enclosures, there was considerable flexibility in matters of cropping and rotations. In 1303 a three-course rotation was evidently practised, for the crops growing in each field were to be the same in three years' time.[9] An average of 173 acres of Thorncroft demesne were sown every year:[10] surprisingly little, which suggests that much of the enclosed land on heavier soil was only sporadically under crop. The demesne livestock, recorded in 1346, included three carthorses, five riding horses, 14 oxen, 11 cows and 250 sheep.[11] The impression is of a

[1] MDLD 80-3.

[2] MDLD 84-7.

[3] P. Brandon, *A History of Surrey* (Chichester, 1977), pp. 47–8, for inventory.

[4] The fields can be identified by reference to a map of 1629, MM 5.28. There are regular payments for scything the two meadows, and scattered references to the arable such as the sowing of 66½ acres in 'Holeburye et la Bocard' in 1282/3 (MM 5738).

[5] Again the map in MM 5.28 provides the key. Specimen earlier references are: cutting down tree between Holberwe and Pyrycroft (MM 5782 m.7); encroachment on demesne between Holeberhge and Briddesgreve (MM 5789 m.3); digging ditch next la Russette and la Merssch (MM 5748); fencing between Little Merssh and Bernett Merssh (MM 5792, court of 22 Hen. VI). For an independent list of Thorncroft demesne fields in 1319 see *Proc. LDLHS*, **3** (10), p. 324.

[6] MM 5690.

[7] MM 5.28 ff. 10, 40: a stated total of '100 ac. at the least', to which a further 500 acres are added in the final total.

[8] MM 5745, 5752.

[9] MDLD 88.

[10] Calculated in Ralph Evans, 'Merton College and its Tenants at Thorncroft and Cuxham *c.* 1270–*c.* 1350', from the accounts covering 1317/18–1349/50. With gratitude to Mr Evans for allowing quotations here and elsewhere from his unpublished paper.

[11] Brandon, *History of Surrey*, pp. 47–8.

farm which was modestly equipped and not one of Merton's biggest, but run to their usual high standards.

Thorncroft also had extensive tenant holdings, numbering 37 in a list of 1279.[1] Some 10 of these were outliers in Newdigate and Mickleham; others were the enclosures east of the Common Field called Colecrofte, Hameldones, Redelande and Paines Grove, and the homesteads or crofts called Apperley Hill, Wollandesdene and Pinchuns.[2] The rest, in the Common Field, amounted to two virgates, 10 half-virgates, and miscellaneous plots totalling 17½ acres. Since the Thorncroft virgate was estimated at 26 acres (in other words two of the old 13-acre holdings),[3] the Common Field evidently contained about 200 acres of Thorncroft tenant land.

Randalls

The main demesne of Little Pachenesham lay along the Mole, between Pachenesham and the town. It was broadly identical with the later Randalls estate: fields totalling 113 acres are listed in *c.* 1330,[4] of which Sevenacre, Kichenmede, la Bottes and la Bradmede, and possibly Mulcrofte, la Bethomeshulle and la Aldecote, can be identified in a Randalls survey of 1788.[5] As described previously (p. 35), other land of this manor derived from Margaret de Montfichet's grant: Bochard (Bockett Farm) and Apelderle in demesne, and Joyesfeld with about 93 common-field acres in the hands of tenants. Other small enclosures and some houses in the town, were held of various lords including those of Thorncroft and Pachenesham. The whole estate amounted to some 400 acres, and there was also a substantial flock: 172 sheep, 101 ewes, five rams and 50 lambs in 1327.[6] The servants paid at Little Pachenesham in 1328 were a drover, two shepherds, a man-servant and a maid.[7] John de Leatherhead and his heirs lived in some style; if not on a level with Hacche, Darcy or the scholars of Merton, they were the aristocrats of their local community.

The Glebe

Another early land-holding was the church glebe. When first founded, the parish church must have been endowed with Thorncroft land. The glebe comprised a block of enclosures south of the church, and common-field land totalling 44 acres when first recorded in 1599.[8] But the

[1] MM 5786ᵛ.
[2] These names appear in later documents, but can be identified with entries in the 1279 list by correlation of personal names and rents. Calcroft in *c.* 1275 (MM 5777c) is Cole Crofts on the 1629 map (MM 5.28); Hameldon Filde in *c.* 1530 (MM 5779c) is Hambledons in 1629; John le Rus's land in *c.* 1275 is Redefeld and Painsgrove in several later entries, and the same in 1629; Wollandesdene appears in 1333 (MM 5779) and 1629; for Apperley Hill see p. 37. For further references to some of these fields see MDLD 260–339.
[3] *EMS*, Ch. III.
[4] *Proc. LDLHS*, **3** (8), pp. 230–3.
[5] P.R.O. C54/6847.
[6] *Proc. LDLHS*, **3** (8), p. 238.
[7] Ibid.
[8] Terrier, Kent Archives Office CCRC T 213.

medieval rectors had little direct influence on the life of Leatherhead since they were absentees and clerks in the royal service until 1345.

The Common Field and the commons

Thus the lands of the manors still lay apart except when they were intermixed in the Common Field. It may be useful to summarise the tenurial composition of the Common Field, in so far as it can be reconstructed from all the various sources:

Manor	Number of acres	Percentage of total
Pachenesham	c. 90	11·9
Thorncroft demesne	c. 300?	39·5
Thorncroft tenants	200·5	26·4
Little Pachenesham (ex Montfichet)	93·75	12·4
Glebe	44	5·8
Unknown	30·5	4·0
	758·75	100

Since both the Little Pachenesham and the glebe holdings were originally formed out of Thorncroft, it appears that almost 90 per cent of the common-field land can be traced back to a Thorncroft origin. So the Common Field was not a fusion of manorial interests, but derived from one manor.

A further sign that township organisation did little to transcend the boundaries of lordship is the fact that each manor had its own commons. A memorandum of 1610 defines the clay to the north as 'a lower common for greate cattell in which every lord's soyle is bounded and knowen', and the Downs to the south as an 'upper common' for sheep where all the lords and their tenants can intercommon without stint.[1] The clay 'lower common' was divided into these blocks by 1300 at the latest, when Little Pachenesham had separate pasture there in la Hoke, la Upcrofte and le Brewer.[2] A perambulation of the Thorncroft common, carefully defining its boundaries between Ashtead eastwards and Pachenesham common westwards, was recorded in 1450/1451.[3] And if the Downs were free for all by 1610, they had not always been so. In 1300 Little Pachenesham had separate pasture on the areas called Kingsdown and Coledown, and its lord could claim that 'the

Walking around Thorncroft Common in 1450/1

Memorandum that the soil belonging to Merton Hall and lying in the west-heath as appurtenance unto the manor of Thorncroft in Leatherhead beginneth at Frothynges corner in the east; and so unto an hawthorn where stood a cross of old time, at the which cross both the processions of Leatherhead and Ashtead were wont to say their gospels in rogation days; and so from that cross into the broad cart-way between the woods, an acre's breadth and from the said cross, and down to the ditch to the end that cometh from Chessington park belonging to Merton Hall, and from Chessington again above Frothynges corner to the utter side of the Barnettes Close in the west; and there is a fair bound, a ditch, and from that ditch to rights to the ditch that lieth between the two Bayhursts in the north from Chessington.

[1] SAC, **xli**, 1933, p. 44.
[2] Proc. LDLHS, **3** (8), p. 232.
[3] Transcript on a rental of c. 1530, MM 5734.

47

people of Mickleham must not common on la Kyngsdone unless they make satisfaction to me, to Maurice de la Grave and to William de Oxenecrofte, for it is ours alone, and so I should have the third part of the fine which they pay for the use of that pasture'.[1]

Status, land-holding and manorial discipline

As usual in Surrey, this division of rights between independent manors meant that controls on the individual peasant were relatively light. Since no one manor represented the whole farming township, no one manor court could dictate township custom. Even in the Common Field, private enterprise had much reduced any early rigidity of holdings or services (see p. 47). Nor is there any evidence for rotations and cropping courses imposed by general agreement. The tenants of strips within each furlong were probably left to agree amongst themselves what crops they would grow from year to year.[2] On all the manors there were more free than villein tenants, and even the villeins were probably in a stronger position than their counterparts in other counties. There is a clear contrast between Thorncroft and, for example, Merton College's other manor of Cuxham in Oxfordshire, where almost all the tenants were villeins whose everyday lives and farming practice were strictly controlled by the manorial court.[3]

It would be wrong, though, to think that manorial discipline was unimportant. All farmers had their land from one or more of the manors, and owed something in return. This is why land was assessed in multiples or fractions of the virgate (*virgata* in Latin documents, 'yardland' in English), for within each manor all virgates may once have borne similar services. By the 1270s freeholders paid money rents which remained fixed thereafter (some of them into the 20th century), but unfree tenants owed labour services as well, and their rents were more fluid. The Thorncroft villeins were one virgater, six half-virgaters and one quarter-virgater, and there were also seven cottagers holding one acre each. The virgated holdings were burdened with a wide range of agricultural services and building maintenance works, whereas the cottagers' duties were mainly confined to the harvest.[4] On the other manors, services seem to have been light and fading away well before the Black Death. At Little Pachenesham in *c.* 1300, Serle le Mouner's villein half-virgate was well on the way to emancipation. He owed 2*s.*

[1] *Proc. LDLHS*, **3** (8), pp. 228–9, 231–2.
[2] *EMS*, Ch. III.
[3] Evans, 'Thorncroft and Cuxham'; P. D. A. Harvey, *A Medieval Oxfordshire Village* (Oxford, 1965).
[4] MM 5777d, analysed by Evans in 'Thorncroft and Cuxham'.

rent 'and must find a man in August every day so long as the lord needs to mow, and the lord will find food for him; and all his other services are remitted in return for land of his own which the lord has taken into his hand'.[1] While Merton College applied its standard policy of maintaining labour services, the other lords seem to have been content to relinquish them in return for land or rent.

The lord's will and the custom of the manor were enforced through the manorial court, which all tenants were supposed to attend. The most important official was the reeve, whose office gave him considerable influence in the manor. Between the 1270s and the 1320s the Thorncroft administration was dominated by Simon de Burford, who was frequently reeve, a regular adviser to Merton College, and tenant of the demesne between 1303 and 1306. Doubtless Burford was useful to the College, but he is a good example of a local official who probably took many opportunities to line his own pockets.[2] Junior to the reeve were the beadle and hayward, responsible for levying distraints and impounding straying animals. Their duties could be hazardous. In 1302, when the beadle visited an outlying villein holding on Mickleham Downs to distrain for non-payment of rent, the tenant threw stones 'and did other enormities to him'.[3]

The officials drew a firm line between free and unfree ('customary') tenants, for the latter were subject to a much wider range of controls. Customary land followed the 'Borough English' custom of inheritance by the youngest son, and its tenants, unlike freeholders, had little scope to vary this custom. If one of them died without heirs, his holding reverted to the lord and was usually granted to some member of another villein family.[4] Merton's policy at Thorncroft was to maintain customary holdings as the economic basis of a distinct villein class; so anything which tended to blur the line, such as the acquisition of free land by villeins or vice versa, was discouraged. Since the court had a considerable capacity to control by means of fines and distraints, status on the manor was still important in determining social status. But the forces of change were too strong for landlords' conservative policies, and gradually the distinctions which they strove to maintain were eroded.

The land-market and social change, 1250–1350

By 1300, manorial tenure is a very poor guide to Surrey freeholders'

[1] *Proc. LDLHS,* **3** (8), pp. 224–5.
[2] This summary of Burford's career is based on Evans, 'Thorncroft and Cuxham'. The demesne lease to him is MDLD 88.
[3] MM 5781 m. 20.
[4] Evans, 'Thorncroft and Cuxham'.

Seals. From the top:
John the Smith, *c.* 1240 (MDLD91, Merton College).
William Viel of Oxencroft, *c.* 1250 (MDLD93, Merton College).
John de Aperdele, 1323 (MDLD101, Merton College).
John son of Elias atte Crouche, 1316 (MDLD274, PRO).
William Randolf, 1379 (MDLD223, PRO).

actual wealth and status. An expanding land-market had fragmented and recombined the old virgated holdings into farms which owed little to manorial custom. Lords, anxious to maintain this custom and the rights which it brought them, still organised their records in accordance with the old divisions. So in a multi-manor community such as Leatherhead, the historian is easily misled. A man who appears in one rental as the humble tenant of half an acre may hold 50 acres elsewhere.

The Surrey market in free land was unusually well developed, and by 1300 had been active for a century or more.[1] This explains the condition of Thorncroft tenements revealed in a rental of 1332. The old 13-acre freeholds in the Common Field had been redistributed in tiny fractions between numerous tenants, more than half of whom held five acres or less. Several new holdings combined fragments of old ones: Gilbert le Glovere had supplemented his compact half-virgate with parcels from the former virgates of Chereburgh, Dru and Boxe, not to mention a messuage and 1½ acres from another virgate held of Little Pachenesham.[2]

In fact, the old notion of intact tenements carrying rights and obligations had been negated by piecemeal sales which paid mere lip-service to manorial custom. The mechanics are described in an entry in the Little Pachenesham rental of *c.* 1300, which begins: 'William le Shepherd holds of the King's fee 3 acres of land in Tibeliesdene and 1½ acres in Shortedene, and on le Whithehulle 3 acres of land. And he has sold of the same free 3½ acres of land lying in a place called la Rudene to William le Pestour [Baker] and Gilbert le Bekere, and 3 acres of land lying on Barerse to Henry Littlewyne and Bartholomew Viron, and 3 acres of land to Richard le Tannere . . .'.[3] The complete entry describes the breakup of some 30 acres between nine tenants. Deeds show one of these men, William le Pestour, acquiring further strips in the Common Field and tenements in the town during 1280–1300 – a process continued by his heir, another William, up to 1345.[4]

The best-recorded case of consistent long-term accumulation is that of the Headley freeholder Richard atte Leghe.[5] Starting with a small estate which his father John had built up in Headley, Walton-on-the-Hill and Epsom, Richard made a long series of small purchases in the adjoining parts of Leatherhead, Ashtead and Headley parishes over some 40 years from the early 1290s. In Leatherhead he concentrated his efforts on the enclosed land east of the Common Field, where the closes called Sepehale, Little Colecrofte, Pinchonesfelde, Pinchonesgrove, Hameldonesfeld, Ponshurstefeld and part of Joyesfeld passed successively into his hands. In 1317 he began acquiring acres and half-acres in Ashtead south common field, and throughout his active life he was slowly building up land in his native Headley. By 1335 he had amassed an estate of at least 70 arable acres, not counting his father's holdings. The impression is of a fair-sized Downland farm, much of it compact and the rest lying within a mile's radius, which could also have supported a sheep flock on the fallow and the surrounding chalk pastures.

All this applies to free land; restraints on villein holdings were much greater. Tenants were forbidden to alienate them in whole or part without their lord's consent, which for obvious reasons was rarely granted. But loopholes could be found. In the early 14th century temporary leases of unfree land were regularly made at both Pachenesham and Thorncroft, either officially (in which case a licence fee was charged) or illicitly (in which case a fine was imposed on discovery).[6] The tighter manorial control meant that customary holdings remained ostensibly more or less intact until the Black Death, but the actual pattern of occupation may have been very different.

The families

Some families rose, other fell. Old names such as Punsherst, Oxencroft and Bradmere fade away during the early 14th century; the piecemeal sale of the ancient Punsherst farm during 1300–1320 is especially well recorded.[7] Other old families, the d'Abernons of Stoke, for instance,[8] bought to consolidate existing holdings. The de Aperdeles, leading local men since the 12th century, now seem more important than ever, constantly buying and selling land in association with their Mickleham relatives, the de Newenhams.[9] The early 14th-century John de Aperdele was a royal bailiff and seneschal of Merton College's Surrey manors, and his son was a scholar at Merton.[10] John and Roger de Aperdele were easily the biggest Leatherhead taxpayers in 1332[11] and Roger's status is emphasised by the perpetual chantry which he founded in Leatherhead church, frustrated after his death through lack of funds.[12] What seems to be this family's swan-song is a grant by William Aperdele in 1366 of a house, 38 acres and 13s. 4d. rent in

[1] For the background see *EMS*, Ch. III; for a good local example see *Fitznells Cartulary*, eds. C. A. F. Meekings and P. Shearman (Surrey Rec. Soc. xxvi, 1968).

[2] *Proc. LDLHS*, **3** (8), p. 226.

[3] Ibid., p. 228.

[4] MDLD 207–22.

[5] MDLD 260–339.

[6] *Proc. LDLHS*, **2** (6), p. 174; MM 5781 m.3, and numerous Thorncroft court rolls.

[7] MDLD 215–22, 227–40, 260–82.

[8] MDLD 15–25.

[9] For instance MDLD 143–53. For the Aperdeles also *VCH Surrey*, **iii**, 297.

[10] Evans, 'Thorncroft and Cuxham'; A. B. Emden, *A Biographical Register of the University of Oxford to AD 1500* (Oxford, 1957–9), **i**, p. 39.

[11] *Surrey Taxation Returns*, Surrey Rec. Soc. pt. xxiii, 1932, p. 76.

[12] MDLD 106.

Leatherhead to Kilburn Nunnery,[1] creating the later 'manor of the Minchin'.

Most other names of the 1320s and 1330s are new: Gilbert le Hore, John Hayward, John Faulkes, Gilbert le Glovere, Nicholas Cornmonger, John de Wolvestone, John Payne and many others.[2] They appear time and time again in deeds and court-roll entries, though their families were unknown or of little account before 1280. These men belonged to a new, broad yeoman class who were neither gentry nor peasants. They held and farmed land on patterns which they had worked out for themselves, and as well as land they had draught beasts and large sheep flocks.[3] If Leatherhead society had changed much since the early 13th century, it was still notably free and prosperous.

After the Black Death

Economic history, unlike political history, has few precise dates; but one is the late summer of 1348 when bubonic plague arrived in England. The first and most savage epidemic, the Black Death of 1348–1350 killed perhaps a third of the inhabitants of England. Later attacks reduced the population to something like half its pre-plague level by 1377, and no long-term recovery came until the 1460s. So for over a century labour was scarce, wages high and prices stagnant. Effects on the landscape and its exploitation were profound. Landlords had to adjust to a harder world, while better and better opportunities opened for the more fortunate peasants.[4]

For Surrey this general picture needs some modification. On the one hand the rise of a rural 'middle class' was already far advanced by 1350. On the other hand, in such 'wood–pasture' areas agriculture and settlement had to adjust less drastically to the new economic scene than in the open, grain-producing Midland zones.

Surrey had never developed the dangerous concentration on labour-intensive cereals. It still had plenty of sheep, pigs, cattle, fruit and timber, all of which needed fewer hands to tend them. Change there was, but much of it an acceleration of changes already in the air.

Removal of direct seigneurial control

A trend which did affect Leatherhead was the withdrawal of manorial lords from direct control of their demesne lands. As labour problems

---

[1] P.R.O. C143/356; *Cal. Pat. R. 1364–7*, pp. 124–5.

[2] All in 1332 subsidy: *Surrey Taxation Returns*, p. 76.

[3] Knowledge of these flocks depends on casual references. See lists of animals impounded at Pachenesham, *Proc. LDLHS*, **4** (1), pp. 12–18. In 1356 Walter le Hore was fined for trespass with 200 sheep in the Thorncroft demesne pasture (MM 5791). The Thorncroft accounts occasionally note the hiring of sheep to manure the demesne, including 120 sheep from John le Heyward and 420 from Gilbert Burgey in 1343/4 (MM 5758), and 160 from Gilbert Burgey and 90 from William le Baker in 1344/5 (MM 5724) . These references from Ralph Evans.

[4] For the general background J. L. Bolton, *The Medieval English Economy 1150–1500* (London, 1980), Chs. 7–8; Platt, *Medieval England*, Chs. 4–6.

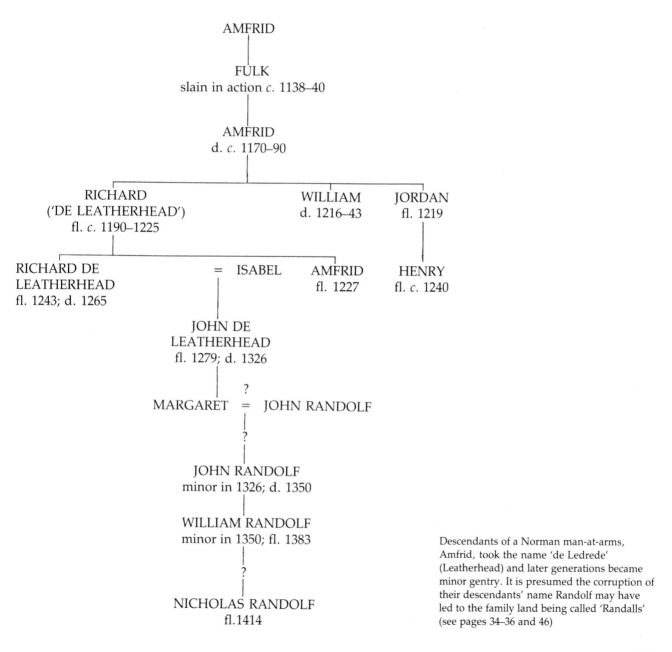

AMFRID

FULK
slain in action *c.* 1138–40

AMFRID
d. *c.* 1170–90

RICHARD ('DE LEATHERHEAD') fl. *c.* 1190–1225   WILLIAM d. 1216–43   JORDAN fl. 1219

RICHARD DE LEATHERHEAD fl. 1243; d. 1265   = ISABEL   AMFRID fl. 1227   HENRY fl. *c.* 1240

JOHN DE LEATHERHEAD fl. 1279; d. 1326

?
MARGARET = JOHN RANDOLF
?

JOHN RANDOLF
minor in 1326; d. 1350

WILLIAM RANDOLF
minor in 1350; fl. 1383

?

NICHOLAS RANDOLF
fl.1414

Descendants of a Norman man-at-arms, Amfrid, took the name 'de Ledrede' (Leatherhead) and later generations became minor gentry. It is presumed the corruption of their descendants' name Randolf may have led to the family land being called 'Randalls' (see pages 34–36 and 46)

Sir Ivo Fizwarren, 1414, a brass on the north chapel wall of Wantage Church.

grew, estate management ceased to be worth the bother. It was easier to negotiate a reasonable yearly rent with a local man who could tackle the problems on the spot and reap the rewards, if any, of his diligence. Thus the aristocrat of late medieval village society was the yeoman with enough cash to take on such a lease and become a 'demesne farmer'. The Thorncroft demesne was leased from 1361, when the account-rolls cease. Drawing a fixed rent, the fellows of Merton College had no further interest in the details of profit and loss. But they took good care that the buildings and capital stock were well maintained, and Thorncroft may have operated as efficiently under Merton's farmers as it had under Merton.

At Pachenesham the story is very different. It is one of discord and dereliction. Care may have been poor during Robert Darcy's later years, since at his death in 1343 the manor-house was said to be 'worth nothing', and it seems that the demesne was already leased out by 1347 (not surprisingly to Roger de Aperdele).[1] Darcy's heir was his son-in-law Sir John d'Argentein, succeeded in 1383 by his own son-in-law Sir Ivo Fitzwarren.[2] In 1386 Fitzwarren and his wife leased the manor-house and demesne for £20 yearly to one William Wimbledon, a newcomer who was to build up wide local interests.

This was a mistake, for like many such tenants, Wimbledon had no links with the manor and his interests were purely financial. In 1393 he defaulted on the rent, and during the consequent litigation the Fitzwarrens claimed that he had dismantled a hall, two chambers, a chapel, two barns, two watermills, two byres, a hay-house and a dovecote to sell the timber, and had felled 110 trees. In fact, the jury found that he had done far less damage; but whether or not he should be blamed for the destruction of the manor-house, it had been reduced to a mere 'site' by the time of Fitzwarren's death in 1414.[3] In any case Wimbledon was a quarrelsome associate, who disrupted the manorial courts and withheld services from a Pachenesham tenement more than 20 years after the lawsuit.[4]

After the Wimbledon affair the Pachenesham demesne was divided up piecemeal between 12 lessees, producing rents of some £11 10s. for the land and meadow, and £4 for the mill, until after 1475.[5] Thus the demesne ceased to exist as a working farm until 1494/1495, when it seems to have been leased as a unit at a £14 rent.[6] With a series of absentee lords[7] and without a manor-house, Pachenesham manor can have meant little to the people of 15th-century Leatherhead.

The Little Pachenesham family survived into the 15th century, though John Randolf himself died in 1349 (presumably of plague) leaving his son William, then a minor.[8] By 1383 William had leased the Bockett Farm demesne to Nicholas Slyfield[9] though keeping direct control of the fields around his house at Pachenesham. The Randolfs seem to have had lawless tendencies. In 1380 William was outlawed for an armed robbery at Oxford, and some 30 years later his heir Nicholas Randolf was accused of menacing one Lawrence West so that he feared for his life.[10]

Most other pre-plague families – even the Aperdeles – had vanished from the Leatherhead scene by 1400. The Leghs, however, continued to rise, first, in 1393, leasing and later buying an accumulation, similar to their own, which had been built up by Laurence le Wyght in Leatherhead and Headley.[11] The combined Legh–Wyght holding was now substantial, and when the Leghs moved to Addington soon after 1400 it acquired the character of a manorial demesne farmed out to local husbandmen.[12]

The new gentry families

Leading families of Tudor and Stuart Leatherhead start to appear during the 15th century. Most seem to begin with outsiders who bought their way in piecemeal, gradually acquiring holdings on the various manors. The Pachenesham rentals of 1418, 1474/1475 and 1509 show a tendency for old smallholdings to become progressively more concentrated into fewer gentry hands.[13] Thus William Wimbledon founded a family which, though based at Norbury Park in Mickleham, appear regularly as Thorncroft and Pachenesham tenants until 1498 when his great-grandson's inheritance passed to the Stydolfs.[14] Thereafter the Stydolfs became more and more important in Leatherhead, and had acquired the whole lordship of Pachenesham by Queen Elizabeth's reign.[15] Other familiar names from the years 1450–1530 are John Rypingden (lessee of the Rectory in 1470),[16] John Trevelyan,[17] and John Richardson (lessee of Thorncroft during 1510 and one of the two biggest taxpayers in 1524).[18] The Skeets, who first appear in 1454, had acquired a major interest in Thorncroft and Pachenesham holdings by 1500.[19] The Randolf estate passed eventually to the Sands family of Shere, who were settled at Randalls by the

A Leatherhead miracle in 1392
'At Leatherhead a fire ran from one part of the town to another, and, leaping over certain houses, consumed almost the whole town, except for those houses which the fire crossed in a leap and which were thus miraculously saved from burning.'

RANULPH HIGDEN'S *Chronicle*

[1] *Proc. LDLHS*, **3** (9), p. 292; **I** (6), p. 19.
[2] *Proc. LDLHS*, **I** (6), pp. 16–19.
[3] *Proc. LDLHS*, **I** (1), pp. 10–11; **I** (2), p. 10; **3** (9), p. 294.
[4] British Library, Add. Ch. 27759; cf. *Proc. LDLHS*, **3** (10), pp. 333, 336.
[5] *Proc. LDLHS*, **3** (10), pp. 335–6, 340.
[6] *Proc. LDLHS*, **3** (10), p. 340.
[7] *Proc. LDLHS*, **I** (6), p. 19.
[8] MM 5791.
[9] *Proc. LDLHS*, **3** (9), p. 272.
[10] P.R.O. C88/52 (121); P.R.O. Cl/4/5.
[11] MDLD 257–9.
[12] Leases of 1428 and 1541: MDLD 330, 338.
[13] *Proc. LDLHS*, **3** (10), pp. 329–46.
[14] *Proc. LDLHS*, **i** (8), p. 15; **4** (4), p. 98; MDLD 124–5, 127. Wimbledon family holdings *Proc. LDLHS*, **3** (10), pp. 329–46; MM 5778 (annotation to 1333 rental).
[15] *Proc. LDLHS*, **2** (3), p. 80.
[16] *Proc. LDLHS*, **2** (4), p. 103; also MM 5778 and 5779c, and *Proc. LDLHS*, **3** (10), pp. 341–2.
[17] *Proc. LDLHS*, **3** (10), pp. 336–40, 344; MDLD 34, 89.
[18] MM 5731; P.R.O. E179/184/143; *Proc. LDLHS*, **3** (10), p. 341.
[19] MM 5779c; *Proc. LDLHS*, **3** (10), pp. 336–40, 341–2; cf. *Proc. LDLHS*, **2** (1), p. 7f.

Etching of the Old Vicarage in 1821 by Harriet Dallaway.

1540s.[1] Another leading family begins with Walter Rogers, the other biggest taxpayer in 1524 and probably lessee of the Rectory. He may have leased Pachenesham too, for in 1550 he is described as 'farmar to Mr Stiddall'.[2] Thus the gentry families of Elizabethan Leatherhead grew out of the old order, both as engrossers of smallholdings and as demesne farmers.

Social change and peasant prosperity

For lesser families too there were wide opportunities. As depopulation left holdings vacant, land became easier to acquire. In the long run, the plague emancipated unfree tenants from the disabilities of their status. Lords found themselves forced to let vacant villein holdings at simple cash rents, and eventually to remit the services of the villeins themselves. Old ties were broken, and formal assessment in virgates was soon replaced by a looser designation of land as 'so-and-so's tenement'. Thus in 1354 Merton College let three Thorncroft customary holdings in Mickleham, called 'Brounestenements', 'Boxereslond' and 'Burfordeslond', to one man on a six-year lease.[3] Eventually the term 'villein' was replaced by the more dignified 'copyholder' (meaning that the tenant possessed a copy of the court-roll entry recording his admission). At Pachenesham all labour services had ceased by 1418, and by 1530 the only trace at Thorncroft was the residual duty of a day's harvesting attached to a couple of holdings.[4]

Yeomen and husbandmen had wide freedom in how they farmed their holdings and managed their crops. It was still usual to have flocks as well as land: thus John Gerard, lessee of the Legh estate in 1428, was accused in 1434 of wrongfully recovering 80 sheep from the lord of Thorncroft's pinfold.[5] Leases of the Legh farm in 1428 and 1541[6] both stipulate the yearly planting of apple- and pear-trees by the tenant – a reminder that 'the art of horticulture and fruit-growing had . . . already made Surrey a land of gardens'.[7]

One important change was the decay of the bond village at Pachenesham. A survey of c. 1380 lists six holdings there north of Gutters Bridge. Two men held 10 acres each, but two others, Robert Camponeye and Roger Blake, had 20-acre holdings, Robert's still containing two houses.[8] Clearly the old 10-acre units were being amalgamated in fewer hands. The destruction of the nearby manor-house must have hastened decay. In 1472 a Pachenesham jury found

[1] *Proc. LDLHS*, **2** (3), pp. 77–9.
[2] MM 5780.
[3] MM 5791.
[4] *Proc. LDLHS*, **3** (10), pp. 334–5; MM 5734.
[5] MDLD 330; MM 5792.
[6] MDLD 330, 338.
[7] Brandon, *History of Surrey*, p. 42.
[8] *Proc. LDLHS*, **3** (9), pp. 296–7.

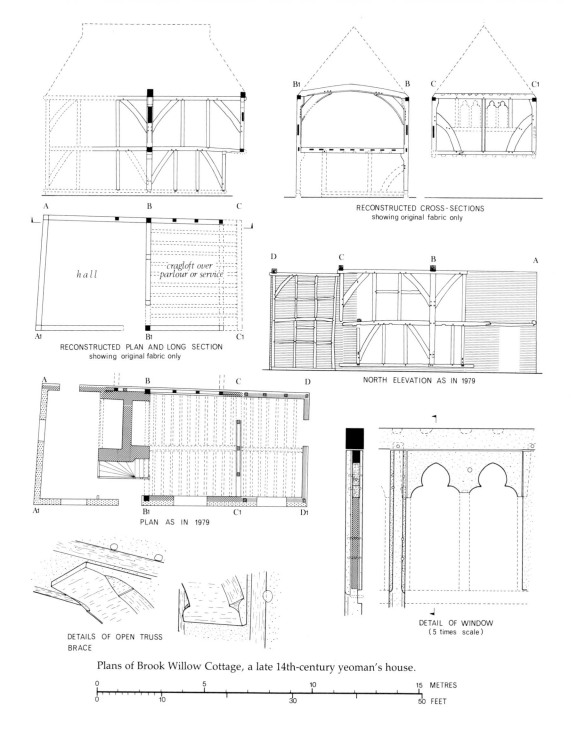

RECONSTRUCTED CROSS-SECTIONS
showing original fabric only

A B C

hall

*cragloft over
parlour or service*

A1 B1 C1

RECONSTRUCTED PLAN AND LONG SECTION
showing original fabric only

D C B A

NORTH ELEVATION AS IN 1979

A B C D

A1 B1 C1 D1

PLAN AS IN 1979

DETAILS OF OPEN TRUSS
BRACE

DETAIL OF WINDOW
(5 times scale)

Plans of Brook Willow Cottage, a late 14th-century yeoman's house.

0   5   10   15 METRES
0   10   30   50 FEET

57

The Vicar of Leatherhead's possessions in 1557

3 beds and fittings	£4. 12.	8
2 chests and a counter table	£1. 0.	0
2 chairs and 2 joint-stools	3.	4
a gown lined with fox-fur	£2. 13.	4
2 gowns lined	£2. 0.	0
2 jackets and 2 doublets	£1. 0.	8
2 pairs of hose	6.	0
3 pairs of sheets	12.	0
a diaper table-cloth	6.	0
a table-cloth	4.	0
2 towels	6.	0
3 table napkins	2.	0
certain old books	–	
2 pots	13.	4
2 pewter pots	2.	4
a brass pot	6.	8
2 kettles	6.	0
24 pewter platters, dishes		
and saucers	16.	0
2 spits with 'coupe'-irons	4.	8
6 latten candlesticks	6.	0
a salt-cellar		6
11 silver spoons	£1. 5.	0
a horse	£1. 0.	0
a cow	£1. 0.	0
3 wether sheep	10.	0
3 ewe sheep	7.	0
Cash	£51. 0.	0
	£71. 4.	2

1 *Proc. LDLHS*, **4** (1), p. 18.
2 *Proc. LDLHS*, **4** (1), pp. 345–6; cf. list of the same holdings in 1418, ibid., pp. 334–5.
3 J. Blair, 'A small fourteenth century cragloft house at Leatherhead, Surrey', *Antiquaries Journal*, **lxi** (2), 1981, pp. 328–31.
4 J. H. Harvey, 'Great Milton, Oxfordshire, and Thorncroft, Surrey', *Journal of British Archaeol. Assoc.*, 3rd ser., **xviii**, 1955, pp. 42–56.
5 W. J. Blair, 'The will of Robert Russell, Vicar of Leatherhead', *Proc. LDLHS*, **3** (8), pp. 244–5.

that they had no cucking-stool, and that the pillory, the stocks and the bridge called 'Goodryche bryge' were utterly ruined through the lord's neglect.[1] By 1509, when the holdings were mostly fragmented or held by absentees,[2] the small village of Robert Darcy's day had dwindled to the three or four farmhouses which still stand near the junction of the Stoke and Oxshott roads.

Fewer tenants meant more land to go round, and more land meant more cash, hence rich peasants started to live in better houses. A relic of these years is a little timber-framed house at Pachenesham (now Brook Willow Farm Cottage) which must have been built on land of the decaying village.[3] Originally it had an open hall, an enclosed lower room, and a first-floor chamber open to the hall through a massive arched truss. The other end of the chamber was jettied out and had a finely carved window. The carpentry, probably late 14th century, is of a high quality although the planning is by contrast crude, for the upper room must have filled with smoke from the hall fire. Was this the home of a newly rich peasant (perhaps Robert Camponeye or Roger Blake), able to afford good materials and craftsmen but wedded to the primitive house-types of his ancestors?

From the late 15th century the population of England rose again and an expanding economy brought new material comforts for all but the poorest. Looking back, Elizabethan observers remembered an increase in personal goods and an improvement of housing. This was the age of the 'Great Rebuilding', when open halls were equipped with chimneys and floored over to provide smoke-free houses and more private rooms.

In 1497 a new timber manor-house was built at Thorncroft, and the accounts show that it had two brick chimneys and a 'loft' over the hall.[4] In farmhouses the open hall survived for another generation, as at the 'Running Horse' (see p. 64); the crosswing of 'Rowhurst', Pachenesham, may have accompanied such a hall.

The old Vicarage, with an upper chamber jettied over Vicarage Lane, was probably built in these years: perhaps by Robert Russell, vicar from 1510 to 1557, whose inventory well illustrates the rising prosperity.[5] Admittedly he was wealthy man by contemporary local standards, but it is doubtful if one of his predecessors a century earlier would have had so many possessions. Russell's inventory symbolises the transition from medieval to early modern Leatherhead.

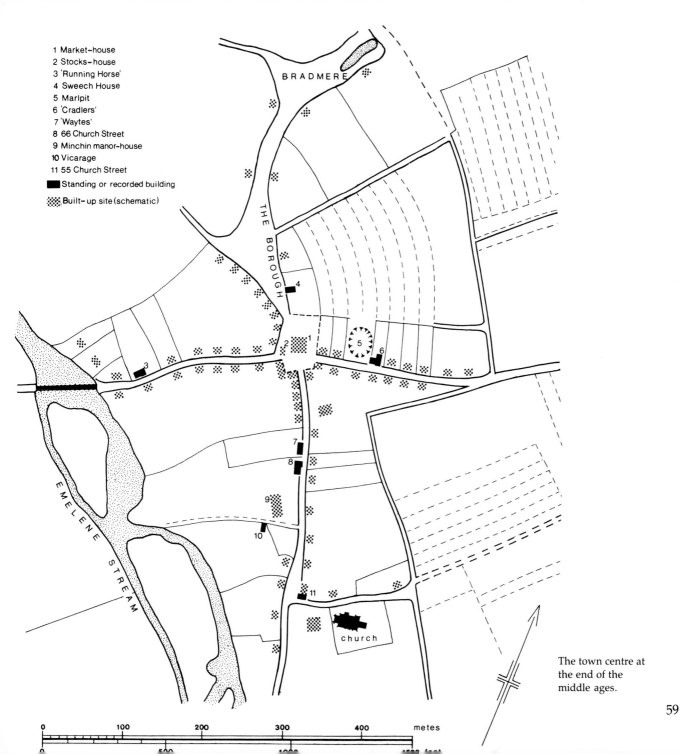

1 Market-house
2 Stocks-house
3 'Running Horse'
4 Sweech House
5 Marlpit
6 'Cradlers'
7 'Waytes'
8 66 Church Street
9 Minchin manor-house
10 Vicarage
11 55 Church Street

■ Standing or recorded building

▨ Built-up site (schematic)

BRADMERE

THE BOROUGH

EMELENE STREAM

church

The town centre at
the end of the
middle ages.

59

0   100   200   300   400   metes

The late medieval town

At the heart of the farming community, both geographically and socially, were the town and its market. Leatherhead has always hovered on the urban borderline, scarcely bigger than such villages as Great Bookham and Cobham, yet marked out as a small town by the special character of its inhabitants and buildings.

Probably the planned town always had a bridge across the Mole. In the 1280s it was said to be maintained 'by the alms of the neighbourhood',[1] and a plot of land at the west end of Bridge Street, between the 'Running Horse' and the river, is described in *c*. 1285 as a tenement 'built at the bridge in the town of Leatherhead'.[2] In 1361 alms were being collected for repairing Leatherhead bridge, and in 1418 an acre in the Common Field was held by the bridge wardens.[3] The Georgian brickwork encases the remains of a medieval stone bridge of 14 arches with chamfered vaulting-ribs.[4]

The town plan is a simple one, based on four main streets meeting at a crossroads. Its extent by *c*. 1300 was evidently no less than at any time before the 19th century. The upper end of North Street, now Gravel Hill, was known throughout the middle ages as the 'Berghe' or 'Borough', and tenements are recorded here before 1300.[5] This could preserve memories of a small Anglo-Saxon fortification (*burh*), though the term was sometimes used in the 12th and 13th centuries for newly planned urban streets. Further north, at the foot of Bull Hill, was Bradmere, home of the family of that name. Simon le Wyte of Bradmere had a house there in the early 14th century.[6] Southwards, the built-up area extended as far as Church Road, where Robert atte Canoune held a tenement at some date before 1418.[7]

The house-plots on the north side of the High Street are strikingly regular. The block may have originated as a common-field furlong containing 13 slightly curved strips of equal width, adapted in the medieval town to make a series of regular tenements fronting on the street. In at least five cases the house and garden were held in the early post-medieval period by the same tenant as the Common Field acre strip abutting its northern end.[8] Most of these plots had houses, but a marlpit (the Swan Pit, obliterated in 1980 by the new shopping-centre) occupied two tenements' width on the street frontage. This may have been the same 'marlyngput' which faced a house held of Pachenesham manor in 1418.[9] By 1629, the pit was disused and contained the com-

[1] 'Per elemosinam patrie'; verdict of Copthorne Hundred jurors, P.R.O. JUST 1/892.

[2] This property was split in two. The deeds granting the northern tenement are MDLD 98–9; its position, and the constant 1*s*. rent, enable it to be traced to modern times. In *c*. 1285 it was held by Richard le Gos, and its later name 'Cradlers' (not to be confused with 'Cradlers' in High Street) derives from John Cradler to whom it was leased in 1414 (MDLD 102). At a court of 3 February 1324 (MM 5781 m.7d) Gilbert Fuller was admitted to 'a cottage at the head of the bridge adjoining the tenement of Richard le Gos'.

[3] *Cal. Pat. R. 1361–4*, 19; *Proc. LDLHS*, 3 (10), p. 333.

[4] D. F. Renn, 'The old bridge at Leatherhead', *Proc. LDLHS*, 3 (6), pp. 165–7; 'The date of the first Leatherhead bridge', *Proc. LDLHS*, 3 (5), pp. 153–4.

[5] Adjacent tenements of Roger Suterich, William de Clendone and William de Ewelle on la Berghe are recorded in *c*. 1280–1300 (MDLD 27; *Proc. LDLHS*, 3 (8), p. 228), and in 1392 Richard Ware of Leatherhead leased a tenement at 'le Berghe de Ledrede' between the road [i.e. Gravel Hill] west, Leatherhead common field, [i.e. the Fairfield] east, and a tenement of William Lude north (MDLD 242).

[6] British Library, MS Add. 5836 f. 147.

[7] Pachenesham rental, 1418: a tenement opposite Leatherhead church once of Robert atte Canoune (*Proc. LDLHS*, 3 (10), p. 330). In the same rental, John Squyer holds a house and 1 acre next Leatherhead church.

[8] *Proc. LDLHS*, 3 (9), p. 311, note 3.

[9] *Proc. LDLHS*, 3 (10), p. 334 (MM 5.28 f.29).

ROBERTVS CHESEMAN .
ANNO . DM

. ETATIS . SVÆ . XLVIII
M . D . XXXIII .

Robert Cheseman (1485–1547) was the son of Edward Cheseman, Cofferer to Henry VII and Henry VIII. Both father and son were royal servants; Robert was one of 120 squires who met Anne of Cleves when she came to marry the king, and as a justice he served on the grand jury at the trial of Katherine Howard and Cardinal Wolsey. In this portrait by Hans Holbein the Younger, the hooded falcon on his wrist implies he was Yeoman Falconer to Henry VIII. He married as his second wife, Alice Dacres, sister of Robert Dacres, a Master of Request. It is possible that at one time Cheseman lived in The Mansion given to him by Henry VIII at the time of the Dissolution of the Priory of Kilburn, who owned it. There is no mention of the house in his will but he did leave an annuity to his sister who was an ex-nun of Kilburn Priory.

Paul Kirwan, *History of the Borough of Southall*,
F. B. Benger, 'Robert Cheseman', *Proc. LDLHS*, **2** (9), 1965, p. 252.

mon sheep pens. Marl (chalk) was vital for enriching the often heavy soils of Leatherhead, and farmers would have carted it to their fields from this open pit in the High Street.

The market-place

It is a long-forgotten fact that Leatherhead once had a market-place. A deed of *c.* 1280 grants to Merton College the rent from 'a certain messuage of the fee of Henry Pinchon which is built between a tenement of Richard Leygat and a tenement of Luke the Tailor in the town of Leatherhead, and . . . a certain shop adjoining the said messuage on the north side'.[1] This shop can be traced through the College estate records and identified with the shop site at the east end of Bridge Street, described in mid-14th century rentals as lying 'within the market-place'.[2] The *6d.* rent paid in 1285 remained constant until recent times. This shows that the medieval market-place was at the central crossroads, perhaps with buildings set back at the street corners and grouped around it. The Merton deed suggests that the shop projected northwards from a building recessed in relation to the Bridge Street frontage.

In 1673, John Aubrey wrote that the market 'hath been discontinued now about an hundred yeares. The Markett-house was remayning here within these fifty yeares.'[3] By analogy with other small towns, this market-house was probably late medieval and built in an existing open market-place. It seems the most likely explanation for the peculiar staggering of the central crossroads. Post-medieval infilling might have incorporated a previously free-standing hall at the present High Street–North Street corner, thus causing Church Street and North Street to be offset in relation to each other. Elias Allen's map of 1629 does in fact show an exceptionally large building on this site, against which the Swan Inn[4] seems to have been built shortly afterwards.

Two other public buildings appear in late medieval sources. The stocks house, first mentioned as a 'tenement called le Stokhous' held of Pachenesham by John Benet in 1418, was a small free-standing building in the market-place. It appeared on the 1629 and 1783 maps and was rebuilt in brick in the 17th century.[5] A reference in 1509 to 'a plot of land next le Chirchehall'[6] reveals the existence of a communal hall for meetings and festivities such as 'parish ales'. Common in

[1] MDLD 95.

[2] The *6d.* rent paid in *c.* 1285 remained constant until recent times. In 1333 (rental, MM 5778), Richard Moriz held 'j schopam in villa de Leddr' citra for' plac'' for *6d.* (with later marginal insertion 'Robert Gerland'). In 1527 (rental, MM 5734) 'Robert Garland holdith one shoppe . . . agaynste the tenement of the foresaide Robert on the est parte and buttes upon the common waye ledynge betwyne London and Guyldford' for *6d.*, which can be traced through to the 'parcel of land where a shop heretofore was . . . on the south part of the West Street in Leatherhead' to which William Hall was admitted in 1778 at *6d.* quit-rent (MM 5.5 p. 65). This was part of the corner site (incorporating the present Westminster Bank and 5 Bridge Street) which William Hall held in 1782 (Gwilt Survey, parcel 535).

[3] Oxford, Bodleian Library, MS Aubrey 4 f. 53.

[4] First mentioned in 1637 (*Proc. LDLHS*, **2** (2), p. 47).

[5] *Proc. LDLHS*, **3** (10), p. 330; *Proc. LDLHS*, **2** (5), p. 128 for drawing.

[6] *Proc. LDLHS*, **3** (10), p. 342.

This tantalising photograph taken about 1900 looking up North Street from the central crossroads shows part of the Swan Inn on the right. It is clearly a late medieval building with jetties facing both the High Street and North Street. Could it have been the old market hall?

Cradlers

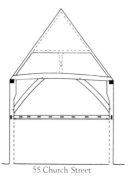

55 Church Street

Running Horse

Cross-sections through chamber ranges of three late medieval Leatherhead houses.

medieval England, such halls often disappeared at the Reformation, and in Leatherhead even the site has been lost.

Farmhouses and shops

The town seems to have contained a mixture of farmhouses and shops. On the one hand, yeomen farming in and around Leatherhead often lived in the town: thus in 1414 Merton College leased its holding by Leatherhead bridge to John Cradler, who was to build an adequate house there within 18 months.[1] On the other hand, late medieval sources mention shops. Reference has already been made to one on the Bridge Street/Church Street corner in 1280, and at about the same date Gilbert Sutor granted a shop in Leatherhead between houses of Thomas Messor and Henry le Polere.[2] A shop 'next the cross of Leatherhead', formerly held by John le Chapman, is mentioned in 1319.[3] 'Newly built corner shops' in le Chirchelane (Church Road) were held of Pachenesham in 1418, and the same rental mentions an empty plot formerly built on with a tenement and shop.[4]

Of surviving buildings, much the most interesting is 33/35 High Street ('Cradlers'), a copyhold of Thorncroft.[5] Carpentry details in its timber frame suggest a 14th-century date. The main range, at right-angles to the street, is of three bays: perhaps a shop on the frontage, a service room in the middle, and a kitchen or private hall behind. Upstairs was a big two-bay chamber; a smaller one at the back covered half the hall/kitchen, leaving the other half open for smoke from the fire to rise to an outlet in the roof. At right-angles to the main range, along the street frontage, was another open hall. As well as this unusual provision of two halls, the alignment of the main range suggests a distinctively urban need to make best use of the precious frontage.

55 Church Street[6] (on the corner of Church Road) is also set end-on to the main street, over which it is jettied. It is of two bays, spanned upstairs by an open truss. This may simply be the crosswing of a destroyed open hall, but there remains the interesting possibility that it repeats the primitive form of Brook Willow Farm Cottage (see p. 57): a hall behind, open both to the roof and to a chamber over the front bay. Perhaps there was also a shop on the ground-floor. Given its location, this might be one of the 'newly built corner shops' of 1418.

The 'Running Horse'[7] in Bridge Street, built on glebeland of

Leatherhead church, has a rather squat open hall aligned on the street and spanned by a moulded truss. The two-bay crosswing, jettied over the street, has an impressive upper chamber with an open truss matching the hall. It seems unlikely that the 'Running Horse' was built as an inn: to all appearances it is a high-quality private house of 1450–1550.

At Sweech House,[8] Gravel Hill, the south range seems to represent a complete small house, with smoke blackening in the roof as evidence for an open hall. This to was aligned end-on to the street, perhaps recalling a time when the east side of the 'Borough' was built up like an urban frontage. So if only 'Cradlers' is distinctively urban, all these four buildings are, for their various reasons, slightly different from ordinary village houses. Such as it is, the architectural evidence supports the impression of a community part agricultural, part commercial.

Craftsmen, tradesmen and farmers

Identifying the people is less easy. With a complex settlement pattern, it is rarely clear who lived in the town and who in the countryside around it. Leatherhead's urban character cannot be defined in constitutional terms, for it had no borough charter or corporate rights. For its trade and industry there is no direct evidence, and the only guide is an analysis of the occupational surnames borne by local people in the 13th and 14th centuries. This is beset with problems, for such names were fast becoming hereditary. The overall pattern in Leatherhead does, however, seem significantly different from that in the villages around it. Even if some names were inherited by their 14th-century bearers, they probably reflect genuine local trades of a generation or so back.

Several occupational names are, naturally enough, of the ordinary rural kind: Smith, Baker, Carpenter, Miller and Shepherd.[9] Others, conspicuously absent in surrounding parishes,[10] suggest a greater economic diversity. Skinner, Tanner, Weaver and Fuller on the one hand, and Shoemaker, Glover and Tailor on the other, point to a clothing trade backed up by production of the raw materials.[11] Commerce at the market, and the outside contracts it brought, are reflected in the names of Merchant, Chapman, Cornmonger and Gaveler (moneylender).[12] Poller (barber)[13] also seems more suited to a town

[1] MDLD 102.

[2] MDLD 23.

[3] MM 5787.

[4] *Proc. LDLHS*, **3** (10), pp. 334–5.

[5] W. J. Blair, '"Cradlers", Leatherhead (33/5 High Street)', *Proc. LDLHS*, **3** (9), pp. 298–312.; J. Blair, '"Cradlers", Leatherhead: a 14th century timber-framed house', *SAC*, **lxxviii**, 1987, pp. 73–7 .

[6] W. J. Blair, '55 Church Street, Leatherhead', *Proc. LDLHS*, **4** (4), pp. 103–4.

[7] W. J. Blair, 'The "Running Horse", Leatherhead', *Proc. LDLHS*, **3** (10), pp. 347–50.

[8] J. H. Harvey, 'Sweech House (Nos. 2, 4 and 6 Gravel Hill), Leatherhead', *Proc. LDLHS*, **3** (5), pp. 146–52.

[9] John Faber, c. 1240–50 (MDLD 91); Gilbert Pistor, c. 1250–60 (MDLD 16); Humfrey son of John Carpentarius, c. 1250–60 (MDLD 93); Serle le Mouner, c. 1300 (*Proc. LDLHS*, **3** (8), pp. 224–5), Henry le Berchier, c. 1260 (MDLD 94).

[10] E.g. in the Copthorne hundred section of the 1332 subsidy (*Surrey Taxation Returns*, pp. 74–9) such names only appear in Leatherhead.

[11] John son of Luke le Skinnere of Leatherhead, 1327 (*Cal. Pat. R. 1327–30*, 205); Richard le Tannere, c. 1290 (MDLD 96), and George Barde of Leatherhead, tanner, c. 1450 (*Cal. Pat. R. 1446–52*, 340); Thomas le Webbe, c. 1327 (*Proc. LDLHS*, **3** (8), pp. 228–9, *Cal. Pat. R. 1327–30*, 205); John le Follere, 1307 (MDLD 231), Gilbert Fuller, 1324 (MM 5781 m.7d), and Ellis le Follere, 1332 (*Surrey Taxation Returns*, 76); Gilbert Sutor, c. 1280 (MDLD 23), and Andrew Soutere, 1383 (*Proc. LDLHS*, **3** (9), pp. 270–1); Gilbert le Glovere frequently from the late 1320s to the 1340s (e.g. *Surrey Taxation Returns*, 76); Hugh Cissor c. 1250–60 (MDLD 93) and Luke Cissor frequently (e.g. MDLD 95).

(*Continued overleaf*)

Engraving of the 'Running Horse' from Brayley's *History of Surrey*, 1850.

12 John the Merchant held a messuage in Bridge Street in *c.* 1280 (MDLD 95), and in the 1280s Richard Gos of Leatherhead, merchant, held the Thorncroft tenement by the bridge (MDLD 99); John le Chapman held a shop in Leatherhead in 1319 (MM 5787, court of Monday after St Peter ad Vincula 13 Edw. II); Hugh le Cormongere, *c.* 1290 (MDLD 96), and the name frequently thereafter (e.g. *Surrey Taxation Returns*, 76); John le Gavelere, *c.* 1300 (*Proc. LDLHS*, 3 (8), pp. 226–7). Note also William Holewey of Leatherhead, mercer (*Cal. Pat. R. 1446–52*, 340).
13 Henry le Polere, *c.* 1280 (MDLD 23).

1 *Proc. LDLHS*, 3 (9), pp. 274–5.
2 J. H. Harvey in *Times Literary Supplement*, 26 October 1946, 521; H. L. R. Edwards, *Skelton* (London, 1949), pp. 115–24.
3 *Proc. LDLHS*, 4 (8), p. 218.
4 *Surrey Taxation Returns*, 76; P.R.O. E 179/184/143.
5 Pitfalls in the use of lay subsidies, see *The Lay Subsidy of 1334*, ed. R. E. Glasscock (London, 1975), pp. xxiv–xxvi.

than a village. Farmers from the countryside around would come to Leatherhead on market-day, buy their shoes and gloves, and perhaps have their hair cut.

Nor would they forget to visit the town ale-house. Agnes Hostilere, mentioned in 1383, presumably kept a hostelry.[1] A much more celebrated Leatherhead ale-wife was the redoubtable Elinour Rumming. John Skelton's comic poem, written in the first quarter of the 16th century, describes her grotesque appearance and the riotous scenes in her tavern. Elinour, long assumed to be Skelton's fantasy, has been proved a genuine local character. In 1525 she was fined 2*d*. in the Pachenesham manor court for selling ale at excessive prices.[2] Exactly where she sold it is, however, unknown (there is no real evidence to associate her with the 'Running Horse'). What may have been another hostelry, a tenement in Leatherhead called 'le George', is mentioned in 1543.[3]

Taxation records give a rough measure of the importance of Leatherhead, and its wealthier inhabitants, in relation to other places around. Unfortunately there is nothing between the Lay Subsidy return of 1332 and that of 1524,[4] and even these exclude many householders, perhaps the majority, whose goods fell below a minimum value.[5] In 1332 the 54 taxpayers certainly exceeded any neighbouring parishes (49 in Ewell, 35 in Mickleham, 29 in Fetcham and 28 in Ashtead), while the average value of goods assessed per taxpayer (£2 10*s*. in Leatherhead, £2 in Ewell and lesser sums in Mickleham, Fetcham and Ashtead) points to somewhat greater prosperity in possessions and stock. If most of these people lived in the town, the basic farming population was evidently swelled by craftsmen and tradesmen with sufficient material resources to qualify as taxpayers. In 1524 Leatherhead's 65 taxpayers still substantially exceeded Mickleham (28), Fetcham (20) and Ashtead (37), though now surpassed by Ewell (70). Averages of the assessments are distorted by the presence of a few very wealthy landowners like the Iwarbeys and Brays of Ewell. A breakdown of the figures suggests that both Leatherhead and Ewell had unusually large numbers of humbler taxpayers with goods valued at £1.

In a recent history of Surrey, Leatherhead is described as 'one of many English places provided with the essentials of a medieval town, in this case four streets meeting in a market-place at the crossroads, which nevertheless failed to grow beyond the scale of a village until modern times'.[1] This is slightly off the mark: it is more a matter of early promise unfulfilled. Medieval Leatherhead was unequivocally a small town, with shops and a market to serve the interests of craftsmen, tradesmen and farmers. A fire there in 1392, and its miraculous character, was noted in a chronicle of national events.[2] The 1418 reference to an empty plot formerly containing a shop (see p. 64) may be the first hint of a slow but steady decline in commercial functions. The 1524 tax-returns show Leatherhead already overshadowed by the rapid growth of Ewell.[3] Soon afterwards the ancient market ceased to be held and the market-place disappeared. So Leatherhead was much more obviously a town in the 14th century than in the 16th. Its prosperity under Elizabeth and the Stuarts had other causes.

Extract from the ballad *The Tunning of Elinour Rumming* by John Skelton, 1529.

> Her lewd lippes twain,
>   They slaver, men sayne
> Like a ropy rain,
>   A gummy glair.
> Her nose somedele hooked
>   And camously crooked,
> Never stopping,
>   But ever dropping;
> Her skin, loose and slack,
>   Grained like a sack;
> With a crooked back.
>   Her eyen gowndy
>   Are full unsowndy,
>   For they are bleared;
> And she gray-haired,
>   Jawed like a jetty;
> And this comely dame,
>   I understand, her name
> Is Elinour Rumming,
>   At home in her wonning;
> And as men say
>   She dwelt in Surrey,
> In a certain stead
>   Beside Leatherhead.
> But to make up my tale,
>   She breweth nappy ale,
> And maketh thereof pot-sale
>   To travellers, to tinkers,
> To sweaters, to swinkers,
>   And all good ale-drinkers,
> That will nothing spare
>   But drink until they stare.

The colloquialism 'Make no bones about it' was used first in one of the stanzas. Centuries later, the ballad was set to music by one-time Dorking composer, Ralph Vaughan Williams.

---

[1] Brandon, *History of Surrey*, p. 89.

[2] *Polychronicon Ranulphi Higden*, ed. J. R. Lumby, **xi** (Rolls Ser. 41, London, 1886), p. 271.

[3] For Ewell's increased importance from the fifteenth century onwards, stimulated by the growth of through traffic, C. F. Titford, 'Medieval Ewell and Cuddington', *SAC*, **lxix**, 1973, pp. 27–35, with critique by P. Shearman, 'The topography of medieval Ewell and Cuddington: a reply', *SAC*, **lxxi**, 1977, pp. 139–44.

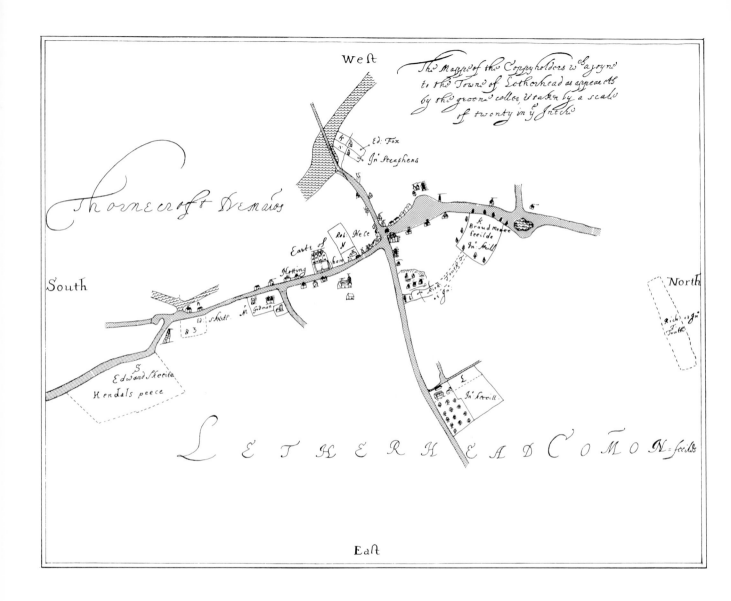

Town centre in 1629 from Elias Allen's survey, Merton College, Oxford.

The Elizabethan and Stuart Period 1558–1714

LEATHERHEAD was a busy little town at this period, growing in size and reflecting perhaps something of the spirit of Elizabethan and Stuart London while everyone, rich and poor alike, looked to the church as the mainstay and centre of parish life. It was a mainly farming community, the home also of courtiers and merchants attracted to the town by its nearness to London. Edmund Tylney, Master of the Revels to Queen Elizabeth, lived in The Mansion and Robert Gardiner of Thorncroft Manor was Sergeant of the Wine Cellar early in her reign. Since Tylney was Censor of plays as well as Master of the Revels, it is thought likely that Shakespeare visited Leatherhead to consult Tylney and may even have named the assistant officer of the watch, Verges in *Much Ado About Nothing* after the local constable, George Varges.[1] Other notable residents included the Earl of Nottingham who was Lord Lieutenant of Surrey for many years; Thomas Sands of Randalls Park who was a member of the Long Parliament and a Bencher of the Middle Temple; the Godmans with wide mercantile interests and lands in Essex and the Rogers family who lived at the Rectory and farmed the church's glebelands. In the late 17th century Richard Dalton was Sergeant of the Wine Cellar to Charles II, his son served in the same department of the Household and Robert Hanbury, Vicar of Leatherhead from 1679 to 1688, was a Royal chaplain. The most famous City man linked with the town was Sir Thomas Bludworth, Lord Mayor of London in the mid-1660s.

The town was often chosen as a meeting place for county affairs

[1] F. B. Benger, 'Shakespeare and the Constable', *Proc. LDLHS*, **4** (7), 1983, p. 171.

because of its central position in Surrey. In 1562 an inquisition was held in Leatherhead on the proper dress for the wives of Surrey's men of substance and in 1599 Surrey leaders met in the town to decide what to do with Catholics who were standing out against Elizabeth's religious reforms.[1] At another meeting some years later the 'prison and prisoners' of Surrey were considered and during the 1580s Leatherhead was frequently chosen for discussions on Surrey's preparations to resist invasion.[2] The Quarter Sessions were held there in October 1593 and in June 1608 there was a meeting of JPs to consider the measures needed to overcome the dearth of corn in the county. The Lord Lieutenant of Surrey reviewed the county militia on Fetcham Downs in November 1625[3] and during the Civil War there were several occasions when Leatherhead played a part in Surrey affairs (see pp. 86–93).

After the Restoration, Leatherhead could not rival Epsom's growing popularity since it was a spa and racing centre but it nevertheless continued to be looked upon as more than just a small farming town. For example in 1661, it was chosen as the collection centre for the Copthorne and Effingham Hundreds of the Free and Voluntary Present to Charles II[4] and it was also host to a meeting of Surrey JPs about this time. In 1680 a conference in the town was attended by Sir William More and Lord Lumley, a leading figure of the Court, notably at Nonsuch, and five years later the election of the knights of the shire for the coming Parliament was held here. The almost daily arrival and departure of a coach to and from London added to the bustle and importance of the town.

The growing town

Like many other towns, Leatherhead increased in population during the Elizabethan and Stuart periods. At the beginning of Elizabeth's reign the town is thought to have had about 300 inhabitants, an estimate based on the lay subsidy returns of 1524–1525, the only comprehensive and reliable source of its kind during the 16th century.[5] This subsidy was levied on all persons with lands, moveable goods or wages of £1 a year or more. In Leatherhead there were 65 taxpayers at this count. To find the total population including wives, children and servants, a multiplier of 4·3 has been taken and on this basis the population numbered about 280 at this time probably increasing

[1] HMC, 7th Report, p. 622a.

[2] Cal SPD (1581–90), pp. 500 and 509.

[3] HMC, 7th Report, p. 676.

[4] PRO E179/257/28, transcribed by C. Webb, W. Surrey Family History Society, Record Series II (1982).

[5] PRO E179/133/122 – W. H. Hoskins, *Provincial England* (1963), p. 185.

slightly by the middle of the century. In 1603, the year of Elizabeth's death, returns made to the Archdeaconry of Surrey[1] give the number of communicants and recusants in the parish as 263 and, adjusting this by one-third to take account of children under 16, the town appears to have grown to 394 – a rise of 41 per cent since the mid-16th century. This is a dramatic increase and judged by the number of its communicants, Leatherhead was at this time larger than its near neighbours, Epsom and Ewell, and much larger than Ashtead, Bookham and Fetcham.

The growth of Leatherhead's population seems to have eased off after 1603, a tax return of the mid-1640s showing little change from the earlier position[2] but the upward trend was resumed after the Restoration. The Hearth Tax returns in 1664 show a marked increase in numbers. This was a tax on households by the number of their hearths and it was paid by the occupier, not the owner. Those who paid neither church rate nor poor rate and had a house worth less than £1 a year and no land or income of less than £10 a year, were exempt from the tax. Leatherhead had 122 entries in 1664, 36 of whom were exempt. This, when multiplied by 4·3 (the ratio used for earlier calculations) gives a figure of 524 as the population of the town at this time. This can be usefully compared with the Church Rate Assessment of 1695; there are 95 entries here and if the same number of exemptions are allowed for this gives a rise to 563, at least by 1695. All this represents a very steady rate of expansion for the second half of the 17th century.

The religious census of 1676, known as the Compton return,[3] is an important source for calculating population but proved a puzzle with respect to Leatherhead. The number of communicants is given as 300 plus three non-conformists and, allowing one-third for children under 16, it represents a substantial dip between the Hearth Tax figures of 1664 and the Church Rate of 1695. This may be explained by the fact that in the 16 years before 1676 (the date of the Compton census) no less than 313 children were baptised.[4] Infant mortality was of course fairly high (40 per cent of children born in 1650 did not survive to the age of 15[5]) but even allowing for this, the figure does suggest a sudden and considerable expansion in the number of children, making them probably more than one-third of the total population. With this assumption the population trend would follow roughly the upward course shown by the other sources.

[1] BL Harleian MSS, 595.
[2] SRO 212/66/7.
[3] SRO 491 (1676).
[4] Parish Registers (from 1656).
[5] Lucinda Beier, *Sufferers and Healers* (1988).

The large number of burials found in the parish registers in the early 18th century seems to confirm that the second half of the 17th century had indeed witnessed a bulge in the population. Excess births over deaths in this period amount to 300 and although those continuing to live here would fluctuate, Leatherhead's population at the end of the 17th century may well have been nearer 700 than 600. This is supported by the Vicar's statement, answering the Bishop's Visitation Articles, that the town had '700 souls and 3 Quakers' in 1724/1725.

The general upward trend in population conceals ups and downs caused, in particular, by illness sometimes in epidemic form, which can be studied only after 1656 when parish registers for the town became available. Certain years, such as 1657/1658, 1662/1663, 1668/1669 and 1686/1687 had exceptionally high burials. A letter dated 1658 refers to 'a world of sickness in all counties round London',[1] an influenza epidemic being the reputed cause which could well explain the large number of Leatherhead deaths at the time. Typhus epidemics in the 1660s and 1680s may also have been the cause of high numbers of burials locally during these years. Since Leatherhead was near to London, it might at various times have suffered as London suffered – plague, smallpox and other diseases. The parish registers show that deaths tended to cluster round spring or late summer but there are no runs of family deaths in the epidemic years, except for two cases of husband and wife dying at close intervals. However, in 1674, the Rogers family lost five members out of the area total of nine deaths and further searches might well provide other examples of a tragic spread of infection.

A look at the town

A traveller in time hastening back some three centuries and more would see in Leatherhead the church on the hill as it is today; the River Mole winding through the meadows and a cross-forked pattern of streets basically the same as now, but simpler and with only a scattering of houses and farm dwellings. A few of these and the main streets are shown on a plan of the town made by Elias Allen in 1629.[2] Street names are given on the Gwilt map which, though made in the next century (1782/1783), probably reflects the position at this period. Church Street was then called Little Queen Street and High Street was Great Queen Street, named, it is thought, to commemorate Queen

[1] C. Creighton, *History of Epidemics* (1965 edn), II, p. 313.

[2] Merton College, Oxford, Muniment 5/28 – John Blair, *The Early Town of Leatherhead* (LDLHS, 1980).

Elizabeth's visit to Leatherhead in 1591 (see p. 75). As today, the church dominated the southern approach to the town but behind it starting at Worple Road was a large open field stretching east to the parish boundary. Pathways led across the field into the town, one of them being the present Elm Road.

Most of Leatherhead's population lived in modest cottages with perhaps a small garden or orchard. There were however some substantial houses like The Mansion, Church House on Dorking Road near the church, the Rectory where Vale Lodge is today, Thorncroft Manor and Randalls Park. Other buildings included Sweech House and three inns, the 'Bull', the 'Swan' and the 'Running Horse' which was probably not residential. The town was a close-knit community and though the manorial courts operated, much of the day-to-day running of the parish was in the hands of the churchwardens, the constables, the overseers of the poor and the surveyor of highways operating through the Vestry, itself a form of town council (see p. 110).

The day's labours

Working the fields occupied most people's day from soon after dawn until early evening with longer hours at harvest-time while others plied trades mainly associated in some way with the land. This was a corn-growing area with cattle, sheep and horses so it is not surprising to find a miller in the town, an oatmeal-maker and a maltster. There were blacksmiths to look after the horses and jobbing work for the farmers was done by carpenters and turners. At least one timber merchant worked here in James II's reign and there were also tanners, cloth-workers, butchers, bakers and brewers. This varied assortment of occupations continued through the century as shown by the returns of the Voluntary Contribution to Charles II in 1661, 17 being listed, repeating those mentioned earlier but adding a collar-maker and a falconer. Other sources at this time refer to a fishmonger, a wheelwright, a glazier and at least two bricklayers. Leatherhead's better-off families would certainly have had servants but their numbers are not known. There were no doctors here early in the 17th century[1] and though two are mentioned in the Church Rate Assessment of 1695, they may not have been medical men. However, a surgeon-apothecary was living in the town later and according to the monument in the parish church, died in 1726.

[1] J. H. Raach, *Directory of English Country Physicians 1603–42* (1962).

Something of the town's character is conveyed by Celia Fiennes writing in William and Mary's reign. She describes Leatherhead as a 'little town where they make much leather and other little trades with many butchers which supply Epsom'.

Sports and pastimes

It was not all hard work in the farms and cottages of Leatherhead. Christmas, Easter and Whitsuntide were times for celebrating with much eating, drinking and dancing except during the Civil War and Interregnum years when festivals were abolished (see p. 108). There was also jollification at the end of the harvest especially if it had been a good one. At other times, particularly in summer, there would be fishing in the Mole, and perhaps a visit by a travelling showman or pedlar. A rather wild game of football was said to be popular as well as 'shuttel-cocke with battel-doore'.[1] Sunday was the most popular day for recreation. James I's Book of Sports issued in 1618 allowed 'dancing, archery for men, leaping, vaulting' but prohibited bear- and bull-baiting and strange to say, bowling. Something of the vigour of life in Shakespeare's London with its wit, rumbustiousness and virility may have filtered into Surrey towns like Leatherhead. At least it is known that the weekly carrier service lodged near the Globe Theatre (see p. 116) and one of the town's leading residents, Edmund Tylney, was Master of the Revels to the Queen. Music in the home was one of the quieter pleasures; a lute was owned and presumably much played by Mary Naldrett who lived at the Rectory with her uncle, Edward Rogers, and there was music at Thorncroft Manor for dancing reported in the middle of James I's reign.

After the Restoration, the fashionable world flooded to Epsom for its spa wells and horse racing and it is possible many of the wealthier people from Leatherhead may have joined them. A falconer was living in the town at this time which suggests that the lord of the manor hunted and hawked (see p. 312). Some of the more adventurous locals may have taken up the new sport of skating in the very cold winters of 1662/1663 and 1683/1684 when most rivers and ponds were frozen.

After a day's sport the local inns the 'Bull', the 'Swan' and the 'Running Horse' would be busy. Samuel Pepys called at one in 1661, writing in his diary: 'We got a small bayt (refreshment) at Leatherhead before going on to Godalming for the night'. Later, in 1686, a survey

17th-century token used in the Swan Inn showing the name of the then-proprietor Edward Shales.

[1] N. Breton, *Fantasticks: The Twelve Months* (1626), p. 20.

was made of Leatherhead's accommodation for men and horses and there were said to be enough beds to put up 11 people and sufficient stabling for 18 horses.[1]

With these facilities, the town was better off than its immediate neighbours.

Some Leatherhead families

Leatherhead society in Elizabethan and Stuart times can only be adequately understood in terms of social status. At this period Leatherhead was the thriving centre of a rural district with more varied and specialised occupations than the neighbouring villages of Bookham, Fetcham and Ashtead. It was an hierarchical stratified community with marked inequalities – gentry, yeoman and artificers or labourers. Nevertheless, the parish seems to have acted as a responsible unit, caring for the sick and poor whatever their status. Social mobility was also a feature of the times: thus, the Rogers, Skeetes and Dalton families originally of yeoman stock, later became gentlemen and in the process acquired wealth, rich profits being available to those with land.

Leatherhead families' fortunes were unsettled and fluid throughout this period. Some, like the Gardiners, faded out after the Civil War; others like the Bludworths were affected by the dreadful Fire of London in 1666. Nor was life secure for the less important families such as the Nettlefolds and the Hudsons, who were relatively substantial and respected members of the Church Vestry. The vagaries of the harvests and the frequent spread of often fatal diseases made all their lives very uncertain.

Edmund Tylney and the Howards

Edmund Tylney, Master of the Revels to Queen Elizabeth and James I, was the town's most illustrious resident at that time and was clearly at the top of the town's social pyramid.[2] He was related to the Howards through his great-aunt Agnes Tylney who married the second Duke of Norfolk. Their son, Lord William Howard, became Lord Howard of Effingham and his even more famous son, Charles of Armada fame, had links with Leatherhead. Howard influence may have helped Tylney to become MP for Gatton in 1572. He came to live at The Mansion in Leatherhead about 1588 and the Queen dined with him

[1] PRO WO30/48 (1686), *Account of Inns and Alehouses in England*.
[2] F. B. Benger, 'Edmund Tylney', *Proc. LDLHS*, **1** (5), 1951, pp. 16–21.

Lanthorn Leatherhead

From 1605 the playwright Ben Jonson was constantly producing masques for the entertainment of the Court where Edmund Tylney was Master of the Revels. Tylney who lived in The Mansion, was also the powerful theatrical Censor. In his play *Bartholomew Fair*, Ben Jonson called one of his characters 'Lanthorn Leatherhead', a ne'er-do-well toyseller, puppet-maker and puppeteer. This may well have been a satirical dig at the Censor.

there on 3 August 1591 during one of her progresses. He was one of the Lay Subsidy Commissioners for the town three years after this visit and was also a justice of the peace. His will of 1610 shows the Tudor preoccupation with charity: 'All my apparel', it reads, 'to be sold at the best value and the money divided between the poore of Leatherhead and Streatham . . . £100 for the reparation of Leatherhead stone bridge'. Despite his involvement with Court life, Tylney obviously cared for the town he lived in.

The Earl of Nottingham

The Howard connection with Leatherhead was not broken with the death of Edmund Tylney in 1610 since the new owner of The Mansion was Charles Howard, son of Lord Howard of Effingham, who became Lord Lieutenant of Surrey in 1621 and succeeded his father as Earl of Nottingham in 1624. His position and rank made him the leader of Leatherhead society until his death in 1642. Little is known about him except that he was a firm disciplinarian. He reviewed the County Militia on Fetcham Downs in November 1625[1] and a few months later, when reporting to London on this he asked for 'exemplary punish-ment' of defaulters. He was made a vice-admiral at this time following the Howard family's long naval tradition. A short time before his death he held meetings in Leatherhead to discuss Surrey's military support for the Parliamentary cause in the Civil War (see p. 86).

The Gardiners of Thorncroft Manor

This family had strong Court connections dating from about 1560 when Robert Gardiner was appointed Sergeant of the Wine Cellar to Queen Elizabeth.[2] He made Leatherhead his home possibly because of its proximity to London and to Nonsuch and Oatlands Palaces. He had been granted a coat-of-arms in 1548 and was obviously a man of substance since he not only held a long lease of Thorncroft Manor granted in 1545 but he also owned London property in the parish of St Martin's-in-the-Fields. His will makes this even more clear, his son Richard being left 'all my armour and weapons and the two geldings I usually keep at Court and my chain of fine gold weighing about thirty ounces or thereabouts'. He made careful provision for his wife Anne saying that should their son marry 'my son's wife shall bear no rule in my said house but under my wife'. Robert Gardiner is remembered by

---

[1] HMC, 7th Report, p. 676a.
[2] F. Bastian, 'Gardiners of Thorncroft', *Proc. LDLHS*, **2** (5), 1961, pp. 135–44.

his monument in the parish church which shows the helmet carried at his funeral and below there is an epitaph by Thomas Churchyard, the Court poet, praising friendly Gardiner's 'merry modde and pleasant speech' who 'served in court with credit' and 'with good regard to all degrees'.

Robert Gardiner's son, the first of several named Richard, continued the family tradition of being in Royal service since he was described as the Queen's Man-in-Ordinary. The second Richard, born in 1578, held no Court position but was important locally being a justice of the peace and Captain of the Trained Bands for the Middle Division of Surrey. This position of authority led to his bitter quarrel with the Brownes of Dorking during the muster at Leatherhead in July 1618. The Brownes at the muster aimed at casting doubts on Gardiner's abilities and later in the day they not only continued their provocation in the town at an alehouse but broke into Thorncroft Manor, which led to fisticuffs with Gardiner's men. The incident was referred to the Star Chamber in London but the result of the case is not known. In the 1620s the Thorncroft estate seems to have suffered financially judging from the sharp fall in Richard Gardiner's lay subsidy assessments, from £20 in 1622 to only £3 in 1629. He continued to live at Thorncroft Manor probably until the late 1640s despite sequestration troubles during the Civil War but in 1649 or soon after, he moved to a more modest house in Fetcham.

After the Restoration the fact that two members of the family in 1663 accepted money for their part in helping the King, suggests that they needed what support they could get. Richard Gardiner, the third of that name, died in 1669 and nothing more is known of the family except that in 1675 his son, another Richard, was granted authority to administer his mother's estate. Ninety years after Robert Gardiner, Sergeant of the Cellar to Queen Elizabeth, had died, the Gardiners were no longer important nor living in the ancient manor house of Thorncroft.

Robert Gardiner's helmet placed on his coffin at his funeral in 1571. Restored under the direction of Claude Blair of the V & A who also took the photograph, the helmet now hangs in the parish church.

The Sands of Randalls Park

The Sands family of a lower social level than Tylney, Nottingham and Gardiner, probably corresponded to what might be called the squirearchy of Leatherhead. They were a 'gentle' family from the time they came to Randalls about 1509.[1] Thomas Sands married Jane

[1] F. Bastian, 'Sands of Randall' *Proc. LDLHS*, **2** (3), 1959, pp. 77–84.

Agmondesham, one of the co-heiresses of an ancient Leatherhead family. Thus the Sands dynasty started as it was to continue, firmly rooted in the local community. For example, Thomas Skeete in 1546 appointed his 'beloved frende' Thomas Sands to be overseer of his will, and in 1550 and 1553 the same Thomas was a sidesman in Leatherhead church, a slightly unusual job for a gentleman. There is also a very homely note to Robert Sands' will in 1598: he left to his wife Anne, among other bequests, 'two cheeses and half the yearly increase of my pigeons'.

Unlike many gentlemen, Robert Sands concerned himself with the detailed management of his own affairs.

The next two Sands, son and grandson of Robert, were slightly more typical of members of the gentry. John Sands, Robert's son, married into the Hatton family of Thames Ditton and attended Balliol College, Oxford, so his perspectives were wider than Leatherhead and reflected the growing fashion for higher education among his class. Often being executor of local wills, he was still very much a part of this community. His daughter Jane married Edward Skeete, member of an important Leatherhead yeoman family. His son Thomas was educated at Oxford and was called to the Bar. He became a member of Parliament for Gatton in 1640 and was active in the Parliamentary cause, serving on several Surrey committees until 1648 when, after Pride's Purge, he had to leave Parliament. He became a Bencher of the Middle Temple in the same year and retired to Leatherhead where he died 10 years later.

The astrologer Wiliam Lilly writing in his Memoirs[1] relates how Sands frequently entertained his friend Bulstrode Whitelocke, his fellow MP in Leatherhead, and trout from the River Mole was served at the table on a number of occcasions. Lilly reported this because he was worried that Whitelocke's trout-eating would lead to an aggravation of the digestive complaint which Lilly had been called in to cure. The Sands family acquired all lands between the Mole, Kingston Road and the Leatherhead Common during the 17th century and in 1658 the extent of their estate was about 300 acres. John Sands, son of Thomas, was still important in 1695 and in 1696 when he featured on the Church Rate Assessment and the Association Oath Roll, but by 1700 he had begun, for reasons that are not altogether clear, to mortgage his land. He died in 1719 and was buried at Leatherhead.

[1] W. Lilly, *Memoirs* (1715), p. 43.

The Rogers of the Rectory

The story of the Rogers family is especially interesting since it demonstrates two important features of Tudor and Stuart life.[1] The Rogers were originally of yeoman status but by 1622 one of the family, Edward, was able to call himself Esquire, a form more prestigious than a Gentleman and they were beginning to break into high society. They had links with both the Court and the merchant oligarchies in London. Edward Rogers, son of the one who had acquired a coat-of-arms in James I's reign, married as his first wife, Joan Coventry, daughter of Sir Thomas Coventry, a judge of the Court of Common Pleas and closely associated with Charles I's Court. This resulted in Rogers taking the Royal side in the Civil War which was no doubt embarrassing for the Earl of Nottingham and Sands, who were for Parliament.

The Rogers family history goes back a long way. They held a lease of the Leatherhead Rectory from the Dean and Chapter of Rochester at least from 1584. As there were so many Rogers cousins, the family tree is complex. Edward Rogers, the husband of Joan Coventry, broke the local connections and entered the wider world. He went to Oxford and also to the Inns of Court. It was both fashionable and wise at a time of frequent land litigation for the sons of important families to study law. Interestingly enough, at this time the Inns of Court were more socially exclusive than Oxford and Cambridge so it is strange that of all Leatherhead men, Edward Rogers, rather than a Gardiner or a Sands, should attend. Edward's legal expertise proved useful to his father in a dispute over tithes with the vicar of Leatherhead, Richard Levitt, in James I's reign (see p. 105) but these skills could not prevent the sequestration of the Rectory in 1646 because of Rogers' Royalist sympathies.

The family never fully recovered from supporting the losing side in the war and though they had a brief revival under Charles II their attempts to recoup losses led to social suicide. Thomas Rogers, the head of the family in 1660, had been brought up in the household of Lord Keeper Coventry and after the Restoration he kept in touch with royal circles through his Coventry relations. His social position was however undermined by unwise speculation of tax funds entrusted to him when appointed the Surrey Receiver for the Hearth Tax in 1664. When the administrative system for the collection of this tax was changed in 1665, Rogers was asked to hand in the money he had

[1] F. Bastian, 'Rogers of the Rectory', *Proc. LDLHS*, **2** (4), 1960, pp. 103–12.

already collected. This he could not do, having spent it or invested it in the stock market. Rogers was ruined and it was agreed that his lands should be sold to pay the King, 'he (Rogers) to have a lease of 100 acres and no more'. By 1673 Rogers no longer lived at the Rectory and in 1679 he died and was buried at Oxford where he had fled to join his brother Edward, who was a Fellow of Magdalen College.

There were many other members of the Rogers family who were very diverse in their activities during the 17th century; lawyers, country gentlemen, merchants and academics as well as brewers (Robert Rogers, one of Thomas's brothers was described as a brewer of Fetcham in 1667). They were all descended from yeoman and tenant farmers. Their story illustrates that social class in England was not a caste system, unlike other European countries where the son of a gentleman could not soil his hands with work if he were to be a gentleman himself.

The Daltons

This family destined for social distinction during the 17th century, made its appearance in Leatherhead through a Rogers connection early in James I's reign.[1] Richard Dalton, a yeoman farmer, married Frances, daughter of William Rogers, also a yeoman. This pattern of marriage within the local community was perpetuated by his son and daughters.

The founder of the Dalton family certainly increased his fortunes considerably. He was assessed at only 20s. in lands for the Lay Subsidies of the 1620s but died quite prosperous 20 years later. In 1639 he had bought a 15-acre freehold estate from Edward Skeete who sold off his property to pay for a series of lawsuits. As a result of this and general prosperity made possible by the rise in agricultural prices, he was able to leave his four unmarried daughters £20 each to be drawn 'from the rents and profits of my lands and tenements'. His son, another Richard, was made Sergeant of the Wine Cellar soon after 1600, perhaps because he claimed to have been active in the plots to restore Charles II (see p. 95). For many years he had the contract to supply Spanish wines to the Court. Pepys refers several times in his diary to Dalton taking over the lease of his house in Axe Yard, Westminster, and having drinks with him. This took place in 1660 and about two years later they caroused again in Dalton's office.

[1] F. Bastian, 'The Dalton family', *Proc. LDLHS*, **2** (9), 1965, pp. 260–5.

Although Richard Dalton may have lived mainly in London, he did have local commitments. For example, he was a witness to Thomas Godman's will in 1652. His family probably ranked with the Bludworths in the social hierarchy of Leatherhead though their chief interests lay elsewhere. Indeed it is thought that to be an office holder was one of the best means of advancement for ambitious families. When Dalton died in 1681 his will showed how wealthy he was. His children, grandchildren and his sister were left amounts varying from 20s. to £300; his wife Mary, received 'his freehold lands and house in Leatherhead' and the lease of another house which included most of its contents. He was clearly a man of substantial means.

The later Daltons led lives enmeshed in the Court circle and yet were still involved in Leatherhead society. The eldest son, another Richard, probably lived out of the area for most of his life since his name does not appear in the Hearth Tax lists or in the Freeholders' Books. Nor is his name on the list of those swearing loyalty to William III in 1696. Yet loyal to the throne he certainly was since he held office under Charles II and William III. He was successively Page, Groom and Yeoman of the Cellar. He made eight separate loans to the Exchequer in 1689 and 1690. Perhaps like others in the Court circle, he found it difficult to reconcile his belief in the monarchy with the confusion surrounding the flight of James II and William III's assumption of power. In any case, he lived out his life prosperously, dying in 1731 and being buried in his native Leatherhead. His son, yet another Richard, was born in 1698 and made Thorncroft his home at least until the mid-1750s. In spite of this, it is hard to establish where his ancestors lived in Leatherhead.

The Skeetes
The Skeete's family history is a vivid chronicle of rise and fall in status mainly due to land quarrels and division among its members. The Skeetes were well established in the district, first being mentioned as early as 1468 when they were husbandmen. Yet by Elizabeth's time they had become yeomen. By 1586 one of the sons was called a gentleman. This same son left in his will a personal estate of £500 as well as nearly 200 acres in Leatherhead apart from lands elsewhere, to his wife Audrey, formerly of the important Bookham family of Slyfield, and to their nine young children.[1]

[1] F. Bastian, 'The Skeete family', *Proc. LDLHS*, **2** (1), 1957, pp. 7–14.

The downfall of the Skeetes began with Edward's death, since soon afterwards in 1599 Audrey remarried, this time to Richard Oxenbridge, an apparently unscrupulous character who used her children's estates as though they were his own. When her son, another Edward, challenged Oxenbridge's rights to harvest his lands, there were violent quarrels with 'bills, swords, daggers, staves and other warlike weapons'. At one point, on 8 August 1612, young Skeete heard that his mother Audrey, was near to death because of her husband's beatings, and a serious clash occurred including Skeete, John Sands, his father-in-law, Thomas Godman and Richard Rogers, the constable of the day. Audrey recovered but the fortunes of the Skeete family did not. Oxenbridge brought numerous cases in the Star Chamber against them and although the results are unknown, Edward Skeete was ruined. He moved to Ewell and the sales of his land in Leatherhead carried on apace.

The name of Skeete is however preserved in Leatherhead to this day there being a block of old people's flats bearing his name in Church Street.

A cousin of this branch of the family, John Skeete, draper and citizen of London, left money to the poor of Leatherhead in 1609 and this charity is commemorated in the parish church and is still administered by Leatherhead United Charities.

The Skeete family history shows that there was considerable social mobility at this time. Although the Skeetes began as husbandmen, became yeomen and finally gentlemen, this process was reversed because of the Oxenbridge affair.

It is also clear that large profits out of owning land could help a yeoman marry into the gentry. Two of the Skeetes did just this by marrying into the Slyfield and Sands families.

Their history further reveals the closeness of the Leatherhead community at this time. John Sands, Edward Skeete's father-in-law, held a pitchfork to Oxenbridge's breast in 1612 in order to arrest him and at a later stage in the quarrel Skeete and Sands were said to have been in the house of Mr Godman 'near adjoyninge to the open street there'. Richard Rogers was also involved in the dispute. This all goes to prove that whatever the apparent difference of status, these men were neighbours and friends. Neighbourliness was an important concept of the time, more important perhaps than kinship.

The Godmans of Church House

The last of the important neighbours in Leatherhead, the Godmans, lived in what Thomas Godman, citizen and mercer of London, described in his will of 1559 'as my mansyon howse in Letherhead adjoyninge to the church'. The house was between the church and the Dorking road as shown on Elias Allen's plan of 1629. Thomas Godman was the founder of the family fortunes but there is a reference to a Godman as early as 1336. The Godmans held the 'Swan' inn in the centre of the town in the 17th century. Despite their mercantile connection, they were a local family. Their story is however much more peaceful than that of the Skeetes and less involved in national affairs than the Gardiners and the Sands.

By 1579 the second Thomas Godman was granted arms and the merchant family had become gentry. He was also a significant member of the local community being the first named, therefore the most important, of the executors of Skeete's Charity. Although Godman helped Tylney in a 1592 lawsuit, he refused to act as his executor in 1610. One wonders why: was Tylney's business too complex for old Godman to handle? He was careful not to get involved in disputes like the Oxenbridge affair and partly because of this his family prospered. Thomas Godman's son, another of the same name, was an attorney for Edmund Tylney's heir in 1616 so the two families remained close.

The Godman family and their descendants, the Dacres, were very much part of Leatherhead life until well into the 18th century. Thomas Godman, the third of that name died in 1661, leaving a widow Olive. She was a lady of some substance as her home, Church House, was assessed at 13 hearths in 1664 and she contributed 40s., more than anyone else in Leatherhead, to a 'Free and Voluntary Present to Charles II' in 1661. Wealthy as they were, however, the Godmans had no male heirs and their lands passed through their daughter Frances to her husband, Francis Gerard and ultimately to a granddaughter, another Frances, who married John Dacres.

Philip Dacres, recorded in the Freeholders' Books of 1698 and 1699 as gentleman and in the Vestry accounts as Overseer of the Poor in 1706, was presumably a great-grandson of the Godmans. A sad record of the births and deaths of his 14 children, a number of whom were called Winifred after his wife, is to be found in the parish registers. Philip himself died in 1725. His wife lived on until 1745 in which year the Godman, Gerard and Dacres link with Leatherhead was broken.[1]

Another Godman daughter Mary had married John Barefoot and although they were landlords rather than occupants of their Leatherhead properties, it is known that they controlled the 'Swan' inn until 1713. Then their grandson John Barefoot was selling the 'Swan' to Edward Toye, and by this time the Godmans of Church House were no longer there.

The Bludworths

This family was closely connected with Leatherhead during most of the later Stuart period. Its members were prosperous city merchants, later becoming country gentlemen who also dabbled unluckily in politics.[2]

Sir Thomas Bludworth, knighted by Charles II in 1660, came to live at Thorncroft because his first wife Elizabeth had been a member of that prolific Leatherhead family, the Rogers. Her father Walter was also a city merchant but retained close links with his family at home in Leatherhead. Elizabeth died young and her children by Sir Thomas predeceased their father. Thorncroft remained Bludworth's country home, though in the mid-1660s when he was Lord Mayor of London, he cannot have been there often. He held this office at the time of the Great Plague and the Great Fire. Even before these dire events, his reputation had been sullied by Samuel Pepys who spoke of him as a 'silly man' and a 'mean man without understanding and despatch of business'. During the Great Fire, Pepys reported that Bludworth panicked complaining 'Lord what can I do? I am spent; people will not obey me. I have been pulling down houses but the fire overtakes us faster than we can do it'. Bludworth's will of 1682 recalls the terrible events of that year 'it having pleased God to lessen me in my estate by that dreadful fire of London'. Bludworth's estate may have recovered but his reputation never did.

After Sir Thomas Bludworth's death in 1682, his son, another Thomas, was a country gentleman. He was a Court servant, still involved in politics but not powerful. His sister Anne married Judge Jeffreys, known as 'the hanging judge' because of his harsh treatment of Monmouth's rebels in 1685, and one of the inner circle of James II's court. Sir Thomas was also a supporter of James. He was MP for Bramber in Sussex and held a minor royal office which he lost after the

[1] F. Bastian, 'Godman, Gerard & Dacres families', *Proc. LDLHS*, **2** (2), 1958, pp. 43–9.
[2] F. Bastian, 'Bludworth of Thorncroft', *Proc. LDLHS*, **2** (6), 1962, pp. 177–85.

Glorious Revolution. He died in 1692 and his uncle Charles Bludworth succeeded to the estate.

The new owner of Thorncroft was also a Tory by conviction and served as Deputy Lieutenant of Surrey in 1702. Earlier in 1696 he thought it politic to subscribe to an oath of loyalty to William III[1] and for a time he was Surveyor of Roads in the parish. After his death in February 1704, the story of this family in Leatherhead comes to an end. The estate passed to a minor Thomas Bludworth who may have been Page to George I in 1726 but as far as Leatherhead is concerned, the Bludworth link was broken.

The Ragges

This is the only family of craftsmen or artificers living in 17th century Leatherhead of whom there is sufficient information to glimpse their way of life.

The Ragges were saddlers and collar-makers making the leather rolls stuffed with rope which hung round the necks of draught horses enabling them to pull great weights.[2] One of the family, Robert Ragge, was a juror at the Manorial Court in the 1650s and he had some connection with Sir Thomas Foote and the Onslows. The Ragges probably lived in Bridge Street. Although they were not men of great substance, being assessed at 6s. 8d. for the Church Rate of 1695, the family was gradually building up its lands and prestige. In 1702 and 1703, Robert Ragge was a Churchwarden and about this time he was active as a moneylender in the local community. He certainly lent money both to John Allingham and Robert Marsh, two other well-documented people, and by 1715 was busy buying land for himself from John Barefoot, a descendant of the Godmans who lived in Essex. The Ragges continued to be Leatherhead residents well beyond this period; indeed their descendants are still living here.

Other Leatherhead families

The families so far described made up only a part of Leatherhead society as it was at this period. Sadly, too little is known about the other families to construct anything other than a partial picture of their lives. There were families such as the Tyrrells after whom Tyrrells Wood is presumably named, the Hudsons and the Nettlefolds to name but a few. The Tyrrell name occurs in the parish registers as early as 1669 and

[1] Association Oath Roll (1696), transcribed by C. Webb (1983), West Surrey Family History Society.

[2] F. B. Benger, 'The Ragge, Lloyd and Walker families', *Proc. LDLHS*, **2** (5), 1961, pp. 144–54.

two of their number were respectively overseers of the poor in 1699 and surveyor of the roads in 1704. The earliest mention of Hudson is the baptism of 'Briggett, daughter of Edward Hudson on October 6th 1623' in the parish register, and a Hudson was churchwarden in 1696–1698. The parish records mention George Page, Clerk to the Vestry, Nevill Reffew, Featherstone Hall and Edward Toye, innkeeper of the 'Swan'. The Nettlefolds had a long-term connection with the Leatherhead district. Robert, son of Richard Nettlefold, was baptised here in 1658, and the last of the family only left the area recently.

The Akehursts were said to own the north transept of the church in 1701 'as attached to The Mansion House estate', where they lived. Their Church Rate Assessment of £1 1s. 1d. in 1695 shows they were among the most affluent families in the town.

CIVIL WAR

On a June day in 1642 Sir Poynings More, Sir Robert Parkhurst and Nicholas Stoughton, Esquire, Deputy Lieutenants of the county of Surrey, rode into Leatherhead to attend a meeting at The Mansion in Church Street. Their host was the Lord Lieutenant of the County, Charles Howard, Earl of Nottingham. The meeting had been called to discuss the 'proper ordering' of the county militia at the time of tension between King and Parliament. The county leaders met again there in August for a similar purpose, in the Lord Lieutenant's words 'to settle the country (county) in a posture of arms (for Parliament)'.[1] Urgent decisions had to be made in a increasingly dangerous political atmosphere and indeed only a few days later Charles I raised his standard at Nottingham. The Civil War had begun.

Less than two months after the Civil War started, the Earl of Nottingham died but Leatherhead maintained a link with the outside world through Thomas Sands of Randalls Park who had been elected to the Long Parliament as one of the members for Gatton, near Reigate. He supported the Parliamentary cause like most Surrey members and Leatherhead probably followed his example even if some families like the Gardiners and the Rogers were staunchly Royalist.

For a time, Leatherhead people went about their business with little concern for the comings and goings at The Mansion and Randalls Park. The national issues which had caused the war were to them of less importance than the harvest returns and the state of trade. They

[1] HMC, 7th Report, p. 677b.

were not involved in any of the armed confrontations which took place in the Thames Valley in 1642, though some Leatherhead men may have been in the trained bands which formed a large part of the Earl of Essex's army facing King Charles and Prince Rupert at Turnham Green in November that year.

The burdens of war

It was during the winter and spring which followed the inconclusive meeting of the two sides at Turnham Green that everyone came to realise that the war would soon become a serious and continuing drain on their pockets. Taxation they felt had been bad enough under Charles I but they were to find it worse under Parliament's rule. The most unwelcome tax affecting all was the Weekly Assessment introduced by John Pym in February 1643; payments based on an assessor's valuation were collected by the parish constable. County committees were set up to deal with this tax and the Surrey committee met in Leatherhead on 1 April 1643.[1] There were 20 members including Thomas Sands and the meeting was probably at his house. Sands was also involved later in the year in the local administration of the indirect tax known as the Excise. This became law in July 1643, and was a form of purchase tax imposing duties on everyday goods such as beer, tobacco, sugar and some articles of clothing (meat and salt were added in January 1644). In the same year an ordinance was passed for the prosecution of delinquents or Royalist sympathisers, though action against those in Leatherhead was slow and not completed for a long time. Richard Gardiner of Thorncroft and Thomas Rogers of the Rectory were both charged after several months' delay and were allowed to retain their property on payment of a fine. In 1646 a third Leatherhead delinquent, a yeoman named William Flood, was fined for once being a lowly member of the King's household.[2]

Royalist troops at The Mansion (September 1643)

Many months after it was thought that all Cavalier activity had been curbed in Surrey, there were reports of Royalist troops making their presence felt in various parts of the county including Leatherhead. They were encouraged perhaps by the Royalist successes against Parliament in the summer of 1643. Whatever the reasons, some of the King's soldiers on 18 September 1643 appeared in Leatherhead during

The Weekly Assessment tax came to be the most unpopular of the new taxes. A ditty of the day, drawing its theme from the Litany, intoned:

> From believing printed lies,
> From the Devil and Excise,
> Good Lord deliver us.

---

[1] HMC, 5th Report, p. 79a; Firth and Rait, I, p. 94.
[2] Cal. Comm. for Compounding (1643–60), p. 1585.

the night and broke into The Mansion where the widowed Countess of Nottingham was living. Nothing more is known about the affair but the troops were probably soon rounded up. There was reported to be 'some scattering of the troops of the King up and down the county' at this time including 'some at Guilford' and 'towards Reigate'.[1]

In addition, a Leatherhead glover named Fox was suspected of arranging for a horse 'to be conveyed to Oxford' (the King's headquarters). So it seems there was some small local sympathy stirring for the Royalist cause.

The Leatherhead mutiny (February 1645)

In the next two years after the incident at The Mansion, Parliament achieved success in the two decisive battles of Marston Moor (July 1644) and Naseby (June 1645). It was between these battles, in February 1645, that an episode of war occurred in Leatherhead which was more than locally important. By the autumn of 1644 the victory of Marston Moor had been dimmed somewhat by the Earl of Essex's defeat in Cornwall, by the inconclusive second battle of Newbury and by disaffection among Sir William Waller's troops. Many of them had deserted because of pay arrears and dislike of campaigning far from their native counties. These happenings led Parliament to consider forming a New Model Army which would be better disciplined, better trained and more regularly paid. The House of Commons agreed to its establishment in January 1645 and the House of Lords' acceptance of the New Model Army ordinance was hastened because the Leatherhead incident showed 'it would be impossible to carry on with a disorganised army'.[2] Waller had been ordered to relieve Weymouth in early February 1645, but delays occurred because about the 12th of the month his cavalry, formerly part of the Earl of Essex's army, and some infantry had mutinied at Leatherhead. This was discussed by the Committee of Both Kingdoms in London on 15 February, Cromwell being one of its members and it reported to the House of Commons:

'. . . the Lord General's horse being come to Leatherhead, an officer came after them and prevailed with them that they would tarry that night till he might come to the Lord General, which they consented to, saying they would rather go under any (commander) who the Lord General should appoint without money, than with Sir William Waller with all the money in England . . . that Sir William

[1] HMC, 7th Report, p. 686a.
[2] S. R. Gardiner, *History of the Great Civil War* (1886), II, p. 75.

Major-General Skippon (left) who was sent to Leatherhead in 1645 to quell the mutiny against Sir William Waller (right).

Balfour and Major-General Skippon are sent down to the horse and foot respectively to appease and quiet them.'[1]

Indiscipline among Waller's troops was not new since a few months previously he had complained to London about it; this had even reached the ears of the Venetian ambassador who reported on 18 November 1644 that Waller had 'fallen into the lowest estimation with his soldiers'.[2]

That two of the leading Parliamentary generals should have been ordered down to Leatherhead to quell the mutiny is indicative of its size and importance. Sir William Balfour had fought at Edgehill and was a renowned cavalry officer; Skippon was also an experienced general being appointed about this time second-in-command to Fairfax in the New Model Army. The House of Commons was most concerned about the Leatherhead affair and ordered Cromwell to report on it to them.[3] Both generals probably came to the town but only Balfour is referred to in the Committee of Both Kingdoms' records of the succeeding days. Thus, on 18 February 1645, three days after the mutiny was reported, there are two references to Balfour, the first instructing him to 'keep the horse together this night' and assuring him that tomorrow they will receive 'contentment' (presumably payment of arrears); the second repeats the assurances of the first referring to a letter from Balfour written from Banstead dated 17 February 1645 which would suggest that by that date the disaffected army elements had moved there from Leatherhead.[4] The number of horse and foot troops involved in the mutiny is thought to have been about 700 which is a considerable body of soldiers and their presence in and around Leatherhead no doubt created a large stir, not least because of the arrival in the district of two generals under Cromwell's orders.

After the troops finally left for the West under Sir William Waller and Cromwell himself, it became quiet again in Leatherhead and remained so until the end of the Civil War which followed the taking of the King's headquarters at Oxford in June 1646.

The troubled peace (1646–1648)

The end of the first Civil War in 1646 was followed by disagreements among the victors about how the country should be run, although Cromwell's close friend, Hugh Peter, spoke in lyrical terms how fine it was 'to see the highways occupied again; to hear the carter whistling to

[1] Cal. SPD (1644–5), pp. 307–114.
[2] Cal. SP Venetian (1643–7), p. 153.
[3] CJ, IV, p. 52.
[4] Cal. SPD (1644–5), pp. 310, 212.

Sir William Balfour, late Lieutenant of the Tower of London, riding in to assist Major-General Skippon. It is indicative of the importance of the mutiny that two leading Parliamentary generals were ordered to restore order.

his toiling team; to see the hills rejoicing, the valleys laughing . . .' If Leatherhead people felt like this at the end of the war, they were soon disillusioned since they and others throughout the country suffered in 1646 and 1647 two bad harvests and the price of wheat soared to record heights. Much of the blame for the high cost of living was put on the government. The feeling was growing that King and Parliament should work together again for the good of the country encouraged perhaps by increasing Leveller influence at this time. There were also complaints that too many units of the New Model Army continued to be based in Surrey even though the war was over and that the soldiers' demands for free quarters and supplies were unreasonable. Plans were therefore made to petition Parliament.

The first of several meetings held to draw up the Surrey petition were held in Leatherhead on 2 May 1648 when great numbers came to the town from all over the county.[1] They recommended that there should be a 'Personal Treaty between His Majesty and Parliament'; that 'the Armies may be disbanded'; and that 'the Arrears of the Armies may be satisfied and paid'. When the talks ended here, the petitioners, people from all walks of life, moved on to Dorking for a further meeting on 8 May. There was a third session at Putney a week later before the petition was finally agreed. The submission to Parliament was made on 16 May by a large body of Surrey men, and there was an affray with soldiers on guard at the House and some fatalities.[2]

Parliament could hardly have been expected to accept in full the Surrey petitioners' requests, but some sympathy was shown to their complaints about the army and Fairfax was instructed that if any of his forces passed through the county, they should 'take care to carry themselves inoffensively to the people'. So the Surrey petitioners had some success.

The second Civil War (1648)

A few weeks before the excitement over the Surrey petition in which Leatherhead played a part, the second Civil War had started with a rising in Wales and soon spread elsewhere. Kent took up arms for the King late in May and Essex followed soon after. Surrey and Sussex joined a month later. The Surrey rising was small in scale and poorly organised starting early in July 1648 and lasting only a few days. Leatherhead was a witness to some of this.

[1] L.J., X, p. 239a; A. R. Mitchell, 'Surrey in 1648', SAC, **LXVII**, 1970, p. 68.
[2] B. Whitelocke, *Memorials of the English Affairs* (1682), p. 305.

On Thursday, 6 July 1648, the quiet of Leatherhead was disturbed at some 500 to 600 troops mainly on horseback passed through the town on their way to Dorking. They had ridden that day from Kingston forming the chief part of the Earl of Holland's Royalist forces assembled a day or two previously in the hope that strong support would be forthcoming from the county. This did not happen and the small force moved south through the Mole valley hoping to join up with Sussex rebels. They were never able to do this since, after reaching Reigate, they almost immediately retreated to Dorking as Parliamentary troops approached under Sir Michael Livesey. The next morning 7 July, the Royalists retreated further and once again passed through Leatherhead, more rapidly this time, pursued by Livesey's men. There was a small skirmish at Ewell, another at Nonsuch and the Royalists finally turned on their pursuers at Surbiton only to be thoroughly defeated. Lord Francis Villiers, son of the 1st Duke of Buckingham and a Cavalier, was killed but the Earl of Holland escaped only to be caught a few days later.

There is an intriguing postcript to the Surrey rising and Leatherhead's part in it. Nearly two years after these events, two Leatherhead men, Robert Nowton and Thomas Rogers, were accused of being associated with the Earl of Holland's forces. Nowton had been 'in arms in Lord Holland's party' and Rogers had 'sent a man on horse armed, and rode himself with the party'.[1] Edward Arnold of Mickleham and Sir Charles Howard of Great Bookham are also said to have helped the rebels. There had therefore been some support for the Earl of Holland in the Leatherhead district.

THE INTERREGNUM (1649–1660)

It is not known how Leatherhead people reacted to the trial and execution of Charles I, the abolition of the House of Lords and the formation of the Commonwealth in early 1649. Uppermost in their minds would be concern on how a republican government's policies might affect their daily lives. They would certainly have known that Thomas Sands of Randalls Park had come back to Leatherhead after being excluded from Parliament by Pride's Purge in December 1648.[2] Some of the town may have supported the Surrey petition to Parliament asking for reforms of the militia, the law and the removal of tithes, presented only a few days after the King's death, to no avail.

[1] Cal. Comm. for Advance of Money, 3, p. 1222.

[2] D. Underdown, *Prides Purge* (Oxford, 1971), p. 384.

Leatherhead people were, in fact, probably less concerned with the goings-on in London than with the recent bad harvest, the fourth in a row, which caused rocketing food prices. Most of the town depended either directly or indirectly on satisfactory returns from the land and a succession of poor years must have led to hardship. Some may have felt a little sympathy for the short-lived Diggers' movement led by Gerard Winstanley at St George's Hill, Weybridge, which in April 1649 bravely claimed the right to dig and grow food on common land.

A few months after the Commonwealth Government had been set up, strangers were to be seen studying the Leatherhead Rectory and inspecting the glebe belonging to it. They were assessing its value under a Parliamentary Commission now that the Deans and Chapters had been abolished by government ordinance in April 1649. The Commissioners' Report[1] refers to Thomas Rogers as being 'the ymediate tennant of the premisses', although he had been sequestered for Royalist sympathies three years earlier (see p. 79). The Rectory's rent of £17 was ordered to be paid to William Robinson, creditor of the Deanery for 21 years. After that, £10 of the £17 was 'to remain on the tithes' perhaps to help the vicar, the remainder to be sold as a reversion. The Rectory building was said to be in a 'very ruinous' state at the time of the survey.

A series of good harvests in the 1650s helped the return to stable living conditions after years of disruptive war. Despite this, there were some in the district who took an active interest in Royalist hopes for Restoration. During Charles' advance into England from Scotland in 1651, Sir Francis Stydolf of Norbury Park, among other Surrey gentry, was said to be sympathetic to a rising in the county but nothing came of this and Charles' defeat by Cromwell at Worcester stilled Royalist aspirations for several years. Although Surrey was not involved in Penruddock's rising in 1655, there were some anti-government rumblings in the county in 1656 and 1657, the only notable one here being in the summer of 1659. This had first started in the north led by Sir George Booth but there was also much activity south of London. The Surrey leader was John Mordaunt, younger son of the Earl of Peterborough and on 13 August 1659 he and his followers said to number about 80 gathered on Banstead Downs awaiting others 'from the direction of Leatherhead'. However, they rapidly dispersed when Parliamentary troops were sighted. It is this assembly of Surrey Royal-

[1] A. R. Bax, 'Parliamentary survey of Church lands', *SAC*, **XVII**, 1902, pp. 83–121.

ists which Richard Dalton may be referring to when submitting a petition to the King on the eve of the Restoration; he declared that he had 'suffered much for being active for the King in the Surrey business'.[1]

A few months before these happenings, Leatherhead had a serious fire. According to Surrey Justices, the fire on 28 April 1659 'consumed and burnt to the ground several dwelling houses with goods and household stuffs . . . and also divers barns, stables, buildings and shops . . . to the utter ruin and undoing of the inhabitants, their wives and children'.[2] The justices appealed for help for Leatherhead to other parishes in the county. Some of the damaged buildings may have been rebuilt by the time the Restoration came just over a year later (May 1660) but because of the fire it is doubtful whether the Leatherhead townspeople were able to share to the full the joyous mood of the country at the return of Charles II.

Farming in a changing world (1558–1660)

At this period, farming was the main occupation of most Leatherhead people. When Elizabeth came to the throne, the harvest throughout the country was the best for many years, so the new reign started well in the farmers' eyes and it was not until the 1590s that there was a run of poor harvests.[3] The farmers followed the traditional practices based on open field and enclosed field cultivation, and the use of common meadows, wastes and woodlands, watched over, as for centuries past, by the manorial courts. Subsistence agriculture predominated though there was often a surplus for sale. Social and economic pressures were leading to changes in farming.

Among the factors making for change was the growth of Leatherhead's population, like that of other towns (see p. 71). The extra food needed had to be produced by increasing crop yields especially wheat and by extending the cultivated areas. Books were being published on how to improve the soil and those by Tusser, Googe and Norden were most widely read. Writing on the eve of the Civil War, Fuller colourfully describes how the yeoman of the day 'improveth his land to a double value by his good husbandrie – some grounds that wept with water or frowned with thorns, by draining the one and cleansing the other, he makes both to laugh and sing with corn'.[4] Leatherhead farming land probably benefited in this way. Early

[1] Cal. SPD (1659–60), p. 426.
[2] Surrey Quarter Sessions (1659–61), p. 7.
[3] W. G. Hoskins 'Harvest fluctuations 1480–1619', *Agric. Hist. Rev.*, **III**, 1964, p. 36.
[4] T. Fuller, *Holy and Profane State* (1642), pp. 106–7.

in the 17th century, Sir Francis Stydolf of Norbury Park tried yet failed to enclose and improve part of the Leatherhead Downs for crop growing but he had been successful in enclosing some Thorncroft manor land. A 1629 survey says that he 'holdeth two enclosed grounds called Radfields, estimated when they laie open at 12 acres',[1] part of nearly 100 acres of Thorncroft land owned by him. Corn growing, fruit cultivation, dairying, meat production and market gardening in the Leatherhead area were being encouraged by increasing local demand and by the rapid expansion of the London market said to have grown five-fold between 1570 and 1638 and continued to grow.

The change in farming habits was gradual and for most the traditional ways seemed to be the best. In the year of Queen Elizabeth's death, fear of the plague added to farmers' worries and trade suffered over a wide area round London. This did not last long because the following year saw the end of the war with Spain which for the wealthier farmers, like Sir Francis Stydolf and the Sands family of Randalls Park, meant a release from some of the burdens of taxation. A run of good harvests in the next three years increased their prosperity.

During the whole of James I's reign there were only four poor harvests in 1608, 1613, 1617 and 1622. The year 1620 came to be remembered as having the most abundant crop returns since Elizabeth came to the throne. There was then a sudden swing to harder conditions, made worse in 1625 by another serious plague. Farming continued to be depressed over much of Charles I's reign up to the outbreak of the Civil War. This was not only due to indifferent harvests but to a fall in wool prices.

Field arrangements and farming practices

A traveller passing through Leatherhead on his way to London at this period would have seen meadows bordered by trees or bushes near the River Mole. On the hill beyond the church was the Common Field, a large open arable field with rectangular strips separated by rough grass verges. This merged into an expanse of pasture ground, the Leatherhead Downs with coppices of woodland. To the north of the town, enclosed fields abutted on to common land and near the Mole there were meadows, one of them divided into strips. This describes in simple terms the field layout as it was, the mixture of open field and enclosures being characteristic of many parts of Surrey.

[1] Merton College, Oxford: Muniments 5/28; H. Lambert 'Some accounts of Surrey manors in the 17th C.', *SAC*, **XLI**, 1933, p. 44.

The Leatherhead Common Field lay on the lower slopes of the Downs like those at Fetcham and Great Bookham and other parishes, along the north-facing chalk hills. It was divided into strips, each individually owned. Shown in detail on the Gwilt map of Leatherhead (1782–1783) there were 374 strips in all including six in the small extension to the Common Field called the Common Fair Field, north of what is now the High Street. The strips were chiefly freehold, most of them under two acres in size. The arable farming practised here was not strictly regulated by the manorial courts in ways such as existed in Midland parishes, since none of the surviving records refer to controls over the crops grown. This suggests that there was no true field system in Leatherhead in which holdings were equally divided between two or three open fields, one field lying fallow every two or three years. It is possible that the strip owners were free to come to some loose arrangement among themselves about cropping. They had however to conform to the ancient manorial rules on common rights. For example, the Thorncroft Manor court imposed fines on those who allowed sheep to graze on the Common Field at the wrong times and the Pachenesham Manor court acted similarly against anyone unlawfully felling trees. Copyholders who held manorial land for life or a specific number of years had to pay a heriot 'at the death of everie tenante' and this used to be 'the best beasts' but it was now normally redeemed for a money payment.[1]

The Common Meadow along the river near the Leatherhead bridge and the 'open' downs well to the south were important to farming at this time providing hay and pasturage for livestock.[2] The manor courts exercised strict control over their use as they did over the common 'waste' on the northern limits of the parish.

In the farming areas of Leatherhead outside the 'common' lands, enclosures were widespread. An old map (c. 1600) shows enclosed 'meads' near the river north of the town forming part of the Randalls Park lands, and a 1629 survey of Thorncroft Manor says that three-quarters of its land was 'in several', that is in enclosed fields and only one-quarter in the Common Field.[3] Other enclosures are shown on the 18th century Rocque and Gwilt maps and the pattern they reveal probably existed as in the 17th century. The Rectory's glebelands close to the church had 34 acres of 'errable closes' and a similar acreage of 'errable peeces', according to a 1649 survey. It is not clear what the

[1] Thorncroft Manor Court Rolls (Abstract), p. vi.

[2] F. B. Benger, 'The Leatherhead Common Meadow', *Proc. LDLHS*, **3** (2), 1968, pp. 53–5.

[3] Merton College, Oxford: Muniments 5/28.

'peeces' were but they may have been unenclosed parcels in enclosed fields. Even though enclosures were so general in most parts of the parish, the traditional farming elements of open field, common meadow, 'waste', woodland and downs continued to be important at this period and for a long time afterwards.

Crops and fruit

Wheat, barley, peas and beans were the main crops grown. In 1595 'the north side of the Downes between Guildford and Leatherhead' was described as one of the 'greatest places for corne' in Surrey.[1] About this time Robert Sands bequeathed to his son '10 acres in winter wheat, now sown in Leatherhead' while Edward Skeete, another local farmer in Elizabeth's reign, left barley to his children and servants.

The crop rotation they followed is not known but wheat, barley and fallow seems a likely sequence in one strip, with rye and possibly oats being included in another, with many variations including a place for peas and beans. On some farms convertible husbandry may have been practised in which arable fields were put down to grass for several years and pastureland ploughed up. This was becoming common in areas like Leatherhead where the open-field system which militated against this, was not rigorously applied.

Wheat was used by wealthy farmers and gentry mainly to make bread and it was probably the chief crop sold at the markets. Among the less well off, barley was the staple corn for bread-making together with rye, though wheat mixed with rye (maslin) was popular as well. Malt and beer were also made from barley. Other crops cultivated may have included hops, since Surrey's 'lowe and spongie ground', like the low-lying lands near the Mole, were said to be suitable for it.[2] Woad for use as a cloth dye may also have been grown. Leatherhead's loss of its market in the middle of Elizabeth's reign[3] may indicate some fall in local trading but Dorking market was not far off and travelling merchants, common enough at this time,[4] enabled the farmers' produce to reach towns like London, ever further afield. An annual fair was held in the town traditionally after the end of the harvest in early August, but in the late 17th century it was said to have taken place on Lady Day, 8 September.

Most farmers had some fruit trees, usually in orchards close to where they lived. The farmers' wives of Surrey took their fruit, mainly

[1] A. R. Bax, 'Parliamentary survey of Church lands', *SAC,* **XVII,** 1902, pp. 106–15.
[2] BL, Add. MSS 31, 853.
[3] J. Norden, *Surveyor's Dialogue* (1607), p. 206.
[4] J. Aubrey, *Nat. Hist. & Antiq. of Surrey* (1718) 2, p. 251.

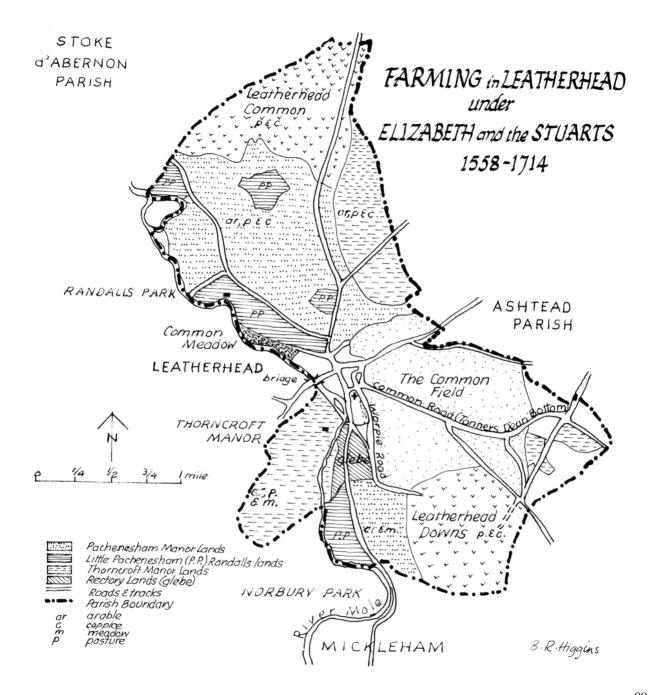

STOKE
d'ABERNON
PARISH

Leatherhead
Common
p.&.c.

FARMING in LEATHERHEAD
under
ELIZABETH and the STUARTS
1558-1714

P.P.

P.P.

ar, p.&.c.

ar, p.&.c.

RANDALLS PARK

P.P.

ASHTEAD
PARISH

Common
Meadow

P.P.

LEATHERHEAD

bridge

The Common
Field

Common Road (Tanners Dean Bottom)

THORNCROFT
MANOR

Worple Road

glebe

N

Leatherhead
Downs p.&.c.

0   1/4   1/2   3/4   1 mile

a.&.p.
&.m.

cr.&.m.

P.P.

NORBURY PARK

River Mole

MICKLEHAM

B.R.Higgins

Pachenesham Manor Lands
Little Pachenesham (P.P.) Randalls lands
Thorncroft Manor Lands
Rectory Lands (glebe)
Roads & tracks
Parish Boundary
ar   arable
c   coppice
m   meadow
p   pasture

99

apples, pears and cherries, regularly to the market serving London. In 1637, these as well as peaches, plums, strawberries, raspberries and gooseberries, were growing in the county.

Livestock

The farmer depended on his cattle and sheep for milk, meat and wool as well as for the manuring of his fields. Some contemporary sources give a rough indication of the number of sheep held. The Assize Records for July 1579, for example, mention that 19 sheep belonging to Edward Skeete had been stolen, presumably only a small proportion of his total flock and in the mid-17th century Edward Hudson is said to have had at least 200 sheep.

Cattle and pig and horse numbers are not known, but every farmer probably had a few cattle for dairying and others for their meat and for draught purposes.

Livestock were allowed to use the arable fields only after the harvest (early August), at other times they used the common 'wastes' and in July after the hay harvest, the riverside meadows. Pasturing rights are referred to in a claim for extending them early in 1610 (see page 97). This described clearly the areas used for pasturing and the rights concerning them.

The Lower Common, meadow land for 'Great Cattell' along the Mole north of the town, was subdivided into individually-owned strips and only thrown open to the whole community after haymaking early in July. The Upper Common, or Leatherhead Downs, high above the town, was for sheep only and there were no limits on the numbers kept there. The shepherds probably managed their flocks with a loose folding system using hurdles which could be moved easily, so ensuring that each part of the field was manured in turn. They also used a staff with a half-horn at its end to hurl stones at wayward sheep.

Wastes and woodlands

Many of the farmers' needs, like wood for fuel, fences and implements, were obtained from the wastes and woodlands of the Leatherhead Downs and the common land adjoining Ashtead, north of the town. Permission had to be sought from the manor courts to cut timber: thus, the Thorncroft Manor court of 29 April 1648 stipulated that no tenant should 'fell any bushes in the Common belonging to

Shepherd with half horn and stone satchel, taken from Sir Philip Sydney's *Arcadia*, 1593. Flocks of sheep were controlled by the dog and the half horn, a cow's horn split and attached to the top of a staff. A stone could be hurled a considerable distance by placing it in the half horn and swinging the staff over the shoulder forwards. Confronted with a barrage of stones, the straying sheep would return to the fold. It is probable that the half horn goes back to even earlier times and with a similar device David may have struck down Goliath.

Thorncroft before they do come to acquaint some of the house of Thorncroft', and the court fined James Arnold 2s. 'for cutting bushes on the common' without authority.

The coppices which formed much of the woodlands are likely to have had a dense undergrowth useful for firewood, and there would also be a number of large timber trees called 'standards' like oak, ash, hazel, yew and birch. Timber sales were obviously an important source of income for farmers with woodland. The building accounts for Ashley House at Walton-on-Thames 1602–1607 show that Leatherhead was one of the main districts supplying timber for the construction work.

Farming after the Restoration

After the Restoration, farming in Leatherhead continued in the same mould, though in time there came to be a partial acceptance of the new fodder crops advocated by many contemporary writers. There was still the large, open arable field close to the church, a meadow divided into strips near the Mole bridge, and many enclosed fields with common pastures and patches of woodland on the north and south outskirts of the parish. Mixed farming was the rule with cereal growing, livestock, dairying and some fruit production, the growth of London providing an increasingly profitable market though farm sales were dislocated for a while in the mid-1660s by the Great Plague and Great Fire. Many of Leatherhead's farm buildings damaged by the 1659 fire (see p. 95) were probably still needing repair at the time of the Restoration and the very bad harvest in the following year (1661) added to the farmers' problems. Harvests improved after this, and they continued to be good for much of King Charles II's reign, but in the 1690s, and again in 1709/1710, they were seriously deficient. In these dearth years, corn prices were very high and food was more than usually expensive. But Leatherhead farmers were not wholly dependent on cereal production, having dairying and fruit interests so that the effect of the bad corn harvest may not have been unduly serious except for the small husbandman, the labourers and the poor of the parish.

Land sales of farming property were common in Leatherhead after the Restoration, as they had been earlier in the century. The consolidation of small farms into larger ones was taking place in many parts of the country, particularly after 1680. The Sands family of Randalls Park had been enlarging their holdings since early in the century, and other Leatherhead landowners probably sought similar benefits but the evidence is fragmentary. There were still copyholders or customary tenants, holding properties for life or a number of years and heriots were paid (now usually in money) on death or at the end of the agreed term. Much land was also held on leases, one of 21 years being referred to in 1688 and there were, in addition, a large number of freeholders listed in the Thorncroft Manor rolls for September 1680 and others in the Pachenesham Manor rental of 1693.

Something of the make-up of Leatherhead's farming at this time may be gathered from local inventories. One of these concerning Edward Lampard, a yeoman who died in 1670, refers to eight acres of barley and peas 'in the ground' and another mentions these crops as well as wheat as being 'in the barn'.[1] Maslin, a mixture of wheat and rye, is mentioned in one of the inventories, which also talks of 'hops in the loft', the first reference (1669) there is to it in the Leatherhead district.[2] The inventories refer to cattle and sheep and horses. One of the farmers had what he called 'the Milk House' in which there were 'eighteen cheeses and butter', so dairying was certainly part of the farming business. Fruit was grown on most farms and orchards appearing in land ownership documents. A 1707 lease referred to one as large as 21 acres. Bee-keeping is also mentioned.[3]

As in the earlier years of the 17th century, the Leatherhead manorial courts concentrated on maintaining common rights without imposing mandatory controls on what crops should be grown in the open arable field. The court records show in particular the pressure to increase the cultivable area by encroaching on common land. At the Pachenesham Manor court of 17 October 1706, three people were fined for enclosing part of Leatherhead Common and this kind of case appears often in other court records. The fines do not seem to have discouraged the encroachers since at subsequent courts the same offenders reappear. Other misdemeanours controverting the manorial rules included allowing cattle and sheep to feed on the meadows or common fields at the wrong times and removing bushes and stakes from Leatherhead Common.[4]

New ventures in farming

The urge to cultivate more land was accompanied by an increasing

[1] PROB 4/3082 (Lampard); PROB 4/277 (Arnold).
[2] PROB 4/5795 (Kirke).
[3] PROB 4/6628 (Reyley).
[4] SRO 59/1/5: Pachesham Court Rolls, 1654–88; 1706–25 (6/17).

interest in new ways to improve crop yields and provide extra for livestock. For many years farmers had been pressed to improve their manuring of the soil and to introduce fodder crops like clover, sainfoin and lucerne. Some clover was said to be sown in most counties of England at this time but it was probably not yet widely used as a rotation crop. Farmers in the Leatherhead area seem to have started to grow this new crop since a 1693 inventory refers to a 'parcel of clover' in the barn and the Pachenesham Court (records for 29 September 1711 say that 'no persons shall bring their sheep upon any clover or other seed grass after Christmas Day'). The new husbandry also encouraged the production of root crops especially turnips which agricultural writers of the day argued would enable the farmer to feed his cattle and sheep throughout the winter. The soil, they said, 'need not be very rich' and two crops could be grown in the year, sowing taking place in April or May and August 'at the wane of the moon'. By the reign of Queen Anne, turnips were said to be found over much of the east and south of England, but it was probably well into the 18th century before turnip cultivation became general in Leatherhead.

The church in the community (1558–1642)

Leatherhead's parish life at this time followed an ordered course as it had always done, determined by the festivals of the Christian year coinciding so often with the seasonal round in farm and field. The unchanging pattern of the seasons masked, but could not let people forget, the alterations made in church practices in the years before Elizabeth became Queen. Many of the ancient rites had been done away with, the church fabric shorn of its images, walls defaced and vestments sold and although there had been a brief reversal to the old customs in Mary's reign, further iconoclasm and other changes were to be expected under her successor.

At the time of Elizabeth's accession in November 1558, the Vicar of Leatherhead, William Walkeden, had been incumbent for little over a year and he seems to have accepted the abrupt introduction once again of the Protestant ethic, first by the need to subscribe to the Acts of Uniformity and Supremacy and then to agree to implement the Queen's Injunctions on the correct church practices. The Prayer Book in English was to be used, homilies were to be read in church 'every Sunday at the least'. Announced beforehand by the tolling of a bell, litany and prayers had to be said on Wednesdays and Fridays; the 'holy table' was to be placed in the chancel during the communion service and the clergy were expected to wear 'seemly dress', avoid alehouses and not play cards or dice. These are only a small selection of the 1559 Injunctions and it is unlikely that William Walkeden managed to obey all. Sermons, as distinct from homilies, could be delivered only by licensed preachers and the Vicar of Leatherhead was not one of these. He had therefore to read the dreary homilies (even if some were written by Cranmer) Sunday by Sunday; to do otherwise, would have risked the Bishop's wrath. However, since almost the whole bench of Bishops had resigned over Elizabeth's religious policy, there was a breathing space of a year or two, though the new Bishop of Winchester did make a Visitation of his diocese soon after his consecration in February 1561.

It was in this year that William Walkeden resigned his Leatherhead living. Although he had stayed on during the early years of the new reign, his resignation suggests an increasing disenchantment brought to a head perhaps by the impending Bishop's Visitation. On the whole, the Bishop found Surrey a conforming county. It is known that Walkeden had recently married, presumably under Elizabeth's recent dispensation, but if he had not sought permission for this he would have courted disfavour. It may have been another factor in his decision to resign. He probably anticipated the Bishop's disapproval. At all events, no other Vicar of Leatherhead took this step, Simon Tysse and John Vaughan dying in office. In 1584, Vaughan was said to be 'a common resorter to alehouses' and given to 'typling and gusling'; one day he had to be 'led home' because of drinking too much. Richard Levitt, who succeeded Vaughan, stayed on until the Civil War.

There was clearly a willingness in the parish to settle down to the established Church of England pattern as ordained by the new Queen in the 1559 Injunctions and in the Thirty-nine Articles of 1563 and church life continued its routine way. On Sundays, morning service started at nine o'clock and everyone had to attend, defaulters paying 1s. to church funds which was a large sum in those days. Let us go into the church. The churchwardens steer people to their proper appointed seats, the Vicar already seated at what looked like a desk in the nave close to the chancel steps and the service began with the parish clerk in the black gown and surplice chanting a psalm. The Litany was read and after a few lessons and prayers, the Vicar delivered a homily, or a sermon, if this was Richard Levitt's time. (The Star Chamber case in which he was involved in the early 1600s refers to his 'painful and diligent' preaching over many years (see below). The service ended with a psalm or hymn and lasted about two hours, leaving time at the end for a chat at the porch and a slow walk home for dinner about midday. There was another service in the afternoon and after this the vicar had to catechise the children for perhaps an hour on their beliefs and to educate them as best he could.

But church life was not only services and learning the catechism. Vestry meetings were held regularly at the church and much day-to-day business was transacted in the church porch. As in the modern parish, fund-raising was a constant preoccupation of the churchwardens and although the church rates levied on all householders helped, reliance was also placed on what they called 'Church-Ales', a lively social gathering usually held about Whitsuntide. Ale was specially brewed, great quantities of food prepared and minstrels and morris dancers encouraged to perform during the feasting which might have lasted several days. Close to Whitsuntide, there was the annual perambulation or 'beating of the bounds' of the parish, ending perhaps with a vestry dinner.

None of these activities helped the vicar to improve his lot and he had to depend on a meagre income from the diocese, reduced by compulsory state subsidy payments from time to time, and supplemented only by what he might gain from fees, tithes and perhaps selling some farm produce. Leatherhead was probably more favoured than some parishes since it had attracted Richard Levitt, the well-educated former Vicar of Twickenham to it in 1590. The glebelands near the church were leased or, more accurately, impropriated to a layman by the patrons of the living, the Dean and Chapter of Rochester. Early in James I's reign, the layman, Edward Rogers, challenged the payment of tithes to the Vicar and also sought his removal from office. The case was heard at the Star Chamber in London but no decision was reached. Its interest lies in the bitter rancour revealed by the litigants over church lands and their ownership. Richard Levitt's tough defence of his position succeeded and he stayed on in Leatherhead until the mid-1640s. In view of the long tenure of his living, it seems likely that he struck a middle-of-the-road attitude to controversial church issues like so many incumbents, conforming to the general rules of the church as directed by London. He probably approved of the Authorised Version of the Bible initiated at the Hampton Court Conference in 1604 and issued to all parishes seven years later.

The fear of Catholic resurgence and of Protestant extremism common throughout the country in Elizabeth's reign, does not appear to have disturbed Leatherhead. The Archdeaconry of Surrey returns in 1603[1] mention only one Catholic as living in the town but the three other non-communicants listed may have been members of one of the several extreme Protestant sects like the Brownists or the Barrowists. Edward Skeete, who died in 1599, may have been one of these since his will includes the unusual request to be buried 'in the place provided for the Christian congregation'.

Church and parish during the Civil War and Interregnum

At the outbreak of the Civil War there were few Leatherhead parishioners who could remember a time when Richard Levitt was not their Vicar since by that time he had been vicar for over 50 years. He was then an old man in his mid-eighties and almost certainly resented the revolutionary religious changes introduced in the 1640s. There had been a foretaste of things to come as early as May 1641 when he and other country vicars had had to obtain from all 18-year-olds and over, their signed promise to defend the 'true Reformed Protestant Religion . . . against all Poperie . . . and also maintain the power and privileges of Parliament'. This was the so-called Protestation Oath.[2] This measure did not perhaps worry the Vicar and his parishioners unduly nor even abolition of episcopacy early in 1643 but they would be concerned about what form of a new church government might take. They had not long to wait for an ever more wide-ranging interference in parish life. Whitehall agents were particularly on the look-out for scandalous behaviour by incumbents and early in the war they suspended the Rectors of Ashtead and Mickleham.[3] Richard Levitt's tenure was also precarious, his case coming before the Committee for Plundered Ministers in London on 22 March 1644 later to be quashed, most likely because of his advanced age. This was taking place about the time when all priests and laymen were required to agree to the

[1] BL, Harleian MSS 595.
[2] H. Carter (Ed.), 'The Surrey protestation returns', *SAC*, **LIX,** 1962, pp. 35–68.
[3] A. G. Matthews, *Walker Revised, The Sufferings of the Clergy, 1642–60* (Oxford, 1948), p. 352.

Solemn League and Covenant and Richard Levitt may well have had doubts about this since by doing so he would have become, in name at least, a 'Presbyterian' minister.

More was to follow to disturb the old Vicar. He may have approved the call for better observation of Sunday worship, but not its rigid exclusion of all sports and pastimes on Sunday. In January 1645, the Book of Common Prayer which he and his parishioners had used all their lives, was replaced by the Directory of Public Worship. Christmas and other Feast Days were abolished and heavy fines imposed for non-compliance.

Richard Levitt was at this time in the process of being replaced as Vicar of Leatherhead by Thomas Mell. It seems likely that Mell had been helping at the church for some years since he was a witness at a Leatherhead ceremony in 1641 and a poll tax of this period refers to him as the 'curate'.[1] He appears to have taken over the parish completely in May 1647.[2]

While changes were taking place at the Vicarage, a new Presbyterian-type church organisation was being set up, at least on paper, in the country. An Ordinance was passed in August 1645 for the election of elders and another, eight months later, for the establishment of a parochial Presbyterian system. The so-called classical system for Surrey, with nominated ministers and lay elders, was first drawn up in February 1647 and sanctioned the following year. It is not known how far Leatherhead and the neighbouring parishes conformed and the churches probably carried on more or less as they were, with only partial compliance to the demands from London.

Thomas Mell was the Vicar of Leatherhead for the whole Interregnum. Since he had been appointed by Parliament in the later 1640s, it is improbable that he was investigated during these years like many incumbents. Because of the way he obtained the living, he most likely followed closely the Parliament's rules on the proper ordering of parish life. The influence of the more vociferous independent preachers was probably felt in the town and the Quakers were known to be active in Surrey. George Fox, their leader, visited Reigate in 1655.

It would be wrong to assume that the Presbyterian influence of Thomas Mell or that of itinerant preachers affected deeply the life of the town, which in the Interregnum period had a population of about 400. The parish church was still the centre of Leatherhead society and

[1] SRO, Ref 212/66/7.
[2] HMC, 5th Report, App. p. 177a; Cal. House of Lords (22 May 1647).

the abolition of penalties for not going to Sunday services contributed to a greater freedom, even though sports and pastimes were still barred. The ban on festivals especially Christmas was strongly disliked but private celebrations were probably carried on at home. These were enlivened by music and dancing since, although both were frowned upon in public, they were not discouraged absolutely. Cromwell himself was known to like music and encouraged composers.[1]

The social change perhaps most resented by Leatherhead people in the 1650s was the introduction of civil marriages. After 29 September 1653, Thomas Mell was not allowed to solemnise weddings in the church. These were to take place before Justices of the Peace and a parish official called a Registrar was charged with making a due record of marriages, births and deaths.

Church and parish after the Restoration

The Presbyterian Vicar of Leatherhead, Thomas Mell, may have thought that radical changes in church life would be avoided in the early months after the Restoration of Charles II, who seemed to favour a Presbyterian/Anglican compromise. This was not to be. In a short time, the High Church clergy secured, with Clarendon's help, a full return to Anglican ways; the Act of Uniformity (1662) required all incumbents to follow the Church of England rubric and in particular to use the Common Prayer Book at services. Those who refused to comply were to be ejected from their living. Mell stayed on in Leatherhead until his death in 1671, so he clearly decided to conform whatever the calls of his conscience. This was a hard decision for anyone of his background since he was now required to accept the Bishop's rulings, wear the surplice, bow to the altar, take the communion service according to the Anglican rite and follow the Common Prayer Book scrupulously instead of the Puritan Directory of Worship. His near neighbours, the incumbents of Ashtead, Fetcham, East and West Horsley and Dorking, felt that they could not compromise in this way and were ejected.[2]

Leatherhead people readily accepted the return to the traditional Anglican rites which most of them were brought up with. Everyone had to go to church on Sundays as laid down in a proclamation of 22 August 1662 and fines were imposed for non-attendance. Feast days and Anglican Communion were restored and the services were

[1] P. A. Scholes, *The Puritans and Music* (Oxford, 1934), p. 130.
[2] A. G. Matthews, *Calamy Revised* (Oxford 1934).

brighter than they had been before the Restoration. Bells rang out again and bellringers were busy. The Leatherhead churchwarden's accounts refer to payment of £1. 7s. for ringing on 5 November 1712, 6 February and 8 March 1713 with news of peace. Accession bells on 29 May 1713 and bells for the Queen's birthday on 25 January 1714 were rung for which the ringers were paid 6s. on each occasion.

Non-conformism in Leatherhead was very limited; Bishop Compton's census of 1676 lists only three in the town. They were no doubt living here when Mell was incumbent and he may have protected them from persecution so common at this time. His successors as Vicar, John Frank in 1671 and Robert Hanbury in 1679, did not have his Puritan background. Indeed Hanbury was a Royal Chaplain. The Leatherhead non-conformists probably attended meetings (or conventicles) in Dorking and, except for a short time in 1672, they always feared prosecution until the passing of William III's Toleration Act of 1689. Three Quakers were reported to be living in the town early in the 18th century.

Shortly before the Glorious Revolution in 1688, James II's Chancellor, the notorious Judge Jeffreys, came to Leatherhead to see his dying daughter. In late November that year he sent his family to Thorncroft Manor, the home of Sir Thomas Bludworth, Lady Jeffrey's brother, to avoid the mounting troubles in London. He is believed to have come here after being told of his daughter's serious illness. He probably stayed until her death and burial on 2 December. Legend has it that Jeffreys came to Leatherhead in flight from London rioters and went into hiding 'in an underground chamber' at The Mansion. There seems to be no truth in this, nevertheless the legend has been repeated many times since it was first mentioned by Manning and Bray and by Dallaway in the early 19th century.[1]

At the time all this was happening, Leatherhead was changing its vicar. This is a story involving Royal patronage and a rather mysterious handover which soon brought the old incumbent Robert Hanbury into a long court case with his successor, Robert Johnson.

The story begins with a letter from James II to the Archbishop of Canterbury dated 13 October 1688 in which the King asked the Archbishop to approve the appointment of one of his chaplains, Robert Hanbury, as Rector of Hemingford Abbots in Huntingdonshire, while continuing to be at Leatherhead.[2] He could not have held

[1] A. T. Ruby, 'The birth of the legend', *Proc. LDLHS*, **3** (1), 1967, pp. 4–8.

[2] Cal. SPD (1687–9), p. 313.

the two parishes for more than a few weeks since he is known to have become Rector of Hemingford Abbots late in 1688 and Robert Johnson came here early in 1689, some months before his reported appointment as Vicar on 19 June in that year. Johnson's arrival much earlier than this date is shown by the records of the court case in which he charged Robert Hanbury with leaving him a broken-down Vicarage. When the case started on 4 February 1689, Hanbury is referred to as 'the late Vicar' so he had clearly left Leatherhead some time before then. Robert Johnson obtained an estimate for the repairs needed and these include bricklayer's and carpenter's work at the kitchen end of the house and mending the roof, the hall, the cellar and the outside wall in several places. There was obviously much work to be done. The case took a long time, extending into 1690, with Robert Johnson successful and Hanbury having to pay £25 'for dilapidations and ruin of the house'.[1]

The Vicarage had probably been in this poor state before but only Robert Johnson seems to have gone to court about it. He was Vicar of Leatherhead from the 1688 Revolution until 1752, even longer than the redoubtable Richard Levitt in the early 17th century. Johnson was by no means well-to-do since in 1707 he was judged poor enough to receive money from Queen Anne's Bounty, a charity set up to assist poorer clergy.

Watch and ward by the Vestry

In the previous period, local disputes and matters of tenure were regulated by the manorial courts. However, from the 16th century, the Tudor statutes including the Elizabethan Poor Law placed the responsibility for administration squarely on the parishes. Vestry meetings took over the handling of local matters which were meticulously recorded in Vestry books. Leatherhead's date only from 1693–1739.

The Vestry members who formed a committee of leading parishioners under the Vicar, played a central part in Leatherhead's parish life. There were two churchwardens, a constable, two overseers of the poor and two way-wardens or surveyors of the highways. These officials were elected yearly and they had a busy time ensuring that the church services were properly attended, the church kept clean and tidy, the church rates duly collected and attention paid to the needs and concerns of the parish.

[1] Court of Arches (B/12/6).

Judge George Jeffreys by W. Claret, 1678. The historian Macauley is responsible for Jeffreys' bad reputation as a 'hanging' judge, due to his harsh sentencing of Monmouth's rebels in 1685. Recently his ruthlessness has been attributed to his suffering from a kidney stone.

The Stocks House in 1822 from a watercolour by Hassell showing the stocks on the road and the lock-up at the side.

Law and order

There was no one in the parish quite so well known as the constable who was responsible for keeping the peace. Though involved with the Vestry work, he was elected by the manor court. When brawls occurred, the constable brought those involved to justice. In 1598 he reported that Henry Stydolf, a member of the wealthy Stydolf family, 'made affray' against Walter Neale and 'broke his head and drew blood'; he also 'shot him in the leg with an arrow and threw punches at him'.[1] Troubles of this kind seem to have been fairly frequent so the constable had his hands full, especially since he was also responsible for taking serious cases through JPs, to the Quarters Sessions or Assizes. Stealing of farm animals, often by butchers, and illegal brewing were common. In addition, the constable was charged with assembling able-bodied men for musters, collecting taxes and getting rid of rogues and vagabonds. These he often kept in the stocks before sending them on their way with a whipping. The nursery rhyme dating from this period makes this all too clear – 'Hark, hark the dogs do bark; the beggars are coming to town; some gave them white bread, some gave them brown; and some gave them a good horsewhip and sent them out of town'. The old stocks of Leatherhead probably stood close to the junction of the present North Street with Bridge Street and in the 17th century there was a building known as the Stocks House near the junction, which may have been a prison.[2]

The records of the Quarter Sessions give perhaps the only accurate flavour of the general social scene. By law, people were obliged to attend church, accept fixed wages and sell their produce in markets at fixed prices. They were forbidden to possess certain books, play certain games, whistle or beat a wife after 9 p.m. As well as enforcing these restrictions, the Quarter Sessions dealt with felonies including larceny, witchcraft, the taking of life, rioting, neglect of hedges, pollution of rivers, purse-picking, tippling and immorality. For instance, in 1663, it is recorded that three Leatherhead men, Robert Rowing, labourer, Nicholas Kent, husbandman, and John Munger, wood-breaker, 'threw a great quantity of dung on the highway called Leatherhead Street'. Richard Cottingham 'kept unpruned his hedge against the highway from Leatherhead to Headley'. In 1665, Richard Stone, yeoman, was proclaimed 'a common swearer, evil speaker and profaner of the name of God', while Richard Gardiner was indicted for

[1] Pachesham Court Rolls, SRO 59/1/4, 28 April 1598.
[2] F. B. Benger, 'The Stocks House', *Proc. LDLHS*, **2** (5), 1961, pp. 129–30.

'allowing his ditches to overflow'. Several men and women in the years from 1669 to 1672 had to give substantial sureties that they would 'keep the peace'.

Two cases of theft were recorded; one involved the stealing of seven silver spoons from Thomas Bellingham, gent., in 1660 while earlier, in 1595, three towels and several tablecloths were stolen from Edward Skeete by John Harris, a cooper from Buckland. There was more than a breath of scandal in two of the entries. One, in 1587 was when Isabel Tenney cut the throat of a baby she had just given birth to in a garden adjacent to the house of her master, John Bramson. She was sentenced to be hanged. In 1602, Anne Woodherst 'conceived and gave birth to two bastards in Leatherhead where she was a servant to Mr Oxenbridge' and the babies were ordered to be supported by the parish. Apart from infanticide, there was only one murder reported. In 1607 a butcher killed another from Mickleham and was duly hanged.

The poor and needy

Looking after the poor, the young and old and the sick and handicapped was an important Vestry activity. The Vestry members showed a continuing concern for the relief of all parishioners who needed help, implementing and adding to the central government's Poor Law measures of 1598 and 1601 which have been called the forerunners of National Insurance, the basis of Poor Law legislation throughout the 17th century. A compulsory poor rate was levied in the parish and overseers of the poor were appointed. Children of poor parents were specially cared for and trained as apprentices. The accounts of Leatherhead's overseers of the poor in William III's and Anne's reign described in detail the help constantly being given. For example, late in 1693 Goody Sherwood was paid for looking after a lame boy for seven months and at the same time half a year's board was given to a 'blind maid' who received regular help until her death in 1705. In 1706 a Mr Burton was paid as much as £6 'for setting Thomas Roakes' leg', the Roakes family receiving 5s. a week during the two months he was incapacitated. They also showed concern for widows, for women with large families, those whom they graphically called 'great bellied' women, and for the very poor.[1]

The same accounts mention donations to seamen, soldiers with passes (distinguishing them from deserters) and 'prisoners from

[1] Lthd. Vestry Books, 1693–8; 1704–12.

H. SHORTRIDGE. S.T.P.

ob. A.D. 1720

The Rev. Hugh Shortridge, DD, Rector of
Fetcham, 1683–1720, whose charitable trust
included the provision for preaching a sermon
on the anniversary of Charles I's execution.

France' passing through Leatherhead at the time of the War of the Spanish Succession. Some were boarded at the Leatherhead alms-house as a charge to the parish.

Private charity was a valuable supplement to the caring work. It was common practice for all classes to remember those less fortunate than themselves in their wills. Edmund Tylney, Master of the Revels to Queen Elizabeth, and the Earl and Countess of Nottingham left money to the poor. Leatherhead parish people also benefited from charitable trusts. For example, in 1608 John Skeete, a wealthy London merchant, left money for the purchase of land and property, the income from which was to be used for the benefit of the poor of Leatherhead 'to be distributed in bread . . . on every Sunday morning after prayer' by the churchwardens and 'four of the most discreet persons in the parish'. Another generous benefactor was Henry Smith who, it was said, was nicknamed Dog Smith, as he had no home of his own and dined always at friends' houses. In his will of 24 April 1627 he directed that the churchwardens 'should meet once a month to consider which of the poor should be in most need of relief' offering to them 'bread, flesh or fish on each Sabbath day'. In 1692 Edward Hudson directed that meat should be distributed on feast day evenings to 'twenty of the poorest inhabitants'.[1] Soon after Queen Anne's death, more help was forthcoming this time for the vicar, a yearly sum being left to him and the vicars of Great Bookham, Effingham and Shalford by Dr Shortridge, the wealthy incumbent resident of Fetcham. In return, prayers were to be said on Wednesdays and Fridays and a sermon preached on Good Friday and on 30 January, the anniversary of Charles I's execution. The money from this trust is still being paid and the sermon is still preached annually in Leatherhead.

Care for the children of the parish included not only charitable offerings from the Vestry and other sources but extended also to their education and training. Sir Thomas Bludworth's will of 1692 left money for his servant to be trained as an apprentice. The Overseers of the Poor Accounts for 1702 refer to a sum of money being given to 'Goody Harrison for schooling'. There is however no record of any true school in Leatherhead at this time, although *Pigots' Directory* of 1832 and 1839 mention a Free School founded and endowed in 1596 for the education of 10 boys; research so far has not traced the name of its founder. There was probably no school building since at that time

[1] Charity Report Commissioners; 13th Report (1825), pp. 492–3.

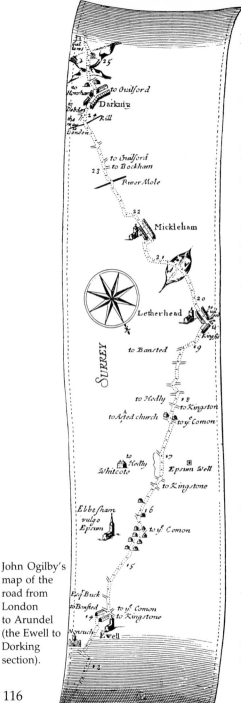

John Ogilby's map of the road from London to Arundel (the Ewell to Dorking section).

schooling usually took place in church with the parish clerk as schoolmaster. The west tower of the church in Leatherhead bears this out with its walls and columns covered with possible schoolboy graffiti; names, initials and dates varying from 1662 to 1729.

In 1712 this school was extended to include 11 girls to be 'taught and cloathed' with a subscription of £22 per annum. It was a remarkable bequest to educate girls from poor families at such an early date and even more remarkable that they outnumbered the boys.[1]

Travel and transport

It is hard to picture how the roads in and around Leatherhead appeared all those centuries ago. They were certainly narrow with rough broken surfaces, dusty in summer and muddy in winter. On week-days, farmers drove sheep and cattle to market along the roads. There were also horse-drawn carriers and packhorses with panniers at their sides and perhaps a two- or four-wheeled horse-drawn wagon. As early as 1594 the roads of the district were being used for moving goods to London and also to and from Guildford.[2]

In the 1630s, there was a regular service on Thursdays from Leatherhead to London,[3] and after the Restoration, a stage-wagon or stage-coach, was to be seen on most days of the week in the town, preparing to take goods, mail and passengers to and from London. The roads serving Leatherhead, north to London and south to Dorking, Arundel and Chichester are shown in J. Ogilby's road survey *Britannia* (1675) and his *Traveller's Road Guide* (1699). Both the wagon and the coach from Leatherhead ended their journey at the King's Head in Southwark. Other Surrey towns with similar connections to London were Epsom, Guildford, Egham, Godalming and Croydon. These towns, including Leatherhead, are also mentioned as principal destinations for carriers by the *Merchants and Traders Necessary Companion* (1715) which suggests that a further increase in services had taken place by this date.

Despite the growth of wagon and coach services, most travelling was on horseback. The Leatherhead Vestry Book includes payment for 'horse hire' for journeys to London, Hampton Court and Kingston.

The traveller by horse, coach or wagon would see groups of men on the road filling in the worst potholes and shoring up any damaged sides with rubble. They were local farmers and tradesmen carrying out their stint of repair work under the watchful eye of one or other of the two surveyors of highways, who had to report three times a year on the condition of the roads and of the bridges to the Justices of the Peace. In 1661 complaints were made at Quarter Sessions that the bridge had been 'out of repair' for several weeks and that the Leatherhead to Dorking road was repeatedly in poor condition. To help matters, the number of horses pulling wheeled vehicles was restricted soon after the Restoration, and the main roads were ordered to be 24 ft wide from ditch to ditch. This provision was repeated in the 1697 Act which also ordered that crossroads should have a 'stone or post' as a direction sign. Nevertheless the real improvements to the roads round Leatherhead had to await the Turnpike Acts of the next century and the improved methods of construction by Telford and McAdam.

Steps towards a navigable Mole

River navigation, including that of the Mole, was much talked about in the 17th century especially after Sir Richard Weston's pioneering work in 1650s to make the River Wey navigable from Guildford to the Thames. Parliament passed an Act in April 1662 ordering that all rivers should be made navigable 'that are capable thereof';[4] an over-ambitious scheme which was in practice whittled down to apply only to a few rivers.

The Mole was once mentioned in an Act of 1664, the plan being to make it 'navigable or passable for barges and other vessels' from Reigate to the Thames. Although this was not proceeded with, the river's navigability was further advocated in 1698 as the Mole was considered 'fit to be made navigable for vessels of twenty tons burthen' and could transport 'good and vast quantities of timber to build ships . . . coals, corn and all other commodities . . . to and from London'.[5] More than one survey was made of the river by Yarranton while another was being undertaken by Ralph Michell.[6]

It was thought Leatherhead's river could rival the Wey, but despite the hopes and recommendations, nothing happened. The Mole remained as it had always been.

The great storm

Early in Queen Anne's reign, Leatherhead and southern England

[1] Linda Heath, *Of Good Report* (LDLHS, 1987).

[2] HMC, 7th Report, p. 661a.

[3] J. Taylor, *The Carrier's Cosmosgraphie* (1637).

[4] T. Delaune, *Angliae Metropolis* (1690), p. 425.

[5] A. Yarranton, *England's Improvement by Sea and Land* (1698), pp. 62–3.

[6] GMR 25/7/1 – Mole Survey, 26 May 1696.

experienced one of the worst storms on record in this country. This was late November 1703 and it lasted for four to five days, during which time the Eddystone Lighthouse was lost. Daniel Defoe who wrote about it in a book appropriately entitled *The Storm*, said that 'most people expected the fall of their houses' and 'no one thought to venture out'. John Evelyn, in his book *The Pilgrim's Way*, describes the peak of the storm on 26/27 November 1703 when with little rain and much lightning, the wind caused havoc to his estate at Wotton, near Dorking, 2000 trees, mostly oak, were 'prostrated like whole regiments fallen in battle'.

Like very many churches in the south, Leatherhead parish church lost its spire, never to be replaced.[1] The town itself suffered badly (an experience to be repeated nearly three centuries later) but after a while, settled down to the routine of country life at the threshold of a new century.

[1] H. Harries, 'The Great Storm of 1703', *Cornhill Magazine*, 1897, p. 579.

The Age of the Georgians 1714–1837

THE PICTURE of Leatherhead in Georgian times is one of a thriving community leading a small-town self-contained life mainly concentrated on the farming year. It had landowners with large estates offering employment to many, a wide spectrum of traders catering mainly for the town's needs and a regular coach and postal connection with the neighbouring towns and London.

The town and its population
A large-scale map of Leatherhead drawn up by George Gwilt in 1782/1783 shows the layout of the streets were basically the same as they were before the new town centre was built in 1982, 200 years later. Only the stretch of the turnpike road from the east end of the town to the church has long since disappeared. In fact, the main change was in the nomenclature of the streets. Great Queen Street became the High Street and Little Queen Street became Church Street. Kingston Road was once Bradmere Lane and Randalls Road, Patsoms Lane. Unfenced tracks crossed the large open Common Field whose boundary was near the church and Worple Road. 'Worple' itself means 'trackway'. There was more common land near Sweech House where Fairfield Road is now and it seems probable that the annual Leatherhead Fair was held there each October.

The lord of the manor was Henry Boulton, one of 17 'gentry' listed in the *Universal Directory* in 1791. In addition to two clergymen and two surgeons, there were 50 tradesmen listed as white- and black-smiths, a

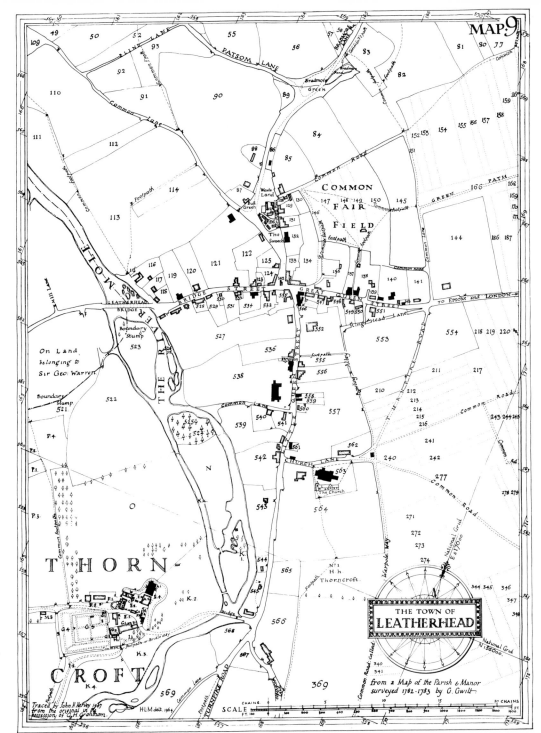

Map of Leatherhead town by George Gwilt, 1782–83.

hairdresser, a plumber and a glazier, a collar-maker, a tanner and miller as well as butchers, bakers, grocers and innkeepers. The population at this period was less than 1000 but by the taking of the first national census in 1801, it had increased to 1078 and in 1831, to 1724. The increase was due fundamentally to better economic and medical conditions which may not have affected the birth rate but which certainly decreased the death rate. Accurate figures allowing a more realistic estimate of occupations and professions did not appear until the 1841 census. Up to then, the majority were employed 'in agriculture'.

Principal families

It is perhaps surprising that very few families prominent in Stuart times in Leatherhead remained so in the Georgian period, although this lack of continuity in family history has been noted before in the chapter on the 17th century (see p. 76). The Gardiners, Sands, Rogers, Skeetes and Godmans disappeared and only the Daltons, the last of the major 17th century families, survived. Even they died out in the middle of this century. The Dacres, connected through marriage to the Godmans, continued to occupy Church House until the mid-1740s and there are no later records of this family. The Akehursts were another prominent family, first referred to in the 1695 Rate Assessment and later as benefactors to the church and owners of The Mansion, though little is known of them after 1730.[1]

Among the new families, one of the most important were the Gores, who took over the ownership of The Mansion from the Akehursts some time during the third decade of the century. Although the house was said to have been rebuilt in 1710, Lt-General Humphrey Gore, governor of Kinsale and a colonel in the King's Own Dragoons, had made further alterations to it. After his death in 1739, the property passed to his son Henry and then in 1777, to Henry's daughter, Catherine, wife of William Wade who became the sole owner when she died in 1786.

William Wade was a figure of note at Court. He was Master of Ceremonies in 1769 at Bath and Brighton and shared with his master, the Prince Regent, a good-humoured liveliness and a love of gaming and of clothes. In fact, he thought of himself as something of a style-setter in opposition to Beau Brummell, as his portrait by Gainsborough

[1] F. Bastian 'Godman, Gerard & Dacres families', *Proc. LDLHS*, **2** (2), 1958, p. 49. James Dallaway, *History of Leatherhead* (1821), p. 8.

Shell bridge at Thorncroft said to be designed by Capability Brown.

shows.[1] He held his post at Brighton until 1808, dying there two years later. William Wade not only owned The Mansion but also Church House, in which Joseph Price lived, according to 1791 *Directory*. Tragically his only son, Gore Wade, his wife, grandson and three infant children were all lost at sea on an East Indiaman, the *John Palmer*, lost in 1813.

Another leading Leatherhead family of this period was the Boultons who lived at Thorncroft Manor and Givons Grove after the last of the Daltons had died in the 1750s. Henry Crabb Boulton was Member of Parliament for Worcester and was a wealthy man. A few years after taking over Thorncroft, he had it rebuilt by Sir Robert Jones, the architect and designer of the Bank of England. The new building in the classical style is substantially the same as it is today. Boulton also commissioned 'Capability' Brown to reshape the grounds and the shell bridge was presumably designed by him. He cut a canal in the river to create Thorncroft Island. When his nephew, another Henry, took over the lease of the property, the family also owned the manors of Pachenesham and Headley. It was he who commissioned George Gwilt to produce the large-scale maps of Leatherhead in 1782/1783. Early in the 19th century, the lodge was added by Colonel Drinkwater-Bethune who lived at Thorncroft and died there in 1844.[2]

Lord Carpenter bought Randalls Park in 1753. His son, created Earl of Tyrconnel in 1761, sold the property 30 years later.[3] It had belonged to the Sands family in Tudor times and for the whole of the last century (see p. 77). There were several ownership changes after the Carpenters gave it up, Sir John Coghill acquiring it in 1802 and Nathaniel Bland in 1810. In 1839 the old house was demolished and a new one built not necessarily on the original site.

The Rogers family who had occupied the Rectory on the site of the present Vale Lodge, no longer appeared in Leatherhead's records, although someone of that name was said to be 'tennant to the parsonage' in the terriers of 1712, 1720 and 1723.[4] He probably only held a sub-lease since a monument in the church makes it clear that at this time and until his death in 1723, Admiral Sir James Wishart obtained the lease from the Dean and Chapter of Rochester. The Rectory House may soon have fallen into disrepair, since there are no later records and Vale Lodge, as it is now called, was built on the site.

Another naval officer of some fame lived in Linden House, now

[1] F. B. Benger, 'The Mansion', *Proc. LDLHS*, **1** (7), 1953, pp. 8–9.

[2] F. B. Benger, 'Thorncroft Manor', *Proc. LDLHS*, **1** (6), 1952, p. 23.

[3] *V.C.H.*, 111, p. 297; *D.N.B.*

[4] F. Bastian, 'Rogers of the Rectory', *Proc. LDLHS*, **2** (4), 1960, p. 109.

Portrait of William Wade by
Gainsborough. Master of
Ceremonies for the Prince
Regent at Brighton and Bath,
William Wade lived in
The Mansion.

Watercolour of Leatherhead Church by J. M. W. Turner in a private collection.

the site of a similarly-named block of flats in Epsom Road. Richard Byron was the brother of Admiral John Byron, renowned in naval circles as 'Foulweather Jack', who was grandfather of the poet. Rear Admiral Richard Byron himself had a distinguished career and commanded the *Belvedere* against the United States of America in the War of Independence. He married Sarah Sykes of Leatherhead in 1801 and had four sons. One son, John, married Mary Richardson whose father owned Belmont Lodge, the former Red House on Bull Hill now replaced by a new building, also called Belmont Lodge. An interesting literary connection was made in the Sykes family when Sarah's niece, Harriet, married John Addington Symonds, the Victorian author and poet.

Some of the town's artistic connections

Jane Austen often visited Bookham where her mother's first cousin lived, the wife of the vicar, Samuel Cooke. It has been suggested that in her novel *Emma*, Highbury is actually a portrait of Leatherhead. The fact that Randalls existed here as a house and in 1761 a Mr Knightly was actually a church benefactor, helps to substantiate the theory.

Many writers came to the area. Apart from Matthew Arnold living at Cobham, Richard Brinsley Sheridan at Polesden Lacey and in the town, John O'Keefe, George Meredith lived at Flint Cottage on Box Hill. Keats, it is claimed, finished his poem *Endymion* while staying at the 'Fox and Hounds', now the Burford Bridge Hotel.

Although not actually resident in the town, artists came to Leatherhead to sketch and paint the surrounding countryside. Cotman, Peter de Wint, Girtin and J. M. W. Turner were among the many young artists encouraged by Dr Monro both at his Adelphi residence and his country home in Bell Lane, Fetcham. Turner said they were given 'half a crown for their sketch and a good supper'. He considered Dr Monro his first patron. Dr Monro and his father were both leading physicians at the Bethlehem Hospital, known as Bedlam, where they studied and treated mental illness. Indeed, it was Dr Monro who certified Turner's mother as insane and committed her to his hospital.

Gerard van der Gucht, one of 40 children born to the engraver of the same name, was a Leatherhead resident, according to his marriage entry in the Richmond parish register in 1759. His brother, Benjamin, was one of the original students at the Royal Academy in 1768. He became a portrait painter and the proprietor of a picture gallery and was accidentally drowned at Chiswick in 1794.

Farming

The majority of Leatherhead's population was engaged in agriculture, either directly as farmers and farm labourers, or indirectly, as traders and craftsmen serving the farming community. Sadly, records of the tradesmen's families are few but it is known that the Ragge family, makers of leather goods, continued their trade in Bridge Street which had started and flourished in the previous century. As farmers became increasingly prosperous and as all coaches using the roads were horse-drawn, there was need for the harnesses made by the Ragges. Consequently the Ragges not only prospered as tradesmen but also bought property in Leatherhead.[1]

This was a century of great agricultural improvement with the growth of root crops and the introduction of new equipment which, together with better rotations, helped to revolutionise crop and livestock production. Some of the new ideas, such as the use of clover and lucerne as fodder crops, had been adopted by Leatherhead farms in the late 17th century (see p. 103). A report made at the end of the century stated that turnip husbandry had been regularly followed in the chalky and sandy loams of Surrey for at least a century. There was a four year crop rotation: turnips followed by barley, then clover and finally wheat.[2] Most farms kept some livestock, sheep and hogs predominating, and cattle for meat and dairy purposes. Wiltshire and Dorset sheep were most commonly bred, as well as pure cross-bred South Down sheep.

Compared with levels in Stuart times, crop production and dairy output almost certainly increased in the Leatherhead area during the Georgian period, but no records of how successful the farmers were have survived. Although there was probably a general upward trend during the century, this was dented by harvest fluctuations; thus, 1740 was a 'dearth' year and although good years followed, there were bad harvests again in 1756 and 1757 when price of food rose and riots broke out in some parts of the country.[3] Nevertheless, the farmers generally prospered, helped by the increased demand for food during the wars in the middle and later years of the century and aided by many new farming implements.

[1] F. B. Benger, 'The Ragge, Lloyd & Walker families', *Proc. LDLHS*, **2** (5), 1961, pp. 144–54.

[2] W. Stevenson, *General View of Agriculture of Surrey* (1809), pp. 170, 187.

[3] W. G. Hoskins, 'Harvest fluctuations', *Agric. Hist. Rev.*, **XVI**, 1968, p. 23.

Leatherhead still farmed traditionally. The town still had the large open arable Common Field and common pasture grounds whose use was watched over by the manorial courts. Pasturing of sheep on the arable land before the crops had been harvested and on the meadows before the completion of the hay harvest, were still common offences as was the encroaching or enclosing of pieces of land. The frequency of such cases suggest something of a land shortage. An Ashtead man was brought before the Thorncroft Manor court in October 1722 for carrying away a cartload of furze, and another from Fetcham was fined for digging up three cartloads of loam from the Common Field. Two years later three Ashtead men were accused of collecting acorns from the waste lands of the manor.

Buying and selling land

When drawing up land leases, it was customary to ensure that the new occupier farmed the land well. No more than two crops were to be grown in successive years on the same field; trees were not to be felled and fences, hedges and ditches had to be maintained. Such concern can be understood since most of the walnut trees so greatly admired by John Evelyn in Norbury Park were felled. Sold to the government to become British Army rifle stocks, they were mainly used in the fight against the colonists in the American War of Independence.[1]

An indenture made in June 1736 shows the continuing ownership of land by Londoners, as in late Tudor and Stuart times. In this, Charles, Lord Baltimore, and Henry, Earl of Uxbridge, sold land to Thomas Paget of Hanover Square, four acres of meadow or pastureland called Keightley Close, north of the road from the town to Leatherhead Common. Landowners were particular how their land let out on lease was managed. An indenture of 24 September 1773 drawn up by a representative of the late Sackville Fox, required the lessee, James Richardson, a Leatherhead brewer, to 'stump out or mark with the letter F all and every piece of land' being leased and to provide 'a true terrier', that is, an inventory of the boundaries.

Among the large number of indentures which have survived, it is heartening to see how often husbandmen, the humblest of cultivators, were able to lease quite substantial holdings. The length of some of the leases is equally surprising; the terms varying from in perpetuity to 500 years and less.

[1] Ronald Sheppard, *The Manor of Wistomble in the Parish of Mickleham*.

Bocketts Farm.

Farms

There were 10 farms outside the area of the Common Field in the Leatherhead area during the 18th century, some long-established like Thorncroft and Randalls, others newly-developed though on old foundations, like Givons Grove Farm.

Thorncroft Manor Farm covered roughly the same area in the 18th century as shown on the 1629 map (see p. 99), west of the Leatherhead–Mickleham road.

Randalls Farm with the Mole forming its western limits, north-west of the town, largely as it was in the 17th century. Later in Georgian times, it was also known as Holme Farm. In 1805 a large-scale map of the farm was drawn and it showed the farm covering 450 acres.

Givons (Gibbons) Grove Farm, astride the road from Leatherhead to Mickleham, and north of the Downs. A new house and farm were built in 1781 when Henry Boulton took over the property with 216 acres of land.

Bocketts Farm, 128 acres, west of the Mole on the Fetcham boundary and shown in the Ordnance Survey map of 1816.

Highlands Farm, adjoining Leatherhead Common Field. Much of its lands were acquired from this field with 635 acres of pasture on the Downs.

Barnett Wood Farm. This is shown on the Gwilt map of 1782/1783 as a narrow, tusk-like area north of Barnett Wood, shown on the Thorncroft map of 1629.

New Pond Farm. North of Leatherhead Common, this was only a small farm with under 16 acres of meadow and shown on the Gwilt map.

Rowhurst Farm, near New Pond Farm. Its stock included two geldings, 54 sheep and lambs, two rams, one pig and chickens in 1817.

Vale Lodge Farm, the successor to the farm on the Rectory or Parsonage Estate.

Sweech Farm at 2 Gravel Hill with barns, sheds, stables and outbuildings.

Leatherhead Fair was held every autumn, possibly in the Fairfield. Normally a bustling rural occasion, according to *The Gentlemen's Magazine*, it became rather more than that in 1803:

'October 11th. Leatherhead Fair, on account of the weather being fine, was attended by almost all of the respectability of the neighbourhood. Very little business was done in the sheep fair; but pigs, being moderate in price, found a brisk sale. A party of the 10th Light Dragoons arrived and began to display their prowess in performing the sword exercise which created some confusion, and drew on the displeasure of the crowd, some of whom attacked them and driving them into a field, assailed them with stones. The soldiers charged the people with drawn swords but the crowds stood firm and proved victorious. One soldier was seriously wounded in the face and eyes. A poor woman received a cut across her arm and breast, but supposed not dangerously. A man had his hand or fingers nearly cut off. Two officers arriving, interfered and put an end to the affray with the assistance of Lord Leslie and Mr Boulton and ordered full amends to be made to the wounded parties. The soldiers left soon after for Guildford.'

Roads and road traffic

Turnpikes from Leatherhead to Epsom, Dorking, Horsham and Guildford were constructed in 1755 and 1758. Acts of Parliament in those years laid down that the maintenance of the turnpikes should be paid for by a system of tolls. The toll-house was in Great Queen Street (High Street) near the present Leatherhead Institute. More money was said to be collected there than at any other toll-house in the area.[1] There was some urgency for the roads to be improved since the Seven Years' War with France broke out in 1756, increasing the need for ready and assured movement of men and materials to the south coast. Hay, straw and oats were stored in magazines in Dorking's chalk and sandstone caves and in Leatherhead between the toll-house and the church, close to the present Magazine Place. Church Road was at one time called Magazine Lane.

Two regiments of Surrey militia were formed at this time and in 1779 recruits for the forces were said to be 'coming in daily' to Leatherhead to join those stationed here.[2]

The pattern of roads in the Leatherhead area at this period is well shown on the John Rocque's map of 1770.[3] Apart from the main roads to Ashtead and Epsom, Cobham, Guildford and Dorking, there are a number of roads connecting with them on the map, and tracks across the Leatherhead Common Field and the Downs near Mickleham. Most of the side roads and tracks would be muddy and pot-holed in winter

[1] T. E. C. Walker, 'Turnpikes to Guildford and Horsham', *Proc. LDLHS*, **2 (10)**, 1966, pp. 286–88.
[2] 'Militia in Surrey in the 18th century', *SAC*, **XXVIII**, 1915, pp. 168–9.
[3] SAC Library, Guildford SAC M2/9/2.

eft) Map by John Rocque 1770,
owing the pattern of roads.

Tollgate cottage 1934, opposite the Knoll, Epsom Road and 20 yards west of the bypass.

and their maintenance probably left much to be desired by the traveller. Sadly, the good intentions of the Turnpike Acts were often unfulfilled.

Because of its importance to road traffic, the upkeep of Leatherhead Bridge over the Mole was a continuing problem to the parish officers as it had been in the past centuries. Early in the 18th century, the bridge was described as 'a fine stone bridge' and as a 'stately fabric of stones and piles laid upon one another'.[1] In the Vestry Minutes of 1695–1739 there are several references to the 3½ acres of land near the bridge, the revenue from which was used for the bridge's maintenance. As much as £4. 3s. 4d. was allotted for repair in 1724. Because of the constant need of repair, the bridge was at this time barred off and reserved only for those paying towards its upkeep in the parishes of Fetcham and Leatherhead; they were issued with their own keys. Most travellers, in fact, used the ford alongside when this was possible.[2] In 1774, the Surrey justices considered that although parts of the bridge were well preserved, other parts were a danger to the public and they recommended that the bridge should be repaired and enlarged. Discussions on what was to be done continued in the parish and at one of the meetings it was even suggested that a new bridge should be built. Nothing came of this and the Vestry of 1778 continued to pay out towards the bridge repairs. The parish was much relieved when in 1782 by an Act of Parliament, Leatherhead Bridge and bridges elsewhere in Surrey, were made the responsibility of the county authorities.

George Gwilt, the county surveyor and mapmaker, rebuilt the bridge in 1782/1783, widening it with small safety refuges for pedestrians and using Portland stone cramped with wrought iron for the parapets. Old bricks from Ashtead Park were used above the arches. This is the bridge to be seen today.[3] The lamp standards which are obviously a more modern addition, were erected in 1963.

Grand Imperial Ship Canal

This was the brainchild of the architect and engineer Nicholas Wilcox Cundy in 1825. He planned a canal 150 ft wide and 28 ft deep, able to accommodate the largest ships afloat. It was to run 78 miles from Rotherhithe to Spithead passing through Wandsworth, Malden, Epsom Common to Leatherhead Bridge and on to Mickleham, Dorking

---

[1] Daniel Defoe.
[2] A. T. Ruby, 'Leatherhead River', *Proc. LDLHS*, **2** (8), 1968, pp. 234–7.
[3] D. F. Renn, 'The Old Bridge at Leatherhead', *Proc. LDLHS*, **3** (6), 1972, pp. 165–7.

and Arundel. Huge locks would raise the canal 127 ft between Ewell and Epsom to the 21-mile long summit level.

The Rennie Brothers surveyed and reported that this route would be a public benefit and was feasible. They estimated the cost at £6½ million, an enormous sum at that time. Other planners thought it would never yield an adequate return. So the great scheme died – never again to be seriously revived.

Coach services

Frequent horse-drawn coach services passed through Leatherhead to and from London and neighbouring towns, continuing what had been started in Stuart times. Later in the century, there was a regular service leaving Epsom, Croydon, Dorking, Guildford and Horsham. With the exception of Sunday, the Brighton coach left Leatherhead at 2 p.m. and the post, arrriving at 3 p.m. daily, left by mail coach for London at 10 p.m. nightly. By 1838 there were daily coaches to Arundel, Bognor and Worthing. Driving a coach could be hazardous and there was often an armed guard alongside the driver. In July 1827 *The Times* reported the waylaying of a mail wagon by two men as it travelled from Dorking to Kingston, just opposite Givons Grove, the home of Captain Boulton. There was a cry of 'The money or your life' and the driver, Cox, although seriously injured by bullets, attempted to return fire and drive on. The sound of all the gunfire brought Captain Boulton and his gamekeeper to the rescue. The mail got through but the assailants escaped and the GPO offered 100 guineas reward for information leading to a conviction.

Most stage-coaches stopped at the Swan Hotel described in 1791 *Directory* as 'a very genteel house with good accommodation, most excellent stabling and good post chaises with able horses for hire'. Trout from the River Mole was one of the specialities served and Pepys recorded earlier having sampled the dish. There was another stage-coach stop at the 'Duke's Head' at the top of Great Queen Street.

A royal accident

On 8 October 1806 there was an accident on the bend outside the 'Swan'. A coach carrying Princess Caroline, the wife of the Prince Regent, to visit her friends the Lockes of Norbury Park, overturned while rounding the corner at speed. The Princess and her ladies were thrown out on to the road and one, Miss Harriet Cholmondeley, was killed instantly. A memorial to her was erected in the parish church.

Church and parish

For the whole of the first half of the 18th century there was only one vicar of Leatherhead, Robert Johnson. He had taken the living as a young man in 1689 and held it for 63 years. He was one of the few elderly people in the parish who remembered the heady days of the Glorious Revolution, and then lived through the early Georgian years when church life was largely free of controversies and had become somnolent. Robert Laxton, a Fellow of St John's College, Cambridge, was the next incumbent, taking over from Johnson in 1752; he improved the vicarage, was a 'worthy vicar' and was killed by a fall from his horse.[1] It was after Robert Laxton's death in 1767 that the parish had to be satisfied for many years with curates taking the church services. The new vicar, Samuel Markham, held the living for 30 years but was often an absentee. It seems he preferred to live in London where he was the evening preacher at the church of St Dunstan-in-the-West.

There were as many as 17 curates appointed to the parish between 1771 and 1779. None of these stayed long, perhaps because of the accumulated amount of work due to the frequent absence of the vicar. Concern over these short tenures is shown in the Vestry Minutes of 24 May 1778 when the churchwardens requested that the new curate should give 'three months notice of desiring to leave the curacy'. Absenteeism among the clergy in the 18th century was not uncommon and so was pluralism. At the end of the century when Richard Harvey took over from Samuel Markham as vicar in 1797, he also held the benefice of Warnham. He was appointed to this by George III and his holding these two positions was approved by the Archbishop of Canterbury. This state of affairs continued even after 1804 when the distinguished antiquarian James Dallaway became vicar, although he chose to live and officiate in Leatherhead.

James Dallaway

James Dallaway was born in 1763 in Bristol, the son of a banker. He was educated at Cirencester Grammar School and Trinity College, Oxford, marrying Harriet Ann Jeffreys in 1780. While a young curate at Rod-

Armorial bearing of James Dallaway. Though not listed in Burke's *General Armoury*, Dallaway was entitled to use these arms.

[1] James Dallaway, *History of Leatherhead*, pp. 9–22.

Portrait of the Rev. James Dallaway, distinguished antiquarian
and Vicar of Leatherhead from 1804 until his death in 1834.

Romanticised etching of the 'Running Horse' by Harriet Dallaway.

borough, Gloucestershire, he edited the memoirs of Ralph Bigland, Garter King of Arms, and as a result was elected Fellow of the Society of Antiquaries in 1789. In 1793 he published *Inquiries into the Origin and Progress of Heraldry in England*. He took a degree of BMed at Oxford in 1794 and was appointed chaplain and physician to the British Embassy in Constantinople for two years. He published a history of Constantinople in 1797 and edited the works of Lady Mary Wortley Montagu whose husband was ambassador to the Sultan in 1716. In 1797 Dallaway was appointed secretary to the Duke of Norfolk, his friend and patron and Earl Marshal of England. In 1799 the Duke gave him the living of South Stoke near Arundel which he resigned in 1803. He took over the vicarage of Slinfold as well as the rectory of Llanmaes in Glamorganshire. It was this post that he exchanged with Robert Harvey for the vicarage of Leatherhead which he held for 30 years with Slinfold until his death. In 1811 he became a prebendary of Chichester.

He is largely remembered for his academic work on Sir William Burrell's manuscript histories of Chichester and Arundel published in 1815 and 1819 although, as an art historian, he published other scholarly work.

It is presumed as secretary to the Earl Marshal the burden of organising the extremely colourful, most elaborate and expensive coronation of George IV fell on Dallaway in 1821. Quite a contrast to the quiet backwater of Leatherhead where, as Vicar with his Vestry, he erected a House of Industry, the workhouse, in the north of the parish where free medical attention was given to the sick.[1]

Between 1820 and 1826, he initiated extensive repairs to the church fabric, particularly to the chancel and the east window which incorporated antique stained glass he had collected in Rouen. He embodied Chi-Rho, an early Christian emblem, in the altar piece he erected and presented a silver chalice hallmarked 1661 to the church.

First printed history of Leatherhead

In 1821 Dallaway wrote the text for 13 etchings by his wife who was a gifted artist. These featured Leatherhead, its vicarage, church, the 'Running Horse' inn and much of the surrounding countryside. Thus it was that the first separate history of the town was written and privately published by Dallaway. He died in 1834 and at his own wish was buried with his friend, author Robert Duppa, in the churchyard.

[1] F. B. Benger, 'James Dallaway, Vicar of Leatherhead 1804–34', *Proc. LDLHS*, **2** (7), 1963, pp. 214–19.

The main lecture given annually by the Leatherhead and District Local History Society bears his name.

The Vestry's care for the poor and needy

The Vestry still watched over Leatherhead's welfare with its surveyors of highways (waywardens) to care for the roads and footpaths and its overseers for the workhouse. The vicar or curate presided over frequent Vestry meetings attended by two churchwardens, four overseers and other parishioners. Many of their meetings were taken up with the state of the local almshouse, the workhouse and caring for those in need.

The rear of the Vicarage with James Dallaway's additions to the left, in an etching by his wife, Harriet.

The Vestry meetings were mainly held in the church except when there was a complaint, as in 1836, when the chimney smoked in the vestry room so the meeting retired to an inn.

The procedure of the meetings differed little from late Tudor times, all aspects of parish life coming within their province and carefully logged. The overseers of the poor were chosen by the ratepayers once a year at a special Vestry meeting and nominations had to be ratified by the Justice of the Peace in Epsom. The overseers were usually tradesmen, though early in the 19th century gentlemen began to take on this responsibility. The trade interests of many of the overseers may have aroused suspicion since 4s. 6d. per person was given to those who contracted to supply the poor with food, drink and clothing in 1829.

The relief of the poor, recommended by the overseers, was dispensed by the churchwardens who also collected the Poor Rate based on the rateable value of property in the town. In 1793, it was 9d. in the pound.

The poor were given fuel, clothes and shoes as well as loaves, this being a national custom. However, bread came with conditions and in 1752 the Vestry ordered that 'those given bread on Sunday must attend church service'. Among those frequently helped were pregnant or 'big-bellied' women who seemed to be passing through on foot. Others, for example '17 sailors and 16 slaves that came out of Turkey' were given 3s. 6d. in 1723. In order to distinguish the vagrants from the parish poor, the Vestry ordered in 1751 that the latter wear a badge. The able-bodied who could work were frequently housed with property holders who were paid to take them on and they were expected

THE POOR MURDERED WOMAN.

[DORIAN.]   [SURREY.]

1.

It was Hankey the squièr, as I have heard say,
Who rode out a-hunting on one Saturday.
They hunted all day, but nothing they found
But a poor murdered woman, laid on the cold ground.

2.

About eight o'clock, boys, our dogs they throwed off,
On Leatherhead Common, and that was the spot;
They tried all the bushes, but nothing they found
But a poor murdered woman, laid on the cold ground.

3.

They whipped their dogs off, and kept them away,
For I do think it's proper he should have fair play;
They tried all the bushes, but nothing they found
But a poor murdered woman, laid on the cold ground.

4.

They mounted their horses, and rode off the ground,
They rode to the village, and alarmed it all round;
"It is late in the evening, I am sorry to say,
She can not be removed until the next day."

5.

The next Sunday morning, about eight o'clock,
Some hundreds of people to the spot they did flock;
For to see the poor creature your heart would have bled,
Some odious violence had come to her head.

6.

She was took off the common, and down to some inn,
And the man that has kept it, his name is John Simm.
The coroner was sent for, the jury they joined,
And soon they concluded, and settled their mind.

7.

Her coffin was brought; in it she was laid,
And took to the churchyard that was called Leatherhead;
No father, no mother, nor no friend, I'm told,
Come to see that poor creature put under the mould.

8.

So now I'll conclude, and finish my song,
And those that have done it, they will find themselves wrong;
For the last day of Judgment the trumpet will sound,
And their souls not in heaven, I'm afraid, won't be found.

(*Sung by Mr. Foster, 1897.*)

This folksong refers to an actual local murder of an itinerant woman in 1834. Her decomposing body was discovered by the Surrey Fox Hounds with its Master, John Hankey of Fetcham Park, while they were hunting on Leatherhead Common. She had a severe head wound and a coroner's inquest was held at the 'Royal Oak' where John Simm was obviously the landlord. The ballad was written by a brickmaker named Fairs from Leatherhead Common and collected by Lucy Broadwood in *English Traditional Songs and Carols* published in 1909.

to do any work required. Thus in 1747, Richard Bushel was given 1s. 10d. a week to clothe and keep Richard Martin in service for four years; his wife undertook for 40s. to look after Sarah Hail for the same number of years, provided she learnt how to milk. Idleness was frowned on by the Vestry and records show that those suspected of it were often threatened with a spell in the House of Correction.

Poor children were farmed out, although late in the century it was a declining practice because of the bad conditions often endured by the children. Orphaned children, until they were old enough to go into service or be apprenticed, were cared for by widows. For this the widows received an average of 2s. a week. Children born out of wedlock and their mother had, by law, to be well supported by the father. Apprenticeship was as common as it had been in the 17th century but unfortunately there are few records relating to it. It is known in 1741 John Geal's son was apprenticed to a fisherman and in 1773, two boys from the Arrow family were apprenticed to a baker and gingerbread maker. In 1795, John Ragge and Daniel Windsor volunteered for the Navy and were paid 6 guineas each by the Vestry.

In 1795, a Watford silk-mill owner named Watson sought Leatherhead's poor children to work in his mills for 1 s. 6d. a week in return for clothing and feeding them. It is not known what came of this offer which initially appeared generous but no mention is made of how many hours the children would have to work.

Care of the sick

The Vestry members were concerned with the sick as well as the poor, but whereas in the 17th century they turned for help mainly to the townfolk (see p. 113), in the Georgian period they sought professional aid. A surgeon-apothecary lived in Leatherhead and died here in 1726. In 1784, Christopher Vine was receiving 7 guineas a year as the parish surgeon and in 1796 Daniel Wilson described as a surgeon, apothecary and man-midwife, received 10 guineas a year.

The parish also gave money to the sick and to those who nursed them. In 1740, Richard Tyrrell received 5s. when he was ill and Elizabeth Arrow 6s. for the month she was sick. Widows, dubbed in the records as 'Goody', were often employed as nurses.

Concern was expressed over the possible spread of smallpox in the town and in 1799, after Dr Edward Jenner discovered the vaccine,

In 1722 the widow of Francis Hailer was provided with the following by the vestry:

One feather bedd and boulster, 2 pillows, 3 blankets, 1 pare of sheets, curtains, vallens and steddle	£1 10s.	0d.
One warming pan	4.	0
3 porringers	1.	6
3 chairs	1.	3
One pare of small andirons	1.	6
One skillett	2.	0
One spitt		10
One pare of tongs		
One pare of pothooks	1.	6
1 frying pan	1.	6
1 porridge pott	5.	0
1 table	1.	0
1 basket and a pare of bellows		6
1 spinning wheel	1.	0
6 trenchers and a wooden bottle	1.	0
1 drinking tubb, 3 crockes, 2 wooden rowles and a tundish	1.	0
1 joynsted chest	2.	0
One round table	1.	6
One candlestick		4
	£2 17s.	11d.

all the poor were inoculated against it. This humanitarian measure may have had an ulterior motive but it is still a good illustration of the sensible use of parish resources to benefit the whole community. Medical treatment for other diseases was also paid for by the parish, even if this meant that patients had to travel outside its limits. In 1741, Elizabeth Peckham and John Lucas in 1779 were both sent from Leatherhead to St Thomas' Hospital in London.

The parish was also responsible for the burial of its poor and a local tradition grew up that the carrying of a corpse for burial established a right of way. Consequently the Swan Hotel charged a penny for permission to bear a body through its yard.

The Leatherhead almshouse was described in 1725 as having six rooms, so it was a fairly substantial building. According to the Vestry Minutes of 1750, an inspection committee was appointed to report on the state of the building and whether or not additions should be made to it in order to maintain the poor adequately. In 1807, it was sold for the large sum of £440 and replaced by a House of Industry, a workhouse, built on the common north of the town and set in two acres of land with a large garden, all donated by Henry Boulton of Thorncroft Manor.

At a national level, there were fears that the poor in the workhouses would be huddled together promiscuously. The Leatherhead Vestry prevented this by paying £160 for a brick wall to be built, dividing the sleeping rooms of the men and women so that, with the exception of meal times, they would be apart both day and night. One sad result of this was that married couples and families were separated. This happened too when only part of a family was put into the workhouse while the other half went into service.

Charities

While the regular financing of the poor in Leatherhead came from the Poor Rate, there were also several charitable bequests, including some for educational purposes.

The Skeete, Smith and Hudson charities set up in the Stuart period (see pp. 115) still benefited the town. These were supplemented during the course of the 18th century by Robert Nettlefold in 1755 who left just over £20 to be distributed to the poor and by Elizabeth Rolfe in 1777 who bequeathed the interest on £400 annually to be given to 10 of the town's poorest families in memory of Dame Catherine Thompson buried in the churchyard. William Denne, a banker, also gave money in 1786 for the purchase of fuel for the poor and Richard Toye, tenant of the Swan Hotel, left the interest from £1200 of gilt-edged securities in 1812 to be paid monthly to six old and poor parishioners. In 1834 Louisa Mary Dickins of Vale Lodge left £1000 for the poor.

Educational charities

The schooling of Leatherhead's children by charitable funding was a new feature. In his will of 1725, David White, a bricklayer of Ewell, provided for the poor children of Epsom, Ewell, Ashtead, Leatherhead and Abbots Langley in Hertfordshire, all parishes with which he had been associated. So far as Leatherhead was concerned, he directed that freehold property to the value of £10 a year should be purchased and the income benefit the town's children. It was paid to the vicar and churchwardens to be used in instructing poor children in reading, writing, arithmetic and religion. Another charity was set up in 1796 by John Lucas, a Leatherhead wheelwright, who left the interest on £400 stock which eventually helped to pay the local schoolmaster's salary of £15 per annum and educate eight poor boys between the ages of 8 and 12.

Education

Free schools for the poor were established in the south by far-seeing London merchants anxious to ensure that by education, Protestantism remained the established religion of the country. In so doing, they laid the foundations for the grammar schools of later centuries.

There had been a free school in Leatherhead since 1596, although it is shrouded in mystery and may for a time have disappeared. Nevertheless it was here in 1832 and , according to *Pigot's Directory*, educating 10 boys. Earlier in 1712 the school had been extended to include 11 girls – subscription £22 per annum. It is remarkable that poor girls should have been educated at such an early date, let alone outnumber the boys. However, by 1818, a day school had been set up for boys alone, the girls' section having failed. This was helped with funds from the White and Lucas charities and Joseph Green was the master. The vicar, James Dallaway, ran a Sunday school for 80 boys and 70 girls on voluntary subscriptions. The curriculum taught was the three 'R's' plus another 'R' for religion. It seems possible that the schoolroom was originally in the west tower of the church. As mentioned in the previous chapter, the walls and columns there are still covered with graffiti of names, initials and dates ranging from 1662 to 1759.

The first private school listed in 1791 and 1798 in the *Universal Directory* was an Academy for Young Gentlemen set up by Thomas Hopkins. Later in 1838, an Academy for Boys under Thomas Hill, who was also the Registrar of Births and Deaths, was listed.

Meanwhile, in 1799 in St George's Fields, Southwark, a school for the blind was founded by four philanthropists, Thomas Boddington, Samuel Bosanquet, James Ware and William Houlston. Up to then it had been thought impossible to educate the blind, but as earlier attempts to train them for manual work had proved successful, the school was established. By 1832 it had 150 resident pupils. It was not until 1901 that it moved to its present site in Leatherhead.[1]

Wesley's visit
Perhaps the most memorable event in Leatherhead in the late 18th century was the visit of John Wesley on 23 February 1791.[2] He was 87 years old at the time and died only a week later. During the visit, he delivered what was to be his last homily in an upstairs room in Kingston House. This was the last of 42,400 sermons he delivered in his ministry and he chose as his text *Isaiah* lv.6. He stayed the night with Leatherhead's curate, Mr Durnford, and travelled to London the following day. A legend grew up that Wesley had given his last sermon beneath a cedar tree outside Kingston House. There is no evidence for this, although he may have given a blessing to the assembled crowd there, when the cedar can have been little more than a sapling.[3]

Time of revolution and social change
When John Wesley came to Leatherhead, the French Revolution was already two years old. It had received qualified approval at first, for with the passing of the Bill for the Abolition of Slavery in 1791 and the publication of Thomas Paine's *Rights of Man*, a national social conscience seemed to be emerging. But when the Revolution's excesses culminated in the execution of Louis XVI, approval quickly turned to

[1] Linda Heath, *Of Good Report* (LDLHS, 1987).
[2] F. B. Benger, 'John Wesley's visit to Leatherhead', *Proc. LDLHS*, **2** (9), 1965, pp. 265–9.
[3] A. T. Ruby, 'The birth of a legend', *Proc. LDLHS*, **3** (1), 1967, pp. 4–8.

John Wesley, who preached his last homily in Kingston House in February 1791. During the demolition of Kingston House many tokens and coins, a plague pipe and an oak cross were found. The cross may have been a medieval gibbet as it has been suggested that the site was once known as Gallows Hill.

This poem was published as a broadsheet in 1803 showing the indomitable spirit of a farmer about to join the musters, awaiting Napoleon's invasion; but first he gets the harvest in.

> So! Bonaparte's coming, as
>   folks seem to say,
> (But I hope to have time to get
>   in my hay).
> And while he's caballing, and
>   making a parley,
> Perhaps I shall house all my
>   wheat and my barley.
> But then, there's son Dick, who
>   is both strong and lusty,
> And towards the French he is
>   damnable crusty;
> If you give him a pitchfork or
>   any such thing,
> He will fight till he's dead, in
>   defence of his King.

disapproval and fear. Then there was alarm when a number of assassination attempts were made on our king, George III, the last in 1800, when two shots fired at the Royal Box in Drury Lane Theatre, narrowly missed him.

In 1793, Britain joined the European Coalition already at war with France, so was herself at war. After Nelson's victory over the French fleet at the Battle of the Nile in 1798, there was an uneasy peace. War broke out again with France in 1803 and as Napoleon massed his armies at Boulogne, invasion was a real threat. The whole country was roused by the danger and parishes like Leatherhead were assessed on how many able-bodied men could be mustered for the forces. Fines were imposed for failing meet the quota.[1] Once more, Nelson was needed and there is a strong local tradition that he spent part of his last night in England here, before the decisive Battle of Trafalgar in 1805. His house at Merton was only 1½ hours from Leatherhead and it is probable he halted at the 'Fox and Hounds', now the Burford Bridge Hotel, to change and water his horses and feed his cavalry escort. Then moving on through Guildford and Liphook, where he drank tea by candlelight at the 'Anchor', he joined the *Victory* at Portsmouth.[2]

The end of an era

Despite wars and bad harvests that caused unrest, particularly in 1830, this period of British history differs from the 17th century because of its essential unity in politics, thought and social development. The foundations of an industrialised society were being laid as the obligations of an agrarian one were beginning to break down. Judging by the 1841 census, Leatherhead itself was slowly becoming part of an urban society for among its normal trades there were watchmakers, milliners, army personnel, chemists, an excise officer and a policeman.

[1] R. Offor, 'Surrey military assessment for 1805', SAC, **L11,** 1952, pp. 60–5.
[2] F. B. Benger, 'Nelson's last journey', *Proc. LDLHS*, **4** (7), 1983, p. 165.

A cottage near Leatherhead painted by Cornelius Varley (1781–1873), brother of John Varley, the artist who with J. M. W. Turner and others was helped by Dr Monro of Bell Lane, Fetcham. This etching was published in 1815. Where can the cottage be and judging from its condition, is it still standing?

A late 18th-century view of Leatherhead from Bull Hill, showing the parish church in the distance.

The Victorian Era
1837–1901

SOME 16 years before Victoria became Queen, James Dallaway, the then Vicar of Leatherhead, observed that the town was rapidly converting itself by a 'multiplication of inconsiderable houses into an appendage of the enormous London'.[1] Leatherhead had long been a favourite place of residence for wealthy Londoners and their numbers greatly increased in the 19th century. Large new houses were built like Tyrrells Wood, Givons Grove, Cherkley Court and Woodlands Park and their estates gave employment to the growing local population of tradesmen and craftsmen. The town's central position in Surrey, on the coaching route from London to Worthing and Brighton and astride the Croydon to Guildford road, contributed to its prosperity, helped further by the arrival of the railway in 1859 which made access to London so much easier. Improved facilities bettered everyone's lot, gas being supplied in 1850 and piped water in 1884, but the installation of electricity, except for the privileged few with private generators, had to wait until Edwardian times.

Despite better communications with the outside world, Leatherhead remained during these years essentially a self-contained little country town with most of its tradesmen catering for all its needs. There was a feeling of belonging to a small community where both the rich and the not-so-rich, the gentleman, shopkeeper and tradesman joined together in very many activities. Class distinction there was, but this did not divide the people in their yearly round of sports and pastimes, concerts and celebrations. The church took the lead in sup-

J. Dallaway, *History of Leatherhead* (1821), p. 10.

147

porting, wherever possible, many ways of drawing people together. Hardly less important were the wealthy benefactors like Abraham Dixon of Cherkley Court who founded and built the Letherhead Institute in 1892, and the owners of large houses, like Edward Budd of Vale Lodge and Wickham Noakes of The Red House who, with other landowners, opened their lovely gardens for exhibitions, promenade concerts and dancing. In 1894, a new era opened for Leatherhead with the formation of the Urban District Council, following the establishment of the Surrey County Council six years earlier. The church's Vestry members no longer held the administrative functions they had had for so long, though the presence of the Vicar of Leatherhead on the Council helped to preserve some form of continuity with the past.

The town and its working life

Leatherhead's population doubled in size in the 40 years between 1841 and 1881 and increased by a further thousand in the last two decades of Victoria's reign. There had been periods of rapid growth before but not on this scale. With the increasing prosperity of trade and industry during the middle and late 19th century, there was general growth throughout the country. The census returns for Leatherhead for the years 1841–1901 are shown below:

1841	1740	1881	3535
1851	2042	1891	4305
1861	2079	1901	4694
1871	2455		

The rate of population growth was highest in 1871–1891 when agriculture was in rather bad shape, yet the loss of farming jobs was more than compensated for by an increase in other employment. A larger population meant that more houses were needed and developers were taking up land wherever possible; for example, in 1872 the large Copthorne estate east of the town was put on the market specifically for housing. The fact that there was a building society here as early as 1883 suggests that house-owning was growing and the numbers of insurance offices being set up – seven in 1882, nine in 1887 – implies a responsible growing population.[1] The opening of an estate agency (Osentons) opposite the Bull Hotel in 1899 prompted the *Leatherhead Advertiser* to observe that the town was slowly but surely pushing

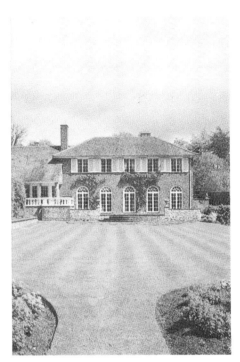

The present Cherkley Court, once the home of Abraham Dixon and the late Lord Beaverbrook and his family.

[1] P.M. April 1883.

ahead as a residential resort – a forecast that became a reality in the 20th century.

Local occupations and trades

Since Leatherhead in the Victorian period was primarily a farming community as it had been for centuries past, most people's work was related directly or indirectly to the land, though how they were employed changed markedly between 1841 and 1881. In that period, those described in the census as 'agricultural labourers' had decreased appreciably, and some may in 1881 have referred to themselves as 'gardeners', a much larger category then than in the earlier census. Other occupations associated with farming included millers, maltsters, carpenters, farriers, blacksmiths, harness-makers and saddlers. The following table shows the changes in selected occupations in 1841 and 1881 in terms of numbers and percentages of the working population:

	1841		1881	
Agriculture	162	(18·5%)	95	(5·4%)
Gardening	12	(1·3%)	84	(4·8%)
Building	20	(2·2%)	90	(5·1%)
Woodworkers	40	(4·5%)	60	(3·4%)
Brick- and tile-makers	10	(1·1%)	23	(1·3%)
Railways	0		34	(1·9%)
Servants	206	(23·6%)	397	(22·7%)

In both years 'servants' were the largest category, suggesting that a significant proportion of households employed maids, grooms, footmen and butlers.

Apart from servants and those in farming, the census returns list about 60 different occupations in Leatherhead. The principal ones are described below.

Building, brick-making and saw-milling

These were prosperous businesses. The population of Leatherhead doubled and the demand for houses not surprisingly doubled also. There was a small brickworks at Woodbridge east of Rowhurst early in the reign, and a larger one, owned by Emanual Marter, which employed 10 men in 1851. By 1881 as many as 23 men were brick- and

Crossing the Mole by the ford at Leatherhead Bridge. Bartholomew and later Thomas Chitty's deserted tanning mill on the left was converted in 1908 into a public swimming bath.

tile-makers and there was a third works called Copthorne by this time. Housebuilders quadrupled in the 40 years from 1841 to 1881 and so the number of joiners and carpenters increased. Timber-yards and saw-mills adjoined the builders in Kingston Road. William Batchelar was the town's leading builder, but his timber-yard and house behind Byron Place were destroyed by a fire in 1893.[1]

Leather traders

Tanning was chiefly in the hands of the Chitty family headed by Bartholomew Chitty from as early as 1826. Their works were close to Leatherhead Bridge. In 1841, a terrace of cottages was built on the north side of Bridge Street presumably to house the employees. This terrace was first known as Tannery Row and later as Chitty's Row. The tannery prospered for many years employing 15 men in 1861 but in the 1870s it fell on bad times and stopped work. In 1888, one barn of the mill was opened as a swimming bath, taken over in 1900 by St John's School. Some of the building survived until after the Second World War when the area was cleared to make way for Minchin Close.

    Boot- and shoe-making in the town diminished in the later years of the century and the number of boot- and shoe-makers fell from 17 to 9 and this in an age when travel was still on foot or by horse.[2]

    One bootmaker, Jeremiah Johns, was to be Leatherhead's first inventor since he patented an apparently effective, if drastic, braking system for railway and other carriages.[3] However, it was not marketed.

    Saddle and harness-making flourished in Bridge Street for some 200 years, first with the Ragges and then in the 19th century, through marriage, with the Lloyds.[4] They lived, working in the finest leather, in an old timber-framed house near the top of the street. The business continued until 1905 after which it only made and sold selected leather goods. Sadly, the building was demolished in 1939/1940 in a Civil Defence exercise.

    Coach-building came to Leatherhead in the early part of Queen Victoria's reign, brought by two families, the Venthams and the Karns. Charles Ventham established his works in Bridge Street in 1835 and after his death in 1879, his sons Edward and Charles continued the business. A scrapbook of trade press cuttings compiled by his youngest daughter Sarah confirms the company's world-wide reputa-

JOHN LLOYD,
Saddler & Harness Maker,
LETHERHEAD & GREAT BOOKHAM.

Carriage, Gig and other Harness warranted of the best Material & Workmanship.

Established in the above building for 200 Years.

John Lloyd inherited this saddle- and harness-maker business from his father who by marriage was descended from the Ragges. Emily Walker (née Lloyd) closed the business in 1905 and moved to other premises in Bridge Street where she sold leather goods until the 1930s. She died at the age of 93 in 1951. There is still a branch of the family living in the area.

[1] P.M. Sept. 1893.
[2] *Kelly's Directory* 1899.
[3] A. Edwards, 'Leatherhead's first inventor', *Proc. LDLHS*, **3** (7), 1973, p. 184.
[4] *Proc. LDLHS*, **5**, 1961.

151

The Swan Inn and the Swan Brewery. The brewery established in 1859, produced very yeasty ale and employed over 25 people.

tion at that time. They built two coaches for the run from London (Hatchetts) to Box Hill, but most of their commissions no doubt came from wealthy people for the supply of private carriages. Following the death of Edward in 1901, his widow, Melissa, directed the company's progress into the era of horseless carriages. Ventham's last two coaches remained in their showrooms until 1929 when one was broken up and the other was bought by Bertram Mills for use in his famous circus.[1] Daimler and Siddeley commissioned Venthams to build coach-work for their motor chassis and about 1909 the company applied to become official RAC repairers.

The second coaching business was owned by the Karn family. They built their carriages in the Fairfield area but they also made wagons and carts and did blacksmith's work in Kingston Road.[2]

Brewing and malting was one of the leading industries in 19th century Leatherhead. The Swan Brewery was established by George Moore of the Swan Hotel in 1859 at what is now the entrance to the Swan Centre. A new steam brewery was set up in 1874. Pale ale was the chief product, but stout and porter was also brewed. The water was obtained from an artesian well 200 feet deep, and in 1857 the beer was described as 'very yeasty and new'. Twenty-five men were employed at one time and the business continued until 1921. Another brewery in North Street was owned by the Start family who owned the 'Bull' and the 'Duke's Head' in 1854 as well as having an earlier interest in the 'King's Head'. In 1872, it was sold to Young's of Dorking and by 1892 had ceased brewing and only malting continued. The premises later became a wine and spirits merchant.

Leatherhead's early records mentioned many beer-houses and beer-sellers, who were cottagers selling home-made ale, once the staple drink. In 1841 there was a beer-house at the top of Gravel Hill run by Joseph Green who by 1851 was described as 'beer-seller and schoolmaster', with as many as 18 travellers and a bricklayer staying at his house, which must have been quite large. In another 10 years, the upwardly mobile Mr Green is described as a 'proprietor of houses'. The 'Jug House', now 1 Church Walk, sold beer and maybe cider, obviously by the jug.

Shopkeepers provided for those living in the town and con-tributed much to its atmosphere. Some, like Hutchinson the coal merchant, still exists today but sadly, most have disappeared. James

[1] Thomas Lewis.
[2] A. J. Ginger, 'Leatherhead in Victorian times', *Proc. LDLHS*, 1953, p. 14.

Hartshorns the butchers of North Street, *c.* 1900–10, display huge joints for sale. The smell and noise from their slaughterhouse was said to distress the children at school behind the Congregational Chapel on the right.

Phillips of Bridge Street was both a grocer and draper, *c*. 1890. The hams hang well above the pavement on the left.

Pullen and later Alfred Blaker had a well-stocked ironmonger's shop in North Street for many years which continued in business until 1936. Ironmonger James Pullen's ledger fortunately survived to give a wonderful insight into the life and domestic appliances of his customers.[1] Late in the century, Duke and Ockenden with premises at Hampton Cottage in Church Street were the largest manufacturers of drilling rigs for water supply in the country. They produced the Norton Tube Well for well-drilling in difficult soils.[2] There was a baker's shop, one of several, at the top of Bridge Street near Miller's grocery and Shoolbred's , the principal drapers. In 1899 Brown and Mercer, the family butchers, proudly advertised that they were 'Purveyors to H.R.H. the Duke of Cambridge'. Other shops included hairdressers, tailors and chemists, a straw hat-maker, a toy dealer, milliners, dressmakers and staymakers, a watchmaker, painters, plumbers and at least one bookseller and stationer. At the end of the century there was a photographer's shop in the High Street.

The shops were open until a late hour especially on Saturdays when wages were paid. At Christmas-time, the High Street was busy with carriages whose coachmen tapped on shop windows with their whips and wares were brought out for the customers to make a choice.[3]

The shops put on exciting displays. In one of Mr Bulpin's windows in Bridge Street there were bonbons, crackers, bottled and other fruits as well as an automatic figure of a lady walking the tight-rope to musical accompaniment. In Church Street, Mr Batten's two shops were crammed with toys, picture books and Christmas cards. Mr Jenden's shop in Highlands Road not only laid out a large stock of seasonal cakes and fancy sweets but was also busy turning out a large quantity of his famed pork sausages.[4]

Prominent families and their houses

Abraham Dixon, who came with his family to Leatherhead in 1871, was a wealthy Midlands industrialist who late in life decided to leave Birmingham and retire to Leatherhead. His wife was friendly with the Brontës of Haworth and his brother George was a Liberal MP. The Dixons quickly made Cherkley Court one of the town's most handsome homes. There were fine yew trees in its splendid gardens which included a large conservatory and a tropical house with water lilies whose size rivalled those at Chatsworth and Kew.[5]

Drawing by A. J. Ginger showing a passage at the side of Lloyd's saddlers shop in Bridge Street leading to a rope walk where ropes for the harnesses were made and stored.

[1] J. W. G. Lewarne, 'Ledger of James Pullen', *Proc. LDLHS*, **2,** 1948, pp. 194–8.
[2] M. Rice-Oxley, *Hampton Cottage* (LDLHS, 1986), pp. 7–8.
[3] Margaret Hayden.
[4] *Leatherhead Advertiser*, 17 December 1898.
[5] *Country Life*, 28 April 1900.

Almost every good cause, whether for the church or for the town, benefited from Abraham's generosity. He gave a substantial sum for the building of All Saints' church in 1888 and for the restoration of the parish church three years later. However, his major contribution was the building of the Institute in 1892.

Its object was to provide for all local working people, education, refreshment and recreation on a subscription initially of 2*d*. a week.

The opening ceremony was in 1893 and the church bellringers rang 1893 changes appropriate for the occasion. The Institute flourished with activities wide-ranging from billiards to pigeon clubs, concerts and whist drives. When Abraham Dixon died in 1907, two of his daughters continued the family's interest by teaching art and cookery there.[1]

The Dixons were also generous with hospitality at Cherkley. In 1873, they held a reception in the grounds for the marriage of their daughter, Edith, to Grosvenor Caliste de Jacobi du Vallon, a kinsman of the Duke of Westminster. There was a disastrous fire when the house was struck by lightning in July 1893 and for about a year the Dixons had to live in Milner House until Cherkley was rebuilt. As growers of exotic plants and flowers, they were particularly interested in the local Horticultural Society, opening their grounds for its annual show in 1896.[2] About this time the famous promenade concerts were held there (as in other big houses in the locality), with dancing on the lawns described as 'green as a billiard table'.[3]

Abraham Dixon had two near-neighbours, Russell Sturgis of Givons Grove and Roger Cunliffe of Tyrrells Wood.

Russell Sturgis of Givons Grove
Givons Grove was owned by the Boulton family during the first half of the 19th century, but in 1859 it passed to Duncan Fletcher, a wealthy landowner, who six years later sold it to Thomas Grissell of Norbury Park. Grissell let the house and its garden of 40 acres to Russell Sturgis, a banker in the firm of Baring Bros. Sturgis later acquired another 116 acres of the estate and the whole property stayed with the Sturgis family until 1919 when it was sold to Humphrey Verdon Roe, the aircraft manufacturer and husband of Marie Stopes. The Sturgis family were keen Liberals and Mr Gladstone is said to have visited them at Givons Grove. They were also enthusiastic cricketers and the Sturgis

[1] G. Hayward, 'The Dixon Family at Cherkley Court', *Proc. LDLHS* **4**, 1979, p. 81.
[2] P.M. Aug. 1893.
[3] Kate Sayers.

The Institute built and endowed by Abraham Dixon for the use of the town in 1892.
At its opening the church's bellringers rang 1892 changes.

name often appeared in the Leatherhead team. Russell Sturgis was a friend of Henry James, the novelist (see p. 185). His son Henry, who succeeded to the property in 1888, married twice, his second wife being the novelist George Meredith's daughter.

Roger Cunliffe of Tyrrells Wood

When Roger Cunliffe, who had banking interests, first came to the Leatherhead district in the 1860s, he lived at Fetcham Lodge. He probably stayed there until Tyrrells Wood house was built to his design in about 1880.[1] The estate then comprised 250 acres, including Highlands Farm, which he let out on short renewable leases. That Cunliffe was knowledgeable about farming is clear from the many letters he wrote complaining about the way Highlands Farm was being managed and how many repairs to outbuildings and fences were needed. He does not seem to have been particularly well known in the town, no doubt due to his long absences in London on business. At Tyrrells Wood he was always loath to release any of his land for housing saying to his land agent in July 1891 that he had decided 'not to humble myself with the letting of land on a building lease'. In September 1896, he was quite prepared to sell a plot for use as a reservoir but only on condition that no buildings were required. His refusal to allow Abraham Dixon to build a road from Leatherhead to Cherkley Court through a part of Tyrrells Wood estate accounts for Forty-Foot Road today being a fraction of the length originally planned.[2] His son, Walter, also a banker and from 1913 Governor of the Bank of England, lived at Headley Court and became the first Baron of Headley.[3]

Cherkley Court, Givons Grove and Tyrrells Wood were rather cut off from Leatherhead by at least a mile of roads, but along the Dorking road and much closer to the town were no less than four large estates, Downside, Vale Lodge, Elm Bank and Thorncroft Manor.

The Tates of Downside

The Tates, who lived at Downside in the late 19th century, were from the family of sugar merchants, Tate & Lyle, who endowed the Tate Gallery. Alfred Tate was a gardening enthusiast and his rose gardens were described at the time as one of the finest in the district. From the verandah of the Italianated house, close to the croquet lawn and the

[1] SRO 99/4/2 (Cunliffe letters); SP 2/20 (Tyrrells Wood Sale).
[2] Soc. Recs. X119.
[3] D.N.B. and Shirley Wilson.

158

tennis court, 1000 roses spread out upon the sloping garden and honeysuckles winding round the many arches filled the air with sweet fragrance.[1] Mrs Tate had a rose named after her and one of the gardeners, William Meuse as well as his wife, gave their name to two varieties of carnation.[2]

Like other Leatherhead houses, Downside grounds were often opened for garden parties and, in the 1890s, for promenade concerts.

Alfred Tate committed suicide in 1913 after a serious throat operation. He was a generous subscriber to every local cause and was one of the first trustees of the Institute.[3]

Edward Budd of Vale Lodge

Edward Budd came to Vale Lodge in 1861, taking over from Edgar Corrie and Thomas Dickens, earlier owners. He quickly made his mark in the town as churchwarden, manager of the local schools and trustee of the Epsom and Leatherhead Friendly Society. He also took a special interest in the Leatherhead Cricket Club.[4] Vale Lodge was sold to Mr Watson in 1886 after Budd's death. The church lectern and two side windows commemorate him. The Leach family became owners of Vale Lodge after 1901.

The Rickards of Elm Bank House

Only Downs Lane separated Vale Lodge and Elm Bank House and their owners, the Budds and the Rickards, were friends with a mutual interest in the church and many good causes. Rickards' son, Lionel, married Budd's daughter, Isabel, in 1882, so the friendship between the two families became even closer. Edward J. Rickards and his family came to Elm Bank in the 1870s. Early in Queen Victoria's reign it was owned by the Clarke family, one of whom, Captain William Stanley Clarke, was an Elder Brother of Trinity House and a Director of the East India Company. He also bought and pulled down the adjoining Church House so that his land extended to the churchyard. By the late 1850s, Reginald F. Remington, a director of the Epsom & Leatherhead Railway Company, had become its owner.

In the Rickards' time, Elm Bank grounds were often open for social functions especially those connected with the church. Edward Rickards was a churchwarden for a long time and was for 19 years Chairman of the Leatherhead Parochial Committee concerned mainly

[1] *Country Life*, 17 September 1898.
[2] Soc. Recs. X3B.
[3] *Leatherhead Advertiser*, 1 February 1913.
[4] Soc. Recs. X3B.

with water supply and sanitation.[1] His wife arranged for the erecting of the church's lych gate in memory of Harriet Millett in 1885.

Thorncroft's many tenants

In the Victorian period there were as many as half a dozen leaseholders of Thorncroft Manor. In 1837, Colonel John Drinkwater Bethune acquired the lease from Merton College, Oxford. He was the author of a military classic *The Seige of Gibraltar* and in 1839 his daughter published a long poem about the River Mole. The house passed first to Alexander Colvin, an East Indian agent and then in 1863 to A. A. Collyer Bristow. There was yet another tenant, Mrs Knight, in the early 1870s, but by 1878 it was taken over by Susan, the widowed Marchioness of Cholmondeley, daughter of the Duke of Beaufort. She lived there until her death in 1886. The next tenant was James Giles but by the late 1890s it was a private school in the hands of Walter Lawrence; he sublet part of the estate to Miss Emily Moore of the Swan Hotel.[2] Arthur Tritton, JP, who lived at The Priory nearby, bought the freehold from Merton College in 1904, ending Thorncroft's association with the College which had lasted over 600 years. Close to Thorncroft Manor but nearer the town centre was The Priory and The Mansion.

Arthur Tritton of The Priory

Before Arthur Tritton took over The Priory about 1880, it had been owned for a few years by Arthur Miller, but by 1879 he had moved to The Mansion. Arthur Tritton was a JP and the first Chairman of the Urban District Council in 1894, and was active in the church. Many local people remembered him best as the presenter of what were called *Mr Tritton's Entertainments*, a mixed bag of solo pieces usually performed by his friends and family on the piano, violin, cornet or banjo, and interspersed with comic readings and songs.

The Mansion: Dr Payne's school and Arthur Miller's house

The Mansion, owned by Colonel W. H. Spicer in the first few years of Queen Victoria's reign, passed in 1844 to Nathaniel Bland of Randalls Park who let it to Dr Joseph Payne for use as a private grammar school (see p. 184). There was a school there for about 30 years which closed in 1878. In the following year, Arthur T. Miller bought the house, which was sometimes referred to (wrongly) as Emlyn House in those years.

[1] S.R.O. P61/6/1.
[2] P.M. May 1882.

He became involved in the affairs of the town, succeeding Edward J. Rickards as Chairman of the Leatherhead Parochial Committee in 1892.[0] He remained the owner of The Mansion until 1916.

There were several other large houses close to the centre of Leatherhead, notably Windfield House owned by the Still family, Kingston House which had John Wesley associations (see p. 143), Elm House where the New Buli Hotel now stands and Linden House, where a distinguished diplomat, Lord Loftus, lived.[1] Early in the century another house on this site was occupied by Admiral Byron, brother of the poet's grandfather.

The largest houses in the north of the town were Belmont Lodge (later The Red House), Randalls Park and on the parish outskirts, Woodlands Park.

Belmont Lodge (later The Red House)

G. F. Richardson and his father before him were the early owners of this house, which stood at the top of Bull Hill, with grounds extending in a noble sweep beyond the present railway lines to the borders of what used to be Randalls Park. Richardson was especially upset by the arrival and proximity of the railway in 1859 which cut across his land, but the property did not change hands until about 1873 when it was bought by Henry Courage of the brewing family. After taking over, he renovated Belmont Lodge and renamed it The Red House.[2] Henry Courage generously subscribed to the new girls' school in 1883 and to the All Saints' fund five years later. He was Chairman of Leatherhead Cricket Club for some years.

In 1892, the Courage family sold The Red House to Wickham Noakes, another wealthy brewer and under the new owner, the house and gardens became one of the main centres of the town's social life. Noakes was an active Conservative and in August 1899 he was host to 350 members of the Primrose League, refreshments were provided in a marquee and an address was given by W. Keswick, the MP for Epsom.[3]

The Hendersons of Randalls Park

Like the Noakes, Mr and Mrs Robert Henderson frequently opened their house and gardens for concerts, dances and receptions, entertaining large numbers of children during the Queen's Jubilee celebrations in July 1897.[4] The Henderson family had been living at Randalls

[1] Soc. Recs. X3B.
[2] Soc. Recs. X63, X88.
[3] *Leatherhead Advertiser*, 5 August 1899.
[4] P.M. July 1897.

Park since 1856 when they bought it from Nathaniel Bland, who had built a new house on the site in 1829.

Soon after taking over the property, Robert Henderson purchased the lands nearby which used to be the Pachenesham Magna estate, so the latter and Randalls (formerly Little Pachenesham) were united for the first time.

A small chapel in the grounds known locally as 'Pachenesham Cathedral', was thought to have been built for the use of railway navvies. There, monthly services were conducted by a Leatherhead curate. The altar could be partitioned off and during the week the building became a social centre for estate staff. There was a sewing circle and reasonably-priced material was obtained by Mrs Henderson who also read aloud to the needlewomen as they stitched.[1]

Woodlands Park – the Smiths and the Bryants

This large house and estate on the edge of Leatherhead parish was owned by the Smith family of London and Shropshire for much of the 19th century, Captain Thomas Smith, RN, living there at the time of his death in 1847.

In the late 1870s it was sold by the Smiths to Frederick Carkeet Bryant, a director and one of the sons of the founder of Bryant & May, the match manufacturers. After a while, he built a new house on the site, completing this in 1885, incorporating the most modern innovations including several bathrooms with hot and cold running water and electric light. Woodlands Park was one of only 11 country houses with this novel method of lighting at that time.

Woodlands Park provided kennels for the Surrey Farmers' stag hounds in the 1890s on land bordered by Oaklawn Road. Bryant, who retired in 1888, the year of the famous matchgirls' strike, died in 1897.

The story of the strike is legendary since it resulted in the formation of the first women's trade union, the Union of Women Matchmakers.

Backed by Fabian reformers and a strike fund with no less than George Bernard Shaw as one of the cashiers, the women won improved wages and working conditions.[2] It is a nice quirk of history that the musical *The Matchgirls* based on the strike story was first performed in Leatherhead's Thorndike Theatre in 1953 before transferring to the West End for a successful run.

[1] Ruth Lewis.
[2] Patrick Beaver, *The Matchmakers*.

Farms and farming

In the early years of Queen Victoria's reign, farming in the Leatherhead area was still very much as it had been in the Georgian period, a mixture of crop growing and pasture land with the Common Field still in use. The quality of the farming at the beginning of the century had been criticised by agricultural experts who complained of neglected pastures, absence of manuring, low yields and poor stock. Their criticisms were repeated in the early 1850s,[1] but things slowly improved in the next 20 years.

Then sadly, from 1870 with its bitter winter onwards, cereal and wool prices fell throughout the country caused by large US imports coinciding with many poor harvests, heavy rains and a serious outbreak of sheep-rot in 1878. Leatherhead did not suffer as much as other large cereal-growing areas. This was mainly because of its fertile land, mixed farming with wheat and oats as the main crops and large flocks of sheep and cattle.

In addition the Leatherhead farmer was sustained by the increasing demands of the growing metropolis for regular supplies of dairy products. The enclosure of the common fields in the 1860s also benefited the farmer. Some landowners added to their fortunes by selling part of their farming land to developers eager to take advantage of the growing need for more houses.

Hassell engraving showing sheep being driven over Leatherhead Bridge *c.* 1823.

The farms

These were mostly held in tenancies from the large landowners like Roger Cunliffe of Tyrrells Wood and Robert Henderson of Randalls Park. In addition there were a number of home farms attached to the big houses worked no doubt by farming staff. Thorncroft, Downside, Vale Lodge and Randalls Park all had home farms close by. Apart from these, one of the largest farms was Highlands Farm (let by Roger Cunliffe) with a farmhouse dating from about 1800, a granary barn and a well-house and in 1873 said to be growing wheat, barley, oats, clover and turnips.[2] Sheep were driven along the roads from the farm to graze in rotation in the field (now Windmill estate) at the back of the Blind School and then moved on to grazing land behind Fetcham church on what was then a polo field, returning to Highlands Farm the same way. Ploughing matches were also held there.[3]

Other farms included New Pond Farm near Ashtead Common;

[1] James Caird, *English Agriculture in 1850–51.*
[2] SRO 99/4/2 (Cunliffe letter).
[3] William Jenden.

Barnett Wood Farm, on both sides of Barnett Wood Lane, owned by Merton College, Oxford, and Bocketts Farm, south of Thorncroft.

All Leatherhead farms were described in some detail by the Tithe Redemption Award dating from 1840 which has been called the Victorian Domesday.[1] The Award was welcomed since it commuted the payment of tithes which had always been a contentious issue.

Enclosure awards

For many centuries Leatherhead had a large open arable field, cultivated in strips and common meadows and wastes. These were compulsorily enclosed in two Awards of 1862 and 1865, the first dealing with the common arable field and the Downs and the second with the north common lands.[2] The Leatherhead Common Meadow was excluded from both Awards since a court case in 1849 had established the public's right to have access to the meadow. George Richardson of Belmont Lodge owned part of the land between the river and Randalls Park. He closed the footpath leading to the Common Meadow, preventing public access. In spite of this, a local inhabitant, Christie, continued to use the path and Richardson took Christie to court in August 1849. Christie won and James Barlow who supported him, arranged a Festival of Celebration in the Fairfield. There was indeed much to celebrate since, as a direct result of the case, the land continues as common land right up to the present day.[3]

Although some landowners gained substantially from the enclosures (Robert Henderson of Randalls Park managing to secure the whole of the northern common wastes), there were many who felt that justice was not being done in the size of the plots they received. Thomas Hersey, a Venthams employee, brought an action against Henderson which was settled out of court. Hersey, very much a village Hampden, succeeded in preserving public rights over footpaths in Fetcham and Ashtead as well as establishing the open market in Epsom High Street.[4]

The enclosure of the Downs created much dissatisfaction as it interfered with the amenities of the neighbourhood and meetings were held in protest but all in vain.[5]

Crop acreages and livestock returns

In the mid-1860s all farmers were required by the government to give

[1] S.R.O. A 9/E.
[2] S.R.O. LA 7/72: 1 and 2.
[3] F. B. Benger, 'Leatherhead Common Meadow', *Proc. LDLHS*, **3** (2), 1968, pp. 52–5.
[4] *Epsom Herald*, 4 April 1934.
[5] S.R.O. 99/4/2.

details of crops cultivated and the numbers of their livestock, and returns like these have been maintained to the present day.

Acres under crops[1]

Year	Wheat	Barley	Oats	Rye	Beans and peas	Potatoes	Turnips	Mangold	Cabbage	Clover and other grasses
1866	381	186	226	16	63	25	177	53	9	294
1876	267	165	236	13	71	67	203	50	24	298
1886	271	159	228	6	26	50	258	80	24	316
1896	206	106	203	25	55	57	155	59	30	98

There was a steady decline in the acreage of most crops though peas, beans, cabbages and market gardens increased in the last two decades of the century. A four-year rotation was the general rule with two grain crops, beans (or roots) and either grass or fallow.

Livestock numbers[2]

Year	Horses	Cattle	Sheep	Pigs
1866	—	162	1410	182
1876	159	256	759	212
1886	136	535	405	127
1896	153	323	501	117

The low cattle figure for 1866 may be ascribed to the serious outbreak of rinderpest or cattle plague which had occurred in the previous year although by 1877 the disease was completely wiped out in Britain.[3] There was a sharp fall in sheep numbers too during this period; the breeds kept were South Down, Wiltshire and Dorsets. Turkeys, geese, ducks and chickens were also reared.

Stage-coaches and turnpikes

Late in the morning on every weekday early in Queen Victoria's reign, there would be a bustling scene outside the Swan Hotel when the coach from London was expected at midday. It was rarely late, and soon in the distance the rattle of harness, the clip-clop of horses' hooves and the sound of a horn could be heard. The stage-coach with

THE SWAN HOTEL, LETHERHEAD.

[1] P.R.O. M.A.C./68/Surrey.
[2] P.R.O. M.A.F./68/Surrey.
[3] R. A. Lever, *Ashtead, a Village Transformed,* ed. A. Jackson.

1847 engraving showing Thorncroft Manor and Bridge Cottage. By the ford below the bridge is a freshwater spring called the Sharnwell. Dorking Road had been widened all down Gimcrack Hill to make way for the stage-coaches (right).

the name of *The Sovereign* boldly emblazoned on it, came into view. Passengers were perched on top with some seated more comfortably inside and its guard and coachmen were smartly uniformed. In the 'Swan' yard, the ostlers changed the steaming horses for a fresh set of four. In less than half an hour, they were away again en route for Dorking and Worthing.

This was a common enough happening in the Leatherhead of the 1830s and early 1840s, when as many as eight stage coaches passed through the town every day except on Sunday.[1] On May Day and other festive occasions, the coachman's whipstock would be decorated with ribbons and flowers and the horses, with coloured rosettes. The coaches which drove through Leatherhead included the so-called *Accommodation* coach, going to Worthing, like *The Sovereign*, but arriving in the town half an hour earlier. There was *The Comet* which went to Bognor from London; *The Star* which left London for Horsham mid-afternoon so did not reach Leatherhead until the early evening and *The Times* which ran to Guildford and arrived in Leatherhead late in the day. Three of the coaches going to Dorking had no special names. All the coaches used the turnpike roads round Leatherhead which, though often difficult in winter and dusty in summer, had been much improved following the recommendations of McAdam and others.

The stage-coaches passing through Leatherhead were brightly coloured in yellow, blue or black with gold trimmings. They carried four inside and as many as 11 or even 12 outside. They had to stop every 10 miles to allow for a change of horse. Their average speed was about 10 mph, and they were renowned for their punctuality so staff at the 'Swan' knew when to prepare the fresh horses and drinks to warm the passengers. The coaches had no proper brakes but on steep hills, an iron plate, a skidpan or drag, was applied to the rear wheels, acting as a primitive form of braking. One may be seen embedded in the wall of the St Mary's Road side of Gimcrack Hill, near the top. It is a modest memorial to a carter, George Clark, who died in a wagon accident there.

All the coaches seen in Leatherhead were owned by the famous London proprietors, William Chaplin and B. W. Horne. The coaches started from the 'Golden Cross' at Charing Cross, the 'White Horse' in Fetter Lane, the 'Old Bell', Holborn, and the 'Spread Eagle', Gracechurch Street. Only the reasonably well-to-do Leatherhead resi-

[1] A. Bates, *Directory of Stage Coach Services, 1836* (1969); *Pigot's Directories*, 1839, 1845.

The Swan Inn, *c.* 1865, was a regular stage-coach stop. Horses were changed in its yard and refreshments supplied to passengers. Now it may seem a romantic way to travel but then it was an uncomfortable and risky experience. Accidents were frequent, breakdowns common, highway hold-ups a hazard and 'coach sickness' inevitable due to poor suspension and appalling roads.

167

Still standing today (1988), the old engine shed from London and South-Western Railway which provided Leatherhead's first service from Epsom in 1859. The station was east of the Kingston road, near the 'Plough'.

dents travelled on these coaches since it cost as much as 5*d.* a mile for an inside seat, though it was slightly cheaper and chillier to ride outside.[1] Booking ahead was usual, half being paid at the start of the journey. The term 'booking office', is said to be a survival of this coaching age.[2]

Coaches continued to serve Leatherhead well into the 1840s and indeed there were still eight a day in 1845, even though by this time railways were reaching out from London into Surrey and to the south coast. There were some new coach names, *The Original* going to Dorking and *The Victoria* bound for Brighton, this being the last going to the south coast.[3] Even these had bowed out by the early 1850s and were replaced by horse-drawn omnibuses which met the trains at Epsom. Nevertheless, private stage-coaches continued and *The Age*, owned and driven by the Duke of Beaufort, was to be seen in summer on its way to Dorking. This was discontinued in 1862. The omnibuses which replaced the coaches for short journeys to Epsom station were drawn by three horses abreast. They were sometimes called Shillibers after the name of the man who first introduced them to London in 1829. Horse-drawn carriers which had served Leatherhead for many years during and before the coaching age, continued their business. Two main carriers were Thomas Bullen and William Poulter, and they with others, provided a daily service to and from London.

The railways arrive

Leatherhead had its first railway service when a line from Epsom was opened on 1 February 1859 by the London and South-Western Railway (LSWR). There had been plans much earlier than this for the London to Croydon line to be extended to Epsom and beyond, using the so-called 'atmospheric' system. The motive power for this was suction in a tube laid between the rails in which a piston ran connected to the train. Brunel and Cubitt spoke in its favour, but steam won the day, and Epsom was reached by rail in May 1847. The railway came to Leatherhead 12 years later and there were great celebrations as there had been in June 1857 when work started on the line.[4] The first station was built on the east side of the Kingston Road. The original engine house which, after 1877, was leased out as a church and school, still exists in 1988.

From July 1859 onwards, the LSWR shared the Epsom–

[1] D. Mountfield, *The Coaching Age* (1976), p. 93.

[2] C. G. Harper, *Stage Coach and Mail* (1903), I, p. 320.

[3] C. G. Harper, *The Brighton Road* (1906), p. 103.

[4] *Surrey Standard*, 6 June 1857.

Leatherhead line with the London, Brighton and South Coast Railway (LBSCR) and shortly after this, trains from Leatherhead reached both Waterloo (LSWR) and London Bridge (LBSCR). There had been links with Waterloo since 4 April 1859 but connections with London Bridge were delayed until 8 August that year. This easy and quick way to travel to London gave a great boost to life in the town, and although tickets in those days were not cheap, it was possible to spend a day in London, a place which many had never seen before.

For a rail trip to the south coast, Leatherhead people had to wait several years, though in the mid-sixties there were navvies beginning to work on the line to Dorking.

This new line, backed by the LBSCR, meant that trains would then be passing through Leatherhead, and it was agreed that the old Kingston Road station would be abandoned and two new stations built adjacent to each other nearer the town. The new stations began operating on 11 March 1867 when the Leatherhead to Dorking line was opened and extended to Horsham on 1 May.[1]

The LBSCR was proud of its Leatherhead station which remained until recently, substantially what it was then. The LSWR station adjacent, with the service road between them, continued to be a terminus until 2 February 1885 when the railway link with Guildford via Bookham and Effingham was completed.[2] By this time, Leatherhead had railway connections not only with London but also with many parts of Surrey and the south coast. When the line to Guildford was under construction, the vicar of Leatherhead invited the Navvy Mission Society to give classes and services probably at Pachenesham (now called Pachesham) to the railway workers or navvies, as they were called. Since navvies then were notorious for their rough language and manners, they were obviously suitable missionary subjects.[3]

Travelling by train was an adventure for most people in those days, and the local Leatherhead papers tempted their readers to try out arranged excursions by train. In August 1881 there was a choir excursion to Brighton and in June 1893 two special trains ran from Leatherhead for an outing to Eastbourne with 800 members of church organisations.[4] The railway also greatly speeded up the postal services and local farmers could market their fresh products more quickly and further afield.

[1] J. W. Turner, *The London, Brighton & South Coast Railway* (1978), II, p. 106.

[2] R. A. Williams, *The London & SW Railway* (1968), II, p. 57.

[3] P.M. Jan. 1885; T. Coleman, *The Railway Navvies* (1969), p. 33.

[4] P.M. June 1893.

1902. The graceful railway bridge to Bookham over the River Mole.

Two adjacent railway stations seen in the mid-1920s. On the right, the London–Brighton South Coast station (the present railway station) and on the left of the road, the London and South-Western Railway station.

The London and South-Western Railway station was abandoned in 1927. Its down side station entrance can still be seen today projecting into Station Road (see above).

Cycling, motoring and more stage-coaches

Roads made a come-back in the late Victorian period mainly because of the popularity of the pedal cycle and the invention of the motor car, though the stage-coach surprisingly also had a small say in this. Modern bicycles first came into prominence in the 1880s and Leatherhead seems to have joined early in the new craze since the Easter Monday sports in 1889 included a one mile and a two mile bicycle race.[1] A Cycling Club was formed by the Letherhead Institute in May 1897 with Abraham Dixon as its Chairman, and in August that year he entertained cyclists at his Cherkley home.[2] Two years later, a bicycle gymkhana was held in Thorncroft Manor grounds with 10 events and prizes presented by Mrs Keswick, the wife of the MP for Epsom. Cycling was not, however, confined to shows and club meetings. It was common practice for youngsters to tear at breakneck speeds through the town, 'scorching' as it was called in the local press. A 12-year-old boy was fined by Epsom magistrates in July 1898 for furiously riding a bicycle in Bridge Street, and the following summer, several constables were on duty on Gimcrack Hill to stop cyclists racing downhill.[3]

During the 1890s, motoring was a luxury for the few, yet the motor car was certainly seen in Leatherhead at this time. A police report in March 1899 complained of motor cars racing through the town on Saturday afternoons and Sundays to the great danger and inconvenience of the residents.[4] The speed limit then was about 12 mph, an improvement on the 4 mph imposed by the Red Flag Act repealed in 1896. The cars in Leatherhead were said by the police to be going as much as 15–20 mph! Abraham Dixon's daughter was one of the first in the town to own a car and it was driven by the family coachman.

Why should the out-dated stage-coach reappear at a time when new machines were all the rage? There were several reasons. First, nostalgia for times past increasingly attracted the wealthy who were prepared to invest in new coaches and provide a private service for their friends as a hobby, indulging themselves by being coachmen. Regular coach services had stopped in the early 1860s but there were occasional private ones operating after that and in the 1880s a summer-only coach is said to have journeyed daily from Hatchetts in Piccadilly through Leatherhead to Box Hill.[5] During the 1890s, coaches with the splendid names of *The Old Berkeley*, *The Rocket* and *The Perseverance*

[1] P.M. May 1889.
[2] P.M. Sept. 1897.
[3] *Leatherhead Advertiser*, 23 July 1898.
[4] *Leatherhead Advertiser*, 4 March 1899.
[5] H. E. Malet, *Annals of the Road* (1876), pp. 165–7.

were reported to have changed horses in the 'Swan' yard; the last two maintained a regular service in summer to Box Hill and Dorking.[1] Another coach, *The Tally-Ho*, ran from Hampton Court every weekday morning through Leatherhead to Dorking and its guard wore a gold-laced red coat.[2]

A second reason for the rejuvenation of coaching was the Post Office's dislike of the heavy dues the railways imposed on parcels. To overcome this, they re-introduced the mail-coach from 1887 onwards, though not on the earlier routes. Leatherhead now was on the one used by the new mail-coach. This is borne out by a court case in March 1899 against a Swan Hotel ostler charged with mishandling the horses of the mail vans which passed through Leatherhead every night to Guildford. However, mail-coaches and stage-coaches were not seen for much longer for with the new century, motor vans and motor cars slowly came to dominate the roads.

Public services

This was the period in Leatherhead when modern water supplies were at last introduced, when gas revolutionised lighting and heating and notable improvements were made in the police, fire, postal and medical services. Only electricity, though much talked about, had to await the early years of the new century to be fully adopted.

Water supplies and sanitation

The steps taken by Leatherhead towards a piped water supply were slow and hesitant. The town had long been fortunate in having water freely available from shallow wells, but as the population grew and land further away from the river began to be developed, deeper wells were necessary. The impetus to provide piped water in 1884 came with the increasing realisation that well water was often contaminated. The Leatherhead and District Water Company supplied water to Leatherhead, Ashtead, Mickleham, Fetcham, the Bookhams, Stoke d'Abernon and Cobham. The main source of supply was a 12-inch bore-hole, 200 ft deep in the chalk sited in the angle between Waterway Road, the River Mole and Bridge Street. From the bore-hole, water flowed to a shallow well from which it was pumped to a service reservoir, now disused but still surviving, close to the top of Reigate Road. The pipes were at first only a little below ground, but after 1895

[1] Murray's *Handbook to Surrey* (1888), p. 91.
[2] *Leatherhead Advertiser*, 1 July 1899.

all mains were lowered to a minimum of 3 ft which is still standard today. A new and larger reservoir was commissioned in 1897 at Highlands Farm and this still remains the service reservoir for the Leatherhead area. A second bore-hole was drilled in 1898 to meet increasing water demands.

Proper sanitation made slower progress than piped water. A Vestry sanitary committee laboured with good intentions from 1868 onwards to improve matters.[1] There were constant complaints about the sewage system in some houses and that most of the outfall through sewers went into the River Mole. Prolonged discussions took place in 1879 about where a sewage outfall might be, considering meadow land near the Mole and possibly a strip of Randalls Park which its owner, Mr Henderson, not surprisingly, objected to. As a temporary measure which however lasted several years, the local Medical Officer of Health, Dr Jacob, recommended in March 1881 the adopting of the Rochdale Pail dry closet system and hundreds of these were ordered.[2] The Vestry committee thought them a great success and in November 1883 they even believed that there was no need for any elaborate or costly sewage scheme for Leatherhead.[3] Eight years later, they were still talking in the same vein but in October 1893 Dr Jacob was now convinced that the only true remedy was the provision of new sewers. Action was however delayed until January 1900[4] and was not completed until early in the new reign.

Gas and electricity

Gas was first delivered in Leatherhead on 3 February 1851. This must have been a magical moment for the shopkeeper, the craftsman in his workshop and the family at home. Now for the first time there was lighting other than candles and oil lamps, and to everyone's delight the streets were lit. The gasworks and the gasholders were north of the town on the Kingston Road near the railway bridge. In the first few years, coal supplies had to come from Deptford Wharf to Epsom by rail, then by road carrier, but after 1859 when the railway reached Leatherhead, transport problems greatly eased. Although street lighting was provided from the start, this was only from the beginning of October to the end of March and even then, not on moon-lit nights. Delicate incandescent mantles replaced the old-style street lamps in 1899. The Gas Company shared offices with the Water Company and

[1] S.R.O. P61/6/1.
[2] S.R.O. P61/6/1.
[3] Ibid.
[4] P.M. Jan. 1900.

there was some overlapping of members on the boards but the two companies remained strictly independent.

Electricity did not come to Leatherhead universally until after the death of Queen Victoria. There had been long discussions about the need for it and on 8 July 1899 there was a provisional order for electric lighting which was not immediately implemented.[1] The stumbling block was almost always how expensive it would be, and doubts were expressed whether the town could afford it. Electric lighting at Cherkley Court and The Red House was being admired by all, so the large private houses with their own generators led the way.[2]

The Police

Law and order in Leatherhead and other country parishes had for centuries been the responsibility of one or more constables selected by the manorial court from good and true local men, approved by JPs. This was all to change during Queen Victoria's reign, though the process was slow and even when proper policemen were in office, traditional constables continued to be appointed, though presumably in an honorary capacity. The spur for change came with the increasing lawlessness after the end of the Napoleonic Wars, and Sir Robert Peel's Bobbies did much to ensure a safer life for all. However, Bobbies were not to be seen in Leatherhead until after 1851, although the County Police Act of 1839 had recommended their appointment. Surrey, for financial reasons, did not adopt them until 1851. Public opinion had been shocked by the murder of a clergyman at Frimley, and conversely impressed by police success in putting down the Chartist riots in London in 1848.[3] Thereafter, Leatherhead felt Bobbies were acceptable and the town had an inspector of police and one or two constables. The police station in the Fairfield[4] had a secure room to keep offenders overnight. The early policemen wore stove-pipe hats, but by the time Leatherhead had theirs, helmets for policemen were coming into fashion in other towns.

Fire services

Leatherhead's firemen in the Victorian period were not full-time professionals like those of today but volunteers who had other jobs. The fire engine, drawn by horses who also drew the dustcart, had been kept in the church tower early in the century and as late as October

[1] *Leatherhead Advertiser*, 8 July 1899.
[2] *Leatherhead Advertiser*, 28 July 1899; *Leatherhead Observer*, 27 June 1891.
[3] T. A. Critchley, *History of Police in England & Wales* (1979), p. 98.
[4] P.O. Directories, 1862, 1870.

1846, the Vestry Minutes emphasised the need to keep it 'in the efficient state'. The clock tower was built for it, close to Sweech House in the 1850s[1] and a new engine was delivered for the 1887 Jubilee celebrations.

The fire brigade held an annual dinner, usually in March, and William Keswick, the MP for Epsom, was present at one of these. Their record fully justified the praise he gave them. In May 1881 they successfully put out a fire in Phillip's grocery business in Bridge Street 'affixing hoses to two hydrants, one by the river';[2] and two years later they extinguished the Cherkley Court fire in July 1893 and the fire which destroyed Mr Batchelar's timber yard and house in Church Road a month later.[3]

Postal services

In the early years of Queen Victoria's reign, letters were delivered only once a day until the mid-1840s and they reached the town during the night on a horse-drawn cart which had picked them up from the Royal Mail coach at Kingston on its way to Portsmouth.[4] By 1850, practically all the country's letters went by rail, but Leatherhead had to wait another nine years before the train sped the mail straight to its door. Until then, the mail was brought to the town by carriers from the Epsom railway terminal. Rowland Hill's penny post of 1840 had greatly popularised letter-writing, and by the 1860s Leatherhead had two deliveries and two dispatches of mail a day, increasing to three in about 1880 and to four in 1899.[5] The Post Office was then in Bridge Street and according to an 1899 report, the number of postmen employed had increased from four to 18 because of the work load.[6]

Leatherhead had a telegraph service at the Post Office, probably from about the middle years of the century and several telegrams sent by Roger Cunliffe of Tyrrells Wood in the 1880s have survived.[7] In the last decade of the century the telephone was taking over more and more from the telegram.

In May 1899 it was reported that many improvements had been effected by the National Telephone Company at Leatherhead and many 'poles and wires have been re-arranged to suit the convenience of the new subscribers'.[8] Telephones were also being connected at this time in Dorking and a public telephone booth had been opened in Leatherhead High Street.

[1] Soc. Recs. X80.
[2] *Leatherhead Observer*, 3 June 1891.
[3] P.M. Aug. 1893.
[4] Henshall's *Twenty-five Miles Round London* (1839), p. 101.
[5] P.O. Directories, 1882, 1899.
[6] *Leatherhead Advertiser*, 3 June 1899.
[7] S.R.O. 99/4/2 (Cunliffe correspondence).
[8] P.O. Directories, 1851, 1895.

The Leatherhead Fire Brigade with their engine at the clock tower which was specially built to house the fire engine. The horses stabled in Bridge Street also drew the dustcart which they would pull to the clock tower when the fire alarm sounded!

Medical services

There had been doctors, or surgeons as they were more often called, in Leatherhead before the Victorian period. The medical services had greatly improved by the mid-19th century and there were never less than two or three doctors working in the town. A veterinary surgeon first appeared in 1851, and two were practising by the end of the century. The doctors were general practitioners, but they were also medical advisers to the Friendly Societies and other welfare organisations.

Dr Jacob, the local Medical Officer of Health, frequently reported the town's health to the Leatherhead Parochial Committee. He occasionally mentioned a few cases of scarlet fever and diphtheria but Leatherhead seems to have been generally free from serious outbreaks of more lethal illnesses.[1] In fever cases the practice was to remove the patient to a London hospital and disinfect the house in which they lived. In January 1887, Dr Jacob suggested that there should be a hospital in Leatherhead for infectious cases but it was not until November 1893 that a cottage hospital was opened at 8 Clinton Road.[2] It had seven or eight patients and a matron trained at Guy's Hospital. Gifts of all kinds were given to the hospital – bundles of linen, an unending flow of books, food and flowers, all gratefully acknowledged in the parish magazine by Mrs Sackville Davis who gave the house and was one of its trustees.

Social services

Looking after the sick and the poor had long been a responsibility of the Vestry committee of the church, helped by the town's general spirit of caring for those in need. The Poor Law Amendment Act of 1834 which established workhouses under a Board of Guardians centred in Epsom, took away some of the caring tasks of the Vestry though their concern for the needy was scarcely lessened. For example, in January 1848 Widow Gardiner[3] was excused the poor rates during the illness of her two daughters and there were many other similar cases documented. The parish charities continued their good work. The Vestry members also strongly supported the allotment scheme for the poor which had been introduced at the time of the enclosing of Leatherhead's common land in the 1860s. Twenty-five acres on either side of Barnett Wood Lane were set aside for this. There

[1] S.R.O. P61/6/1.
[2] P.M. Nov. 1893.
[3] S.R.O. P61/6/1.

178

were 110 allotments altogether and the holders paid a low monthly rental. Allotment wardens were appointed by the Vestry to supervise the allotments.[1]

In the 1870s the Vestry arranged for District Visitors to call on poor families and report any cases of sickness or distress. In Leatherhead, there were as many as 15 District Visitors, mostly the wives of well-known local families like Mrs Budd, Mrs Rickards and Mrs Courage, and even the Headmaster of St John's School, the Rev. E. C. Hawkins.[2] The church also sponsored a Provident Coal Club subsidised by wealthy parishioners to help those who could not afford winter coal. Only a nominal sum was paid for tickets which were honoured with coal in November each year.[3] In the very first Parish Magazine of January 1880 the Vicar strongly advocated the use of the Penny Bank and the Post Office Savings Bank. Then there were the 'slate' clubs, also designed to encourage the savings habit, set up for the most part in public houses but there was also one in the Parish Room in the Fairfield. About this time, a Leatherhead and District Co-operative Society was founded and their general store based on the profit-sharing principle[4] was opened in North Street. There was an almshouse for old people in Church Walk.

Other social arrangements included the Epsom and Leatherhead Friendly Society, the Ancient Order of Foresters and the Oddfellows Society, all of which helped their members in times of sickness and accident. There was a Girls' Friendly Society, a Young Men's Institute, supported by Abraham Dixon, and a Church Lads' Brigade, some of whom represented Leatherhead at a Royal Review in Hyde Park on 14 July 1897 when they were inspected by the Duke of Connaught.[5]

The National Schools
There had been some very limited schooling in Leatherhead during the 18th and early 19th centuries, but it was not until Queen Victoria's accession that true progress was made towards giving children the rudiments of education. The initiative for improved schooling came from the Vicar of Leatherhead, the Rev. Benjamin Chapman, who founded its first National School in July 1838. These were Church of England schools set up throughout England and Wales, financially supported by the parishioners and aided by the National Society for the Education of the Poor in the Principles of the Established Church.

[1] GMR: Parish Report, 1871/72.
[2] P.M. (various).
[3] Ibid.
[4] Soc. Recs. X205.
[5] P.M. 1897.

1895. All Saints' Church built by Canon Utterton in 1889.

This Society, founded in 1811, was known more generally as the National Society and the schools they aided were known as National Schools. The Leatherhead School was in Highlands Road and it originally consisted of one classroom to take 80 boys. In 1839, the year after it was built, another classroom was added and this was the Girls' School. Ten years later, yet another room was constructed to provide an Infants' School for boys and girls from three to seven years old. However, this gradually became more and more overcrowded, so in 1865 a separate school, known as the Infants' School on Gravel Hill was built in what is now Upper Fairfield Road. This building still exists, next door to the British Legion Hall, but the playground, which sloped down Gravel Hill behind the school, has been cut away to form part of what is now Leret Way. The Infants' School and the Boys' School in Highlands Road remained as schools until 1912.[1]

Another infants' school, the future All Saints' School, opened in July 1877. The school was in the then-disused engine house off the Kingston road, which doubled as a Sunday School and a Mission Church. This shed can still be seen beside the railway line at the Kingston Road bridge. An early entry in the school logbook for 1879 presents a vivid picture of conditions in the school at that time: 'Oct. 18th. The attendance worse, the children are so sad, their coughs and colds so bad that it is quite painful to hear them . . . On Friday, Mrs. Rickards came and kindly said she would make a mattress for the babies (the three-year-olds) to lie down upon when they were sleepy, and also a coverlet for them.'

After All Saints' Church was completed in 1889 it was decided to raise funds for a new building for the Infants' School which was known as All Saints' School by this time. On 25 April 1900 the new school was formally opened in the building which in 1978 was to become the North Leatherhead Community Centre. So, after nearly a quarter of a century in the old engine shed, the school moved into its new home. It was there for another three-quarters of a century.

Many years before all this, the Boys' and Girls' Schools in Highlands Road had become more and more overcrowded, and in 1882 a site was purchased on which to build a separate school for the girls. The building which later became Poplar Road Church of England First School, was erected as the National School for Girls and opened on 10 January 1884.

[1] Linda Heath, *Of Good Report* (LDLHS, 1987).

There was no Roman Catholic school in Leatherhead in Victorian times, but there was a Nonconformist one at the back of the old Congregational Church in North Street. This was known as the British School because it was aided by the British and Foreign School Society, the Nonconformist equivalent of the National Society. There was a British School here as early as 1818 but it was always short of funds and probably closed and re-opened more than once. A list of these schools compiled at the end of the 19th century refers to the one in Leatherhead as founded in 1861 or 1862.[1] A critical report in 1901 by the Board of Education architect[2] led to the closing of the school in 1902, though the Sunday School continued. Among other things, it pointed out the insanitary conditions and the distress caused to the children by the smell and noise of the neighbouring slaughterhouse.

Towards the end of the 19th century the influence of both the National Society and the British and Foreign School Society declined as government became more directly concerned with education. A law making education compulsory for children under 10 years was passed in 1876, but the historic milestone occurred in 1891 with the introduction of free education. From then on, education was to pass more and more into the hands of the state. Finally in 1902, an Education Act was passed abolishing the old School Boards which had been set up in 1870. On 1 July 1903, two years after the death of Queen Victoria, the four National Schools in Leatherhead were taken over by the Surrey County Council and the age of state education began.

St John's School and other private schools

St John's School came to Leatherhead in 1872 from St John's Wood, London, where it had been founded in 1851. When the school arrived here, the headmaster was the Rev. E. C. Hawkins. At the start there were about 65 pupils, but the school expanded considerably during the next 30 years and by the turn of the century there were nearly 300 boys attending the school.[3] The Rev. A. F. Rutty was Headmaster from 1883 to 1909 and much of St John's progress was due to him.

About the same time that St John's moved to Leatherhead, another boarding school for boys was opened at the corner of Grange Road and Leatherhead Road. This was a school for boys from 8 to 13 years old which was later to become Downsend School but at this time it seems to have been known simply as the Leatherhead Road Board-

[1] British & Foreign School Society Archives.
[2] P.R.O. (Kew).
[3] E. M. P. Williams, *The Quest Goes On (St. John's 1851–1951)* (1951).

Construction workers *c.* 1871 resting on the site of St John's School which was completed the following year.

ing School. The Headmaster was the Rev. A. T. Scudamore and the house, which accommodated the 14 boys attending the school, was called Gateforth House. By 1890 the school had the name of Gateforth House Preparatory School and five years later it became Downsend School with 25 boarders and 25 day boys.

There were a number of other private schools which came and went and have left no records, but the one at The Mansion (now the Library) lasted for quite a long time. It was known as The Mansion Grammar School for Boys and was started about 1846 by Dr Thomas Payne. He taught the then-advanced Jacotot system of education based on the principle that because all men have equal intelligence received from God, they have the faculty of being able to instruct themselves in everything. This Jacotot method implied a freedom in education which many Victorians must have found shocking. The school was a boarding and day school for about 50 boys from 10 years upwards. Dr Payne was succeeded by one of his assistant teachers, Robert Ibbs, in 1866 and the school appears to have continued until some time during the 1870s.[1] In the 1890s Thorncroft Manor was also a 'High-class preparatory school' under Walter Lawrence.[2]

Technical education

During the 19th century there was a strong movement towards technical education for those most in need of it. Leatherhead, like so many other places, had a Mechanics Institute which was in North Street and it probably ran courses for a moderate fee on all kinds of practical subjects.[3] Evening classes were also being held in the Institute and sometimes in one of the local schools. The subjects covered included history, arithmetic, chemistry in everyday life, carpentry, dressmaking, civics and shorthand.[4]

Literary and artistic associations

The Brontë family, especially Charlotte Brontë, had close connections with Abraham Dixon of Cherkley Court since his mother, Letitia Taylor came from Gomersal in Yorkshire not far from the Brontë home in Haworth. Her niece, Mary Taylor, went to the same school as Charlotte and they were friends. The Taylor family is portrayed in Charlotte Brontë's novel *Shirley*. In 1843, Dixon, then a young man in his late twenties, met Charlotte Brontë in Brussels when she was

[1] F. B. Benger, 'The Mansion', *Proc. LDLHS*, **1** (7), 1953, p. 11.
[2] *Kelly's Directory*, 1895.
[3] *Kelly's Directory*, 1862.
[4] P.M. November 1882.

studying French and in 1849 she was invited to spend Christmas with his family in Birmingham. It is curious that long after Charlotte's death, there was a concert on 28 November 1881 at the Swan Hotel in Leatherhead given entirely by members of *a* Brontë family. No less than six Brontës, Mr and Mrs F. Brontë and their four children, Constance, Ernest, Minnie and Edith took part. They danced a quadrille and a polka, sang duets, played a trio for flute, violin and piano and the whole family rounded it off with a performance of Haydn's *Surprise* symphony.[1]

Edward Lear, the artist and writer of humorous verse and limericks, was associated with Leatherhead through his sister Eleanor who lived most of her married life in Church Street and died there. She was married to William Newsom, a director of the Bank of England. Eleanor Newsom wrote regularly to her brother when he was travelling abroad and he visited her often in Leatherhead. In 1874 when in India, Lear wrote home to say that the cool of the Ootacamund Hills reminded him of Leatherhead.[2] One of Edward Lear's brothers, Charles, was a missionary in West Africa and after marrying a native girl, Adjouah who nursed him during an illness, they both returned home and went to live for many years with the Newsoms in Leatherhead. Eleanor and her husband grew very fond of the black girl who went to school here for three years although it is not known which school she attended.[3] After a while the couple returned to West Africa. Eleanor went blind and deaf in the mid-1870s and Edward Lear wrote to a friend in 1877 'after a happy day with the Tennysons, he had gone to see poor Ellen'.[4] She died in 1885.

Henry James, the novelist, had no family links with Leatherhead but he liked to visit his friend Russell Sturgis of Givons Grove. He stayed with Sturgis on at least two occasions taking a fly or a trap from Leatherhead station to his friend's house. These visits in late summer 1879 and 1881 were when James was being lionised by society. He had just published *Portrait of a Lady*, a book as admired by his readers as his conversation was, by his hosts.[5]

George Meredith and Robert Louis Stevenson probably knew Leatherhead well. Many are the stories of Meredith's strenuous walks over the Mickleham and Leatherhead Downs from Flint Cottage under Box Hill where he lived and wrote for over 40 years.[6] Swinburne, Hardy and Sir James Barrie used to visit him there. Meredith's daugh-

[1] P.M. January 1882.
[2] V. Noakes, *Edward Lear* (1968), p. 269.
[3] A. Davidson, *Edward Lear* (1938), p. 6.
[4] V. Noakes, op. cit., p. 276.
[5] Leon Edel, *Life of Henry James* (1953), I, pp. 614, 642.
[6] E. E. Green, *The Surrey Hills* (1915), p. 87.

ter married one of the Sturgis family of Givons Grove. Robert Louis Stevenson, like Meredith, was very much an outdoor man and in the 1870s he stayed the whole of one summer with his mother at Burford Bridge.[1]

Neither Thackeray nor Conan Doyle may have known Leatherhead but both wrote about it. The Rev. John Honeyman is a Leatherhead curate in Thackeray's *The Newcomes*; and in Conan Doyle's *The Speckled Band* the action takes place near Leatherhead. Sherlock Holmes and Dr Watson take a train from London to Leatherhead and on arrival they hired a trap at the station inn and drove for a few miles through the lovely Surrey lanes.

The novelist Anthony Hope, was the son of the Rev. E. C. Hawkins, Headmaster of St John's School. He wrote *The Prisoner of Zenda* in 1894 and *Rupert of Hentzau* two years later. He died in 1933 and is buried in the churchyard.

The most famous of English painters, J. M. W. Turner, must have known Leatherhead in his youth since he often stayed with Dr Monro in Fetcham. His sketch of the church tower is on page 124.

William Holman Hunt famed for his *Light of the World* and a leader of the Pre-Raphaelite school of painting, found romance in Leatherhead. Through the sculptor Thomas Woolner, he became friendly with and married Fanny, one of the beautiful daughters of Dr George Waugh. Hunt and his wife went to live in the Middle East where she died, leaving him with a child. He later married her younger sister Edith.[2]

Another painter with Leatherhead associations was Edward Wilkins Waite who was born here in 1854, son of the town's Congregational minister and one of eight children. Three of his brothers became artists and two musicians. Edward Waite conducted the Abinger choir which won at the Leith Hill Festival in 1905. He was educated at The Mansion Grammar School in Leatherhead. After two years in Canada, he returned to take up painting seriously. He died at Fittleworth, Sussex in 1924. Public interest in his paintings, described as poems of the English countryside, has revived and there was an acclaimed exhibition devoted to his work at the Burlington Gallery in London in May 1987.[3]

Other, less familiar, painters who were living in the town in the late Victorian period included Henry Grey, a landscape artist and

[1] *The Times*, 13 November 1950.
[2] Diana Holman Hunt, *My Grandmothers and I.*
[3] *Leatherhead Advertiser*, 10 April 1987.

Henry Hall Knight[1] and William Snow who worked in both oils and water colour. Unlike these, Cecil Aldin was known for his sporting paintings. In his mid-teens while a student at the Royal College of Art, he received a commission from Miss Emily Moore, the proprietor of the Swan Hotel, to paint her terrier. He stayed in the town for about six months, getting commissions from local people to paint their pets. In later life he exhibited at the Royal Academy and lived on until 1935.[2]

There were also musicians; the Middleton brothers, Alfred and James lodged with their families in Highlands Road and were professors of music while a third brother, George, in Church Walk, was the owner of travelling marionettes.

Other residents were Matthew Moggeridge, journalist and editor of *Social Notes* and George Ryder, the naturalist.

A look at the parish
Leatherhead in the late Victorian period was far busier and larger than it had been at the start of the reign, but nevertheless there was still the feeling of being in the country. There were many inns; the 'Swan', the 'Duke's Head' and the 'King's Head' in the High Street, the 'Bull' in North Street, the 'Running Horse' in Bridge Street, and the 'Plough', the 'Royal Oak' and the 'Railway Arms' in Kingston Road (see pp. 291–305). The way of life of most Leatherhead people improved greatly with the provision of domestic gas in 1851, and after 1859, the freedom to travel came with the railways. Many joined friendly societies and social clubs both to improve their lot and as security against ill-health and poverty. The parish church continued to play an important role in the town's affairs and Leatherhead was fortunate in having a trio of vicars so devoted to the welfare of their community.

Benjamin Chapman, the first vicar of Leatherhead in Queen Victoria's reign, came of a distinguished Yorkshire family mentioned in *Burke's Landed Gentry*. Soon after leaving Christ's College, Cambridge, he was Rector of Westley Waterless in Cambridgeshire for seven years before being appointed to Leatherhead in 1836.[3] Chapman quickly became well known in the town by his active sponsoring of the first National School for Boys and later of other schools. The Vicarage was brimming with children for he had three sons and seven daughters. One of his sons born in 1838, was called Arthur Drinkwater Bethune Chapman,[4] no doubt a godson of the owner of Thorncroft Manor. The

Emily Moore drawn by the artist Cecil Aldin, 1870–1935, who dedicated his book *Romance of the Road* (Bracken Books) to her for three reasons; 'Firstly she is a very charming old lady; secondly because for 40 years she was the hostess of that old coaching house, the Swan Inn at Leatherhead; and lastly, many, many years ago she befriended and gave a very shy and very red-headed youth his first commission, the result of which was the terribly bad picture which now hangs in her dining room'.

[1] *Kelly Directory*, 1881 et seq.
[2] Roy Heron, *Cecil Aldin* (1981), p. 16.
[3] J. A. Venn, *Alumni Cantabrigensis* (1947), II, p. 110.
[4] A. C. Fox-Davies, *Armorial Families* (1929), p. 350.

Three Vicars of Leatherhead. From the left; the Rev. Bernard Chapman, 1837–71; the Rev. Thomas Griffith, 1871–76; and Canon Frank Utterton, 1876–1908. Canon Utterton had two outstanding curates, the Rev. Jourdain and the Rev. S. N. Sedgwick who wrote *The Legends of Leatherhead*, first published in the *Leatherhead Advertiser* and later in book form. He is largely responsible for most local legends.

Vicar was a highly cultured man with wide interests who had spent part of his early life in Sweden, and had written biographies of Gustavus Adolphus and Gustavus Vasa. At Cambride he won the Porteous Gold Medal for the best theological essay and his sermons had a quality few preachers attained.[1] He made some improvements to the church, started a fund to renovate the organ and established the choir in its modern form.[2] He died in 1871 and the church's altar reredos was erected in his memory.

Thomas Thompson Griffith was vicar of Leatherhead for only five years (1871–1876) but in that time he built a new Vicarage (which is still standing but now used for other purposes) and supported a major restoration of the church. He had been at Clare College, and was Precentor of Rochester Cathedral for 11 years. After Griffith left Leatherhead in 1876 to become Rector of Seale, he continued to show an interest in his old parish and in January 1884 he was one of many who attended the opening of the new Girls' School here.[3] Fifteen years later, he and Canon Utterton took the marriage service at Winchester Cathedral of Griffith's son, also in Holy Orders, to Miss Collins, a niece of Canon Utterton.[4]

Frank Ernest Utterton, vicar from 1871 to 1907, was in many ways one of the most remarkable men in Victorian Leatherhead. He went to New College, Oxford, and was Rector of Seale before coming here, so he exchanged livings with the previous incumbent.[5] His father was Archdeacon of Surrey and Bishop Suffragan of Guildford. Utterton was only 31 years old when he came to Leatherhead, but later in life he grew a long white beard. It was this which old people of the parish recalled, one saying that, as a young child in the 1890s, she always thought that 'he looked like Moses'. He was keenly interested in all aspects of parish life. In church affairs he had never less than two or three curates to assist him plus a licensed reader. He arranged for yet another church restoration and was the chief force behind the scheme for the building of All Saints' Church and school. He was also the enthusiastic supporter of the annual choir festivals of the Leatherhead Deanery which in 1884 took part in the Winchester Cathedral Triennial Festival. A new church banner worked and presented by Miss Rickards, was used for the first time at this festival.[6]

Apart from being chairman of the Vestry committee, Utterton was a member and often chairman of many other groups including that

[1] Soc. Recs. X187.

[2] P.M. December 1914: obituary of the choristers.

[3] P.M. February 1884.

[4] *Leatherhead Advertiser*, 29 July 1899.

[5] J. Foster, *Alumni Oxoniensis* (1968), III, p. 1,461.

[6] P.M. July 1884.

Eccentrics

'Happy Jack' lived in the lodging house in Brickbat Alley in the 1890s. He loved horses and always tried to help at the Epsom Races. He appeared at Epsom Court charged with using bad language and the magistrate said, 'You were here a few weeks ago and I warned you then it was your last chance'. 'Happy Jack' promised if he was let off he would go right out of the country. 'Where will you go?' enquired the magistrate. 'I'll go right to the other side of Bookham', he replied!

Jimmy Edwards, the son of a wealthy butcher who lived in the Withies, himself lived rough and when he died in 1925, was found to have owned property in the town.

About that time 'Mr Green Fields' also lived rough under the Waterway Road iron bridge. 'Fetcham Ciss' who always wore gloves was given a meal daily at the Knoll by Mr Harry White. 'Dong' came from Epsom selling brushwood and was so nicknamed by the children because he always carried a clock.

[1] *Leatherhead Observer*, 30 May 1891.
[2] P.M. September 1894.
[3] Lord Alverstone and C. W. Alcock, *Surrey Cricket* (1902).
[4] P.M. Aug. 1893.

190

which ran the Institute. With his wife, he was forever giving parties at the Vicarage for the choir, the Mother's Union, the Sunday Schools and other schools, the Girls' Friendly Society, the Temperance Society and other good causes. He encouraged the provision of soup kitchens to help the poor during the cold winter months, showed continual concern for the success of the Mission Church in North Leatherhead and, in the same area, opened the Rose Coffee Room as a social centre. The Parish Room in the Fairfield was also watched over by him. He founded the parish magazine in 1880 and it is still published today.

Utterton loved travel and there are fine descriptions in the parish magazine of his visits to the Holy Places. He was a physically active and fit man as shown by his account of how he and the church's architect Sir Arthur Blomfield in May 1891 walked the whole length of a beam to examine its timber, high above the nave.[1] He even dived into the River Wharfe in Yorkshire in August 1894 to save the life of a boy who tried unsuccessfully to jump across The Strid, a notorious danger spot. For this heroic rescue, he was awarded the medal of the Royal Humane Society.[2] A few years before this, he had been made a Canon of Winchester and he was later appointed Archdeacon of Surrey. He was one of the first members of the newly-formed Urban District Council in 1894. He died in 1907 and the stained glass in the church's east window is to his memory.

Sports

Cricket was as popular in the Victorian period as it is today. The Leatherhead Cricket Club was founded in 1850, but the game would certainly have been played before. There is a record of a match in August 1843 at which plans for a revived Surrey County Club were discussed.[3] In the 1880s Leatherhead played teams as widely apart as Sevenoaks and Wimbledon and there were on average 32 matches in the season. Every August there was a cricket week, Leatherhead playing the MCC in 1892 and the next year a team grandly called 'The World'. They drew with the MCC but easily beat 'The World'.[4] St John's School played some fine cricket at this time and one of its old boys, L. T. Driffield, took a sensational seven wickets for seven runs when playing for Cambridge University v. the MCC in 1900. Cricket of a more modest nature was played by the Young Men's Institute, the Fire Brigade and the Town Band. The cricket grounds used were a

Fishing at Leatherhead Bridge, *c.* 1880. The daughter of the Rev. Sir Edward Graham Moon, Rector of Fetcham, with her net.

recreation area next to Kingston Road and a field in St John's School.

Football was probably taken up in Leatherhead in the late 1870s and early 1880s when County Associations were being formed, backed by the Football Association. The town's football club was founded about 1887, taking its name Leatherhead Rose from the Rose Coffee Rooms in Kingston Road which became its headquarters. It usually had a full season of fixtures, meeting clubs as various as Epsom, Guildford and Banstead. In April 1892 it played Battersea Albion at Hackbridge in the final of the Herald cup and won 3–1, so the early years were very successful.[1] The club ground was in the Kingston Road area, but for some years in the 1890s it played at Thorncroft Manor.[2] St John's School fielded rugby sides when it first came to Leatherhead in 1872 but soccer was really its main game after 1883 and so it continued until 1919.

Athletics became popular after the formation of the Leatherhead Athletic Sports Association in 1888. It held its annual meetings on Easter Monday in the St John's School grounds. The events included a tug-of-war, a steeple-chase, a mile cycle race and an obstacle race. In the 1890s gymnastic classes were given for teenagers in Victoria Hall.

Tennis was not widely played in Leatherhead at this time, though many of the larger houses had their own courts. A Girls' Tennis Club was formed in 1895, their courts being at Thorncroft Manor. In 1901 the Institute had at least one tennis court in use.[3]

Swimming was at the baths built in 1888 in one of the large barns of the Mill on the River Mole.[4] Local boys, many of whom had no bath at home, swam in the small bathing hole near Randalls Park and often took soap and towels with them.[5]

Hunting in Leatherhead and district at this period was closely associated with the Surrey Union Hunt, whose kennels for many years were at Fetcham Park, the home of the Hankey family.[6] The hunt met at the 'Bull' in 1852 and on Leatherhead Downs in October 1857.[7] Late in the century, the kennels of the Mid-Surrey Draghounds were at Downside in Leatherhead.[8] The Surrey Farmers' Hunt had a celebration at the Swan Hotel in December 1891 attended by the recently-elected Lord Mayor of London, Sir David Evans, who was presented with his portrait in recognition of his five years' mastership.[9]

Other sports included **polo** played at Hawks Hill in Fetcham by many from Leatherhead's hunting fraternity; a form of amateur **horse-**

[1] *Surrey Advertiser*, April 1892.
[2] P.M. May 1901.
[3] P.M. July 1901.
[4] P.M. July 1888.
[5] Kate Sayers.
[6] R. Greaves, *Foxhunting in Surrey & Sussex* (1962), p. 39.
[7] *Surrey Standard*, 31 October 1857.
[8] J. C. Cow, *Surrey* (1903).
[9] *Leatherhead Observer*, 3 November 1891.
[10] Jean and Pat Read.
[11] A. J. Ginger, 'Leatherhead in Victorian times', *Proc. LDLHS*, **1** (7), 1953, p. 12.
[12] Kate Sayers.

racing on Epsom Downs in winter, the races being known as the Leatherhead St Leger and the Leatherhead Derby. There was **fishing** in the Mole rich in trout so it attracted many anglers, and **golf** was said to have been played on the Downs near Cherkley Court and privately at Polesden Lacey.[10] **Shooting** in the Highlands Farm area was referred to by Roger Cunliffe in 1871 and this was probably a common enough sport among farmers and sportsmen. Indeed many landowners employed their own gamekeepers.

Pastimes and celebrations

Sport was only one of the many ways in which Leatherhead people spent their leisure hours. On Saturday nights the town was full of late-night shoppers while listening to the town band which played outside the 'Duke's Head' in the High Street or in front of the clock tower in North Street. There had been a town band since 1881 and though decimated by the First World War after which it was disbanded, the Silver Band has recently been revived and renamed in 1974 the Mole Valley Silver Band.

In Victorian Leatherhead, there was plenty of street music, buskers and other itinerant showmen, hurdy-gurdy men always with monkeys, performing bears, Italian organ-grinders. There was even a mini-Speakers' Corner at the square below the town clock where 'anarchy and atheism was preached from a soap box'. On May Day, young men and girls fixed nosegays of cowslips and other spring flowers on poles and danced round them through the day.[11] In early June the town would be full of excited racing people going to and coming from the Epsom races, especially on Derby Day. In the autumn, usually on 11 October, there was a fair which everyone attended. Only a few weeks later there were the jollifications of Guy Fawkes night with fireworks and bonfires, followed by Christmas and the New Year. On New Year's Eve, the townspeople danced to the Town Band in the street and sang 'Auld Lang Syne' in the gaslight under the town clock at midnight.[12]

Gardening and the display of flowers at annual exhibitions were not surprisingly, as popular as they are now. Consequently the Horticultural Show, usually held in marquees in the gardens of one of the large houses, was one of the best supported events of the summer. There was a fine flower show at Elm Bank in July 1886 with the added

Col. William Holme Sumner, Master of the Surrey Union Foxhounds from 1858 to 1866.

Bridge Street bedecked for Queen Victoria's Jubilee, showing Ventham's shop on the extreme left with the walnut tree felled years later to provide access for the petrol pump (now in the Museum).

interest of a display with bees at work in hives under glass. Givons Grove, Downside and The Red House were also hosts for these events. The Town Band usually played and the day once more ended with dancing.

Late in the 19th century, photography became increasingly popular. A Camera Club was formed in Leatherhead in 1897 and monthly competitions were held.[1] The following year, the editor of the *Amateur Photographer* judged the entries.[2] A professional photographer, Richard Huck, was living in the town doing extensive commercial work. One of his photographs appears on p. 183.

The cinema was too new to be more than a curiosity, yet a cinematograph show was given at the Institute in October 1898. There was another at the Victoria Hall early in the following year and in October 1900, still South African Boer War pictures were shown.[3] There was also some interest in gramophone recording, or the phonograph, as it was called. At a lecture in October 1897 given by a representative of the Edison Bell Company, Canon Utterton made a short speech into a machine which repeated it 'with startling accuracy'.[4]

Leatherhead was prone to dress itself up at the slightest provocation. Concerts, processions and celebrations of many kinds provided plenty for the people to organise and perform in. There was a delightful open-air concert for the Mothers' Union in the Vicarage grounds in July 1898 when the curate and the whole Utterton family took part, and afterwards there was rowing on the Mole.[5] Indeed there was much memorable boating at a Water Carnival in July 1901. The Town Band played on the island in the centre of the river while circled by a stately procession of illuminated boats.[6]

Many entertainments were held in the hall of the Institute and on one occasion the popular music hall star, Albert Chevalier, appeared.[7] In quieter moments, draughts, whist and bagatelle were played here, and there was a circulating library regularly supplied with the latest books which still operates today. Penny Readings, a modest concert form for charity, with songs, music and recitations were often held. In April 1893, the Royal Nubian Minstrels performed, the ancestors of our own Black and White Minstrels, and in October of the same year the Royal Handbell Ringers entertained.[8] The Church Lads' Brigade produced two operettas in May 1900 in the Institute and the

[1] P.M.
[2] P.M.
[3] P.M.
[4] P.M.
[5] P.M.
[6] P.M.
[7] *Leatherhead Advertiser*, 29 January 1898.
[8] P.M.

'Duke's Head', *c.* 1850, described then as 'a commercial inn and posting house' but concealing beneath its rendered façade a timber-framed 17th-century building.

Emily Moore of the Swan Hotel on the left with her friend the actress Ellaline Terriss, wife of Sir Seymour Hicks. Previously it was thought to be Emily Moore with another of her friends, the actress Ellen Terry.

Leatherhead Orchestral Society gave a concert at the Institute in May 1897.[1]

Victoria Hall, later to become the Leatherhead Theatre in the High Street, was another place for entertainment. The Girls' Friendly Society had a Winter Festival at the hall in January 1896, including Tableaux Vivants (pointing a moral) and a very pretty maypole dance wound up the evening.[2] Their annual summer festival was of course out of doors and in 1900 this was at Randalls Park, tea being served in a marquee and a boat was available for use on the river.[3]

The Assembly Rooms at the Swan Hotel were the most used and most prestigious of the meeting places in the town. Emily Moore, the proprietress of the 'Swan', was famed far and wide for her sumptuous table, providing food for the yearly horse sales at Hampton Court attended by the Prince of Wales (later King Edward VII) no less. She was a close friend of Jenny Lind and Ellen Terry, the actress, and was highly respected. Many sought references from her before employing servants – as a guarantee of their sobriety.[4]

Royalty came to Leatherhead on three occasions in the 1880s and 1890s, and each time it was the HRH the Duchess of Albany who twice came over from Claremont to present the prizes at St John's School, on 28 July 1887 and 27 July 1898. The third time was on 16 July 1895,[5] when she opened perhaps the most splendid of the many fetes Leatherhead had held. It was at Thorncroft Manor and lasted for three days, with flower and sweet stalls, a doll stall and a fish pond and paintings were on display in a gallery. There were concerts on the lawns and more boating on the river.

The celebrations at these fetes were as nothing compared to the way the town threw itself into the Jubilee days in June 1887 and 1897.[6] On 21 June 1887 the streets were decorated with bunting, loyal banners and portraits of the Queen. At 7 a.m. the church bells rang a celebratory peal and there was a huge procession to the church for morning Thanksgiving Service after which there was lunch for 269 people at the 'Swan'. This was followed by a children's treat at Randalls Park, about 775 sitting down to tea and cakes and going home each with a Jubilee mug. After dark at about 10 p.m., large crowds thronged Highlands Road on their way to its highest point near the reservoir. There, after the Leith Hill rocket gave the signal, Leatherhead's rockets were fired and a huge bonfire was lit.[7]

[1] P.M.
[2] P.M.
[3] P.M.
[4] P.M.
[5] Bert Powell.
[6] P.M.
[7] P.M.

B 30.732^

Home Office,
Whitehall,
15th Feb. 1901.

Sir

I am commanded by the King to
convey to you hereby His Majesty's thanks for
the Loyal and Dutiful Message of the
Urban District Council of Leatherhead,

on the occasion of the lamented death of Her
late Majesty Queen Victoria

I am, Sir,

Your obedient Servant,

Geo. S. Ritchie

The Chairman of the
Urban District Council
Leatherhead
Surrey

The 1897 celebrations were similarly jolly and so impressive that the local paper likened the town to Venice at carnival time.[1]

The mood was soon to become sober with the outbreak of the South African Boer War at the end of the century. With Lawrence Potts as Chairman of the LUDC, Leatherhead made its contribution to comforts for the troops and put its music into concerts for disabled soldiers and their families.

Then, early in 1901 Queen Victoria died.

There were black borders round the Parish Magazine and muffled church bells to mark her passing after a reign which lasted 60 years.

[1] A. J. Ginger.

THEN &NOW

Much of the appearance of the town changed little during the first half of this century. The following pages show the drastic changes within the last 20 years. These photographs reveal a more prosperous Leatherhead but at the cost of losing some of its charm.

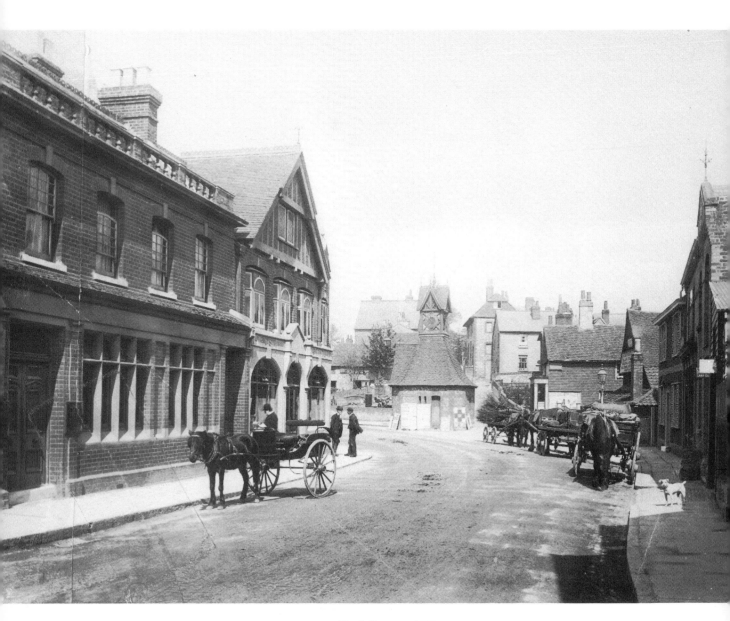

North Street, *c.* 1895.

North Street 1988.

High Street 1895 before the disastrous fire in 1908 at Moulds (third shop blind from right).

High Street showing 'Cradlers' restored.

Sweech House on Gravel Hill *c.* 1902 showing the clock tower.

Sweech House on Gravel Hill 1988. The clock tower was demolished in 1952.

Bradmere Pond at the bottom of Bull Hill on the north side of Park Rise, 1903.

Bradmere Cottage in Kingston Road viewed from the same position, 1988.

Parish Church *c.* 1912 with the clock at seven minutes past four.

Parish Church 1988 with the clock at seven minutes past four.

Bridge Street *c.* 1912.

Bridge Street 1988.

Church Street with raised pavement 1913.

Church Street with buildings in foreground still intact 1988.

The Swan Hotel and High Street seen from the crossroads *c.* 1926.

High Street seen from the crossroads with street market and clowns performing under the clock 1988.

Looking down Church Street from The Crescent to the 'Swan' 1928.

Church Street from the Crescent to Pimms 1988.

1894. Beatrice Welling with her class from the First National Girls' School built in 1884 in Poplar Road.

The Twentieth Century
1901–1988

LEATHERHEAD changed more in this century than in any other, the small country town of Edwardian times becoming modern and newly planned, a haven for commuters and a base for industry. These changes were slow in coming in spite of some of the larger estates being broken up after the First World War. Perhaps the first sign of threat to traditional Leatherhead came in the mid-thirties when the Swan Hotel, a 300-year-old hostelry at its centre, was pulled down and redeveloped and Kingston House where John Wesley delivered his last homily also disappeared. Yet the character of the town was not basically changed until after the Second World War when, attracted by its nearness to London and the country, there were even more increases in the number of daily commuters. Naturally, house-building increased also in areas where there had been fields, though the post-war Green Belt Act attempted to restrict house growth in open country. Even today, large areas of beautiful country can still be enjoyed just outside the parish boundaries. While conserving the country, there was a slow-growing awareness of the need to preserve what remained of the town's old buildings and many like Sweech House and Cradlers have been restored with conspicuous success.

In the last few years, the most radical changes to the town came with the closing of Church Street and the High Street to road traffic, the building of a shopping precinct, the Swan Centre and the Leisure Centre and the circling of Leatherhead with the M25 motorway. All these will take time to absorb and evaluate the effect on the town.

Chronological events are adapted from the *Leatherhead Advertiser,* verified by interviews and tape recordings. Sources other than the *Leatherhead Advertiser* are given.

219

Nevertheless much of old Leatherhead remains; the criss-cross of the four main streets, the ancient 14-arch bridge over the River Mole, Thorncroft Manor and the parish church standing on the hill overlooking the town, as it has done for over 900 years.

Edwardian times and the prelude to war (1901–1914)

In the first year of Edward VII's reign, Leatherhead continued to send comforts to the troops still fighting in the Boer War. When it ended in May 1902, the town's celebrations were quickly followed by preparations to mark Edward VII's Coronation. This was intended for 26 June but the king had appendicitis and national celebrations were postponed until 8 August.

It was about this time that Leatherhead decided a fitting memorial to the late Queen Victoria would be a new hospital, the Cottage Hospital in Clinton Road having closed in April 1902, £130 in debt. Walter Cunliffe of Tyrrells Wood gave the land in Epsom Road and the foundation stone for the Queen Victoria Memorial Hospital (now Victoria House) was laid by Mrs Alfred Tate of Downside in October 1903. The hospital was opened two years later and served the sick of Leatherhead for nearly 40 years.[1]

The School for the Blind came to Leatherhead and completed their building in 1904. Accommodation was provided for 250 pupils and with 15 acres of ground there was room for expansion. Reputed to be the finest school of its kind in Europe, with King George V as its patron, it became the Royal School for the Blind.

There was much new house-building in the 1900s mainly in the Fairfield, Kingston Road and Highlands Road areas. Queen Anne's Gardens, off Linden Road, was built in 1903 and in the next few years the lower part of Copthorne Road was developed for housing with Woodville Road, Kingston Avenue, Clinton Road, Reigate Road and St Nicholas Hill. All the new houses had electricity which the Town Council in 1902 had at last agreed to and it was installed by Buchanan and Curwen. The Leatherhead and District Electricity Supply Company was formed and their works established beside the River Mole.

This spurt in housing was mainly due to the increase in the town's population. Between 1901 and 1911, it grew from 4694 to 5491, double the rate of the previous decade. This may have led to an over-full labour market since in 1903 there were 100 unemployed, perhaps 10

[1] Dr R. G. Gilbert.

per cent of the total working population. Leatherhead and District Commercial Association was formed in 1908 to improve trading which was not helped by a serious fire in Mould's High Street store early that year. It began late at night in the large warehouse next to the shop and quickly enveloped both. There was an huge explosion caused by gunpowder and cartridges, stored on the top floor, igniting. The Leatherhead, Epsom and Dorking fire brigades spent most of an exceptionally cold night trying to put out the flames. Water from the hoses froze on the High Street, making it sheet ice and difficult for the horses drawing the fire engines to reach the site.

More headlines were made when a four-year-old boy, George Dench, fell from Thorncroft Bridge and was saved from drowning by postman Harry Dancer who later was decorated with the Royal Humane Society medal. George Dench lived to found 1st Leatherhead Scout Troop in 1921; joined the church choir in 1914 and is still a member, singing bass for over 74 years. George Dench's brother, Sidney, was chosen as one of the firing party at the Cenotaph for the inauguration of the Tomb of the Unknown Warrior.[1]

During the winters of 1908, 1909 and 1910, the parish church ran a soup kitchen for the poor and distributed 120 pints of milk and 60 loaves a day for three days a week. There was also a popular Coal Club at the church and for a small monthly subscription, winter deliveries of coal were made to those in need.[2]

The poor, disabled and aged welcomed the imaginative Lloyd George-inspired Insurance Act of 1911 which protected them from hardship through illness or unemployment by creating the doctor's panel and the insurance stamp. The Act was explained at a meeting at Oddfellows' Hall at which the Vicar of Leatherhead, the Rev. T. F. Hobson feared that the work of the Friendly Societies would be weakened. However, it supplemented rather than eliminated their work and Leatherhead was one of the first towns to claim maternity benefit under the Act. With pensions for the old granted in 1908 and the introduction of the weekly half-holiday in the Shops Act of 1911, this proved to be a period of great social benefit and a small first step towards the welfare state of the 1940s.

On festive days and public holidays, many took excursions by train, or went motoring or cycling. At least two shops in the High Street sold petrol and did cycle repairs. As early as 1912, a man in

MISS DORA GIBSON
DRAMATIC SOPRANO

Dora Gibson, Mrs Van Thol, lived in later life on the Tyrrells Wood estate.
In 1901 Marconi succeeded in transmitting and receiving signals by wireless telegraphy across the Atlantic from Poldhu in Cornwall to St Johns, Newfoundland. In 1902 he invited Dora Gibson, a professional contralto who had sung under Toscanini at La Scala, Milan, to sing 'Land of Hope and Glory' at Poldhu. This was transmitted and received loud and clear by the liner SS *Mauretania* steaming 700 miles away at sea.

[1] George Dench.
[2] P.M. May 1912.

ALFRED G. VANDERBILT.

Alfred Vanderbilt and his personal stage-coach 'The Venture' reaching Burford Bridge Hotel on its way from London to Brighton as it did most summer weekends. Vanderbilt lost his life when the *Lusitania* was sunk in 1915.

[1] P.R.O. ASSI 31/51.

Clinton Road advertised he could teach anyone to drive a motor car.

The first bus service between Leatherhead and Guildford began when the First World War started, and there were other bus services to Clapham via Epsom and Ealing via Kingston. Indeed, there had been a bus service to Kingston as early as 1911. The railways with their inexpensive excursions to the sea were increasing in popularity, yet a few well-to-do still travelled by private stage coach. *The Venture*, owned by the American millionaire Alfred Vanderbilt often called at the 'Swan' on its way from London to Brighton and was driven by Vanderbilt himself. He lost his life when *The Lusitania* was torpedoed in May 1915. Three years earlier, there was another marine tragedy when the *Titanic* went down on her maiden voyage and a Mr Harvey Collyer from Leatherhead was drowned but his wife and young daughter were rescued.

In 1911, Keith Prowse and Co. proposed plane flights from Brooklands to Dorking and were looking for a suitable landing field in Leatherhead. The LUDC proposed a site on the Cherkley Court estate but nothing came of the whole venture. As abortive were the proposals in 1913 to build electric tramways to Leatherhead as an extension of London's tram system. Watford Council asked Leatherhead to join them to oppose putting trams on the roads and consequently the idea was dropped.

This was hardly a topic to make the headlines in 1913, but the arrival of a leading suffragette in the town certainly was. On 24 February 1913, Mrs Emmeline Pankhurst was held overnight in Leatherhead's new police station in Kingston Road. Accused of conspiring and procuring certain persons to place gunpowder in Walton Heath Golf Club tea pavilion, frequently used by Lloyd George, she had already been found guilty of a similar offence. She had attempted to blow up a bedroom in a house being built for Lloyd George, then Chancellor of the Exchequer. For this she had been sentenced at the Old Bailey to three years' penal servitude. Her committal to the Surrey Assizes after a night in Leatherhead, where it is said the Chief of Police gave up his bedroom for her, led to the dismissal of this particular case.[1]

Mrs Pankhurst was not the first suffragette to brave Leatherhead. Four years before, in 1909, a meeting of the Women's Freedom League (Suffragettes) had been held in the square before the Old Bull Inn.

Local supporters were outnumbered by mostly male hostile demonstrators. Two of the suffragettes, a Mrs Despard and a Mrs Grieg, were on a proselyting tour of the southern counties and were travelling in a horse-drawn van, with the legend 'Votes for Women' on its chassis, in which they slept. The crowd of between 400 and 500 was so noisy when the open-air meeting began that the ladies could not be heard above the catcalls and the ringing of a loud handbell. They moved the meeting to the relative safety of Victoria Hall where entrance was for ticket holders only. Even so, the mob scaled the roof and the whole activity bordered on a riot with the police outnumbered and the meeting cancelled. But Leatherhead suffragette supporters were not put off by such scenes and only a short time afterwards, Letitia Dixon, daughter of Abraham, chaired a presumably peaceful meeting on the merits of women's franchise.

On the outskirts of the town, another game of high politics was being played by Sir Max Aitken, later Lord Beaverbrook, who lived and died at Cherkley Court. This ebullient ambitious Canadian, the MP for Ashton-under-Lyme in 1910, dominated the newspaper world in the first half of this century. Cherkley Court was his main country home until his death in 1964. It was an ideal place for politicians of the day to meet, manoeuvre and plot. Herbert Asquith, Prime Minister for the first part of the First World War, Bonar Law, F. E. Smith (Lord Birkenhead) and Lloyd George were frequently entertained there.[1] In spite of his friendship with Asquith, Beaverbrook succeeded in bringing down his government and replacing him with Lloyd George. For this he was given a peerage and became Minister of Information and later Minister of Munitions in 1918. In 1918 he launched the *Sunday Express*, the *Evening Standard* and a number of Scottish newspapers. He continued in politics and through his newspaper, he advocated Empire Free Trade and in the 1960s campaigned against Britain's entry into the Common Market. The emblem of the Crusader, so personal to him, first appeared at the top of his front pages in 1930. Chains, proclaiming his lack of faith in the Conservative Party, were added to the emblem in 1951.[2]

Leatherhead in the First World War (1914–1918)

In the first few weeks of the war, many of the town's young men joined the colours in response to Lord Kitchener's vigorous appeal. Indeed,

[1] A. P. J. Taylor.
[2] Record Office, House of Lords.

University and Public Schools Battalion (UPS) of the Royal Fusiliers at Randalls Park. Most of them were billeted in and around the town and were virtually wiped out in the First World War at the battle of Delville Wood.

most of St John's school leavers went straight into the forces. Their school had been completely gutted by fire in 1913 but by 1914 had been rebuilt.[1] It was not until September 1914 that the town felt the real impact of war. An Emergency Relief Committee was set up; the postal services were alerted and had issued a circular in early August declaring that the Leatherhead signal station would maintain day and night telegraphic communication with Dover.[2] The reservoir was guarded by Boy Scouts by day and the Church Lads' Brigade by night. By September the town council rightly thought boys aged 9–11 were far too young for such an onerous task and the Water Company took over the responsibility.

At the end of September there was a great upheaval in the town when several hundred soldiers of the Universities and Public Schools battalion (UPS) of the Royal Fusiliers arrived to be billeted locally. King George V inspected them on 17 October and later Lord Kitchener and the French War Minister on Epsom Downs in January 1915. Those stationed in Leatherhead left shortly afterwards for Epsom and thence to France, promising to write to their hosts. Tragically few survived the battle of Delville Wood to do that.[3]

The town was also receiving wounded Belgian soldiers, 30 of them coming on 28 October to The Red House which had been converted into a Red Cross hospital and convalescent home, still run by its owner, Mrs Burton. More wounded were expected, and a Belgian Refugee Aid Committee chaired by the Rev. E. A. Downes, headmaster of St John's School, was set up. Three houses were made available for the duration of the war and by March 1915 over 25 Belgian refugees were living here.

Early in 1915, more soldiers came to Leatherhead, 13th Battalion London Regiment (the Kensington Rifles) but only for a month; time enough for their brass band to give a concert at the Forty-Foot Road recreation ground.

During 1915, two Leatherhead men received posthumous awards for bravery; an old Johnian, 2nd Lieut. J. H. Woolley of the Queen Victoria's Rifles (TA) was awarded the Victoria Cross in April, the first Territorial in the war to receive it. The Albert Gold Medal was awarded to 2nd Lieut. Grey de Lisle Leach of the Scots Guards who died on 3 September 1915 from wounds received in a grenade accident in France while saving the lives of his own men. He was the son of C. F. Leach,

[1] Linda Heath, *Of Good Report* (LDLHS, 1987).
[2] P.O. Circular, August 1914.
[3] Col. Pettifar, R.F.A., and Margaret Hayden.

later to be president of the Port of London Authority, and very much a major benefactor of the town described as 'one big family with Mr Leach as father'.[1] He gave the land for both the war memorial and the new Leatherhead Hospital in 1940, which he endowed. A ward was named after him there and another after Dr Von Bergen, a much loved local physician who served on the hospital board. C. F. Leach was a somewhat austere man in appearance whose many interests included exotic birds housed in a magnificent aviary at his home, Vale Lodge.[2]

By midsummer 1915 there were said to be over 400 Leatherhead men serving in the forces and a plea for medical supplies and sandbags to be made by those at home, brought a response and workrooms were opened. Mrs Leach forwarded new-laid eggs weekly to London hospitals for wounded soldiers and by the end of 1915, over 4680 eggs had been dispatched.[3] Miss Brown of Church Terrace was enterprising enough to take family photographs to be sent by relatives to the forces overseas.[4]

In the middle years of the war, soldiers were said to be 'marching through Leatherhead with guns all day' and aircraft flew over the town daily.[5] Indeed, one came so low in 1915 that the pilot was able to ask the way to Brooklands! Later that year, Lieut. Maurice Le Blanc Smith, a Royal Flying Corps pilot, paid an unorthodox surprise visit to his parents and landed, damaging his plane on the Forty-Foot Road recreation ground.

There was the first white Christmas of the century in 1916, yet little joy came. Fear of enemy air attacks led to the official banning of external lights after dark and fines were imposed for non-observance. Dr Marie Stopes, then living at Craigvara in Belmont Road with C. Aylmer Maude, was one of those prosecuted.

Leatherhead's high casualty rate led to an early call for the fallen to be commemorated and on 21 March 1917 the Bishop of Winchester dedicated a war shrine on the wall of the clock tower in North Street. The shrine was a triptych of fumed oak carved by C. E. Grantham from a design submitted by the donors, the women of Leatherhead.[6] This was later moved to the parish church and the present memorial unveiled in 1921.

The last spring of the war was black with the Allies severely pressed and there was no real hint of peace to come. In War Weapons Week in June, the Lord Lieutenant, Lord Ashcombe appealed for

[1] Tom Locke.
[2] Charles Simmonds.
[3] P.M. October 1915.
[4] P.M. July 1915.
[5] W. S. Ekins.
[6] P.M. March 1917.

'The Old Bull', 1905. Mrs Thayer and her daughter who owned it, organised a nosegay competition on May Day when wild flowers were gathered and posies made by children for prizes. The three elms on the left were set alight in 1918 by the Armistice Night bonfire.

funds for the forces. Other simple comforts like letters from home were somewhat restricted since, after 75 years, the penny post for letters was raised to 1½d.[1]

Nevertheless, a few months later the war was miraculously over and on Armistice Night there was a huge bonfire outside the old Bull Hotel.[2] The final mattress to burn managed to set fire to three large elm trees and yet the crowd happily sang, cheered and danced, for peace had returned to their lives.

Between the wars (1918–1939)

With the demolition of historic landmarks like the Swan Hotel and the death in 1925 of the last town crier Joseph Longhurst, Leatherhead began to change a great deal.

There was much council house building, new roads and schools and the growth of many new industries. It was the start of the long transition to the town of today, only partly interrupted by the Second World War.

Prelude

There was naturally general relief that the war with its high casualty rate was at last over and advertisements began to appear in the local Press announcing the return of many of the town's tradesmen. Pirate buses built on ex-service vehicles were run by enterprising demobilised soldiers.[3]

The Belgian Refugee Aid Committee was wound up and The Red House reverted to private ownership and became an hotel. A War Pensions Committee was formed to help returning men and war widows. In all, 983 Leatherhead men had served and 163 gave their lives.

On 19 June 1919, the day chosen for the whole country's peace celebration, 350 returning servicemen were given a grand lunch at St John's School. Afterwards, a procession 2000 strong led by the Vicar of Leatherhead and the Council Chairman, made their way to Randalls Park. There were sports and tea for all and dancing until dusk when the Silver Band led the way to Yarm Court for the lighting of a bonfire and fireworks; the time-honoured way for the town to celebrate.[4] In this case, the euphoria was short-lived as the reality of hard post-war years came with the twenties.

---

[1] H. Robinson, *Britain's Post Office* (1953), p. 239.
[2] Arthur Rapley.
[3] Eric Trunkfield.
[4] P.M. July 1919.

Peace celebrations were held countrywide on 19 July 1919. The procession of 2000 with the Silver Band ended at Randalls Park where there was sports and dancing until dusk and in the evening the band led the way to Yarm Court for a bonfire and fireworks.

Dedication of the war memorial. The high local casualty rate led to the early dedication of a shrine in the clock tower in 1917. This was later removed to the church and the present memorial with all the names of the fallen was unveiled in 1921.

The Twenties

Support for the Labour movement had grown with unemployment in the country, and the Leatherhead branch held one of its first meetings at the Victoria Hall in November 1920. Unemployment in the town had reached 200 by 1921 and was rising. The local party actively supported Dr Somerville Hastings who stood for Epsom in the General Election the following year, but lost heavily to the Conservative, Sir Rowland Blades.

Housing

The Leatherhead UDC was as much concerned as the Labour activists with the high cost of living which, according to the Board of Trade, had risen one and a half times since 1914. The Council believed the way to alleviate some of the hardship would be to provide and manage cheap rented houses for those on low incomes. This led to the first council houses being built early in 1921 in Poplar Road. In all, 59 houses were built and preference was given to ex-servicemen and their families. It was another four years before the second group of 90 council houses were built, this time in Kingston Road. There was of course plenty of private house building as many of the large estates were broken up. Elm Bank, opposite Thorncroft Manor, was sold by Mrs Rickards in 1924, and the house and fine gardens were eventually demolished and developed into the St Mary's Road housing estate. Likewise Tyrrells Wood, formerly the home of Lord Cunliffe and Major Keswick, MP, was also put on the market. The Golf Club took it over in 1924 and two years later further building plots were for sale.

Another large house and grounds to come under the hammer was Givons Grove. Its owners, H. V. Roe, the aircraft manufacturer and his wife, the sex educationalist and birth control pioneer Dr Marie Stopes, moved to Hindhead. Dr Marie claimed she needed 'intelligent youth, Leatherhead being too grown up for her'. She later returned to live at Norbury Park.[1] In another part of the town, in Ermyn Way, The Long House, the home of Sir E. F. O. Gascoigne was sold to the Ex-Service Welfare Society for the Mentally Disabled and renamed Frederick Milner House; it still houses a number of old soldiers.

In 1923 the town's first Roman Catholic church was built in gothic revival style in Garlands Road. It was donated by Sir Edward Hulton who lived at Downside. Born in 1865, he joined his father's newspaper

[1] Ruth Hall, *Dr. Marie Stopes* (André Deutsch).

business in Manchester in 1885 and produced the *Daily Sketch* in 1909. He was knighted in 1921; sold his four publications for £6 million and retired in 1923 with a reputation of producing commercially successful publications quite free from political interference. His son, also Edward, was raised in Leatherhead and succeeded his father, becoming chairman of Hulton Press. With the closing in 1957 of his most brilliant experiment in photo-journalism *Picture Post*, he also was knighted.[1]

The break-up of the large houses and their estates was taking place when living conditions were at a low ebb for many in the town because of the country-wide industrial troubles which culminated in the 1926 General Strike. Like every other town, Leatherhead had difficulties with supplies and distribution of food during the strike. The few trains and buses that were running were driven by volunteers. Leatherhead found 300 volunteers to drive lorries and other vehicles. The strike began to crumble in just over a week.

It was in the year of the General Strike that Leatherhead opened its first purpose-built fire station in River Lane to house its first motor fire engine. The previous machine had been housed in the clock tower in North Street and was drawn by horses stabled in Bridge Street who also drew the dust cart. The new fire station was opened by Sir Rowlands Blades who lived in Grange Road and was shortly to become Lord Mayor of London. The fire engine, then the latest in fire-fighting appliances, was named after Sir Rowland's daughter Margaret, and took proud part in his Lord Mayor's Show in London. However, when it came to have its baptism by fire, so to speak, the engine took a quarter of an hour to start. A new Fire Committee was set up and arranged that the Gas Company call the Fire Brigade by sounding a hooter when the fire alarm bell rang in the Post Office.[2]

After the General Strike

The town's population was now increasing at a rate even higher than in Edwardian times, with new inhabitants arriving weekly.[3] By 1931, there were 6916 people living in the town. New industries set up, like the Rayon Manufacturing Company in Ermyn Way employing 300 and the Cable Manufacturing Company in the Kingston Road. On a smaller scale, Lady Zoë Hart-Dyke began silkworm farming at her home, The Wilderness at the entrance to Tyrrells Wood, in 1932. She

[1] *D.N.B.* and Edward Hulton, *When I was a Child*.

[2] S.R.O., LA7/7.

[3] P.M. January 1928.

The High Street *c.* 1920 showing the 'Duke's Head' and the 'King's Head' which was demolished in spite of protests. Frank Benger described the rear view of the 16th-century building as 'one of the beauties of the town' and it seems a pew was reserved for the 'King's Head' in the parish church.

and her husband first bought 5000 silkworm eggs which hatched and silk threads from the cocoons were spun on a large hand-reeler in their garage. Eventually more space was needed and a small out-factory was opened near The Warren, Epsom Road. This had to close, mainly due to an injunction taken out by a neighbour, Lady Duckham who complained that silk-making produced a very unpleasant smell. Eventually work was transferred to Sir Oliver's ancestral home Lullingstone Castle and the silk made by the Hart-Dykes has been traditionally used for Royal coronation and christening robes ever since.

Farming

In spite of all the new industry, for most people the farm and its life never seemed far away. Even in the mid-1920s there was a farrier and harness-maker in Bridge Street, another farrier in the High Street, millers in North Street and Randalls Road and a wheelwright in Kingston Road.[1]

Farming itself had changed over the years. The in-filling of Bradmere Pond at the foot of Bull Hill in 1905 was perhaps a hint of changing times, although a horse trough to replace it had been thoughtfully presented by a Mrs Braybrook.

Horse ploughing continued up to the Second World War and up to 1925, there was still a pound for stray animals near the 'Plough' at Barnett Wood Lane – a shilling to claim an animal back.[2]

The once labour-intensive harvesting was certainly revolutionised by the rapid reaping, threshing and baling of the combine harvesters and by the general use of tractors. As a result, the need for only one or two men to carry out in hours what had previously taken several days, inevitably reduced the numbers of agricultural labourers needed.

Leatherhead continued mixed farming with a balance between cereals and livestock. Some old farms, like Prewetts in Cleeve Road, were ultimately taken over by Unigate but others, like Bocketts Farm and Highlands Farm, carried on independently. Early in the century, Highlands Farm began harvesting mint and lavender and the town was filled with its scent as it was carted to Mitcham for the making of mints and lavender water.[3]

The Mizen Brothers who were well-known Surrey market gardeners, had extensive land by the mill pond in Fetcham in 1921. There were eight acres of watercress beds and 15 acres of glasshouses where

[1] *Kelly Directory,* 1925.
[2] Arthur Sydney Anderson.
[3] William Jenden.

Horse ploughing continued in Leatherhead up to the Second World War and ploughing matches were regularly held at Highlands Farm.

939 'Leatherhead' is the nameplate of the last of the 40 Schools class locomotives named after leading public schools. No. 939 was 'St John's' and is on display in the school entrance hall.

asters and ornamental ferns were cultivated on the largest scale in England at that time.[1] In war-time, salads and tomatoes were grown but after the Second World War, the business slowly declined and ceased trading in 1957. The Leatherhead Bus Garage and the Water Board took over part of the Mizen's land. It was near the site of the present fire station in Cobham Road, Fetcham, that in 1929 during the digging of celery beds, finely worked bronze Saxon objects were unearthed (see p. 23). For most of this century, wheat and oats were the main crops grown in the area, but in the last 20 years, barley has easily taken first place.

Services

The Leatherhead and District Water Company was taken over by the East Surrey Water Company in 1927 and an Act of Parliament provided for the water to be softened. In the period up to 1939, the new water managers built the present pumping station with its four large boreholes deep in the chalk, and the Elmer softening plant on Hawks Hill. Today with even more sophisticated equipment, Leatherhead's water continues to be maintained to a high bacteriological and chemical standard; no fluoride has been added.

Improved transport was an important factor in the growth of Leatherhead's population. The Southern Railway soon after its formation in 1923, began an electrification programme. In July 1925 the Waterloo to Effingham Junction line as well as the Waterloo to Dorking line, both via Leatherhead, were electrified while steam trains continued to run to Dorking and beyond until the mid-1960s.[2] There were at least three steam engines named 'Leatherhead'; LBSC 5a 1872–80, LBSC 178, 1890–1912 and SR 939, 1935–61.[3] No. 939 'Leatherhead' was the last of the 40 Schools class locomotives named after leading public schools; 939 was 'St John's, Leatherhead'. One of the original nameplates from the engine is on permanent display in the entrance to St John's School.

With the Southern Railway formed and operating, the LSWR station was no longer needed and was closed down on 10 July 1927, leaving Leatherhead one station where it is today. Railway excursions to London and the South Coast resorts intensified to compete with cheap charabanc tours. For shorter journeys, there were at least half a dozen bus services operated by the East Surrey Traction Company

[1] Piers Mizen.
[2] V. Mitchell and K. Smith, *Epsom to Horsham* (1986), p. 4.
[3] E. W. J. Crawforth.

Steam engine shed with twin water towers at Leatherhead station, 1925, and the station today in 1988.

Aerial view of Leatherhead 1930

with pick-up points in the High Street at the Swan Hotel and outside the Bull Hotel.

It was early days for most people to take to the air but Sir Alan Cobham, the best known airman of the time, went a long way in 1929 to persuade the LUDC that the town should have its own airfield. Nothing came of his initiative since the Council were really more concerned with how to cope with increasing motor traffic. The main streets were often packed with cars at holiday time and in 1928 at Easter, there was a two-mile-long queue on the Ashtead–Leatherhead road. Traffic lights were considered and a by-pass to divert traffic away from the town and both materialised within the next few years. The Council sought to control the town's development and showed foresight in suggesting that there might be, among other things, a town hall, a swimming pool, a theatre or cinema, a bandstand, more houses and an industrial area near the railway. There was a growing awareness for the need in all this development for open spaces and in 1929 this prompted Frank Benger to found the Countryside Protection Society, which has done much to preserve the town and its surrounding country ever since.

The formation of Leatherhead's Chamber of Commerce in 1929, with Stephen Mould as its first President, superseded the Commercial Association founded 21 years before. Ironically at a time when the town's fortunes might have expected to flourish, the financial collapse on Wall Street heralded another period of world depression which affected the town seriously.

The Thirties

During the early thirties, living conditions were hard for all and the unemployment rate in Leatherhead was probably higher than it had ever been since the First World War. In order to help alleviate this, the LUDC set up a special committee in January 1933 which proposed that everyone should pay a shilling (5p) a week towards the cost of public works to be put in hand. This also applied to Ashtead, Fetcham and the Bookhams, since in April 1933 they became part of the Council's remit and each sent representatives to the committee. This unemployment support scheme gave jobs such as making a car park on Bull Hill and resurfacing St Nicholas Hill. Money was also set aside to supplement the state unemployment payment. The Council declared that no mar-

Queen Elizabeth the Queen Mother when as Duchess of York she opened the Queen Elizabeth Training College in 1935.

ried man should have less than £2 a week to live on. This is a fair indication of how low the standard of living was for Leatherhead's poorer residents. Even so, in 1934 Surrey adopted Jarrow, a northern distressed area and Leatherhead scouts and guides collected and sent gifts to Jarrow for Christmas.

Low trade turnover in the town led to many shop closures including Shinners, the drapers established in Leatherhead for 30 years. Some shops stayed empty for many years. Granthams, the furniture-makers with their own store, was still operating although in May 1933 its head, Charles E. Grantham died. A trustee of the Institute, he was also the founder in 1906 of the Leatherhead Operatic Society. Its first performance was *The Pirates of Penzance* in Victoria Hall in 1907. Its most memorable was probably an open-air production of *Merrie England* in Randalls Park in 1922 and again in 1937. 'Queen Elizabeth I' arrived by river on the state barge and in 1922 her progress was limited by a real thunderstorm in the first act.[1] The Operatic Society has now been in existence for over 80 years. A founder member C. J. (Corny) Hooker, the parish church organist who died in the organ loft, was for 27 years its musical director. His elder son Bernard, was chorus master and then for 28 years, honorary secretary, chairman and finally president. His wife, who was born a Grantham worked as wardrobe mistress and his brother Stanley and his wife Daphne were also performers. He later became production secretary and she, choreographer and producer.[2]

The town's spirit was indomitable even in hard times and in January 1932 the Leatherhead Rotary Club was formed to lend a charitable hand. In March 1934, the British Legion founded here in 1921, set up a relief committee in Leatherhead to assist needy ex-servicemen while the disabled were heartened by the Cripples' Training College acquiring Leatherhead Court School building in Randalls Road. It was opened in November 1935 by the then Duchess of York, now Queen Elizabeth the Queen Mother. Fifty years after, she opened a newly-built women's hostel in July 1984. The College took her name in 1942 and became Queen Elizabeth's Training College for the Disabled. The founders were Dame Georgiana Buller and Stanley Evans, an orthopaedic surgeon with whose help the disabled rose above their disadvantages. The founders' work led the way for many of the social services which are nowadays taken for granted. The students today

[1] Joan Burnett.
[2] Bernard Hooker.

240

range from young people, often with congenital handicaps, to those who are older who may have had serious illnesses or disabling accidents. The Queen Elizabeth's Foundation includes the training college and Dorincourt Estates. These consist of Banstead Place, an assessment centre for handicapped teenagers and a mobility centre, Dorincourt itself, with workshops, residential hostel and arts centre, and Lulworth Court, a holiday home at Westcliff.[1]

Following the death of King George V a year after his Jubilee in 1935, Leatherhead dedicated the memorial gardens on Bull Hill to him. A tree was planted to mark George VI's Coronation as well as a colourful procession through the streets while the church bells rang a Coronation peal. A few weeks later, the Royal train sped through Leatherhead from the Naval Spithead Review at Portsmouth and the crowds just glimpsed the King and his daughter Princess Elizabeth. The King and Queen as Duke and Duchess of York, had spent their honeymoon at Polesden Lacey, the home of the Hon. Mrs Greville who later as Princess Margaret's godmother, named Leatherhead's newest fire engine after her in 1932.

Throughout the 1930s, Leatherhead was changing dramatically in appearance. Many buildings were torn down regardless of their age and despite pleas from the Countryside Protection Society. Kingston House, bought by the Council in 1930, was demolished three years later and what is now called Wesley House, was built in its stead. Since 1922, the Council offices had been at Surrey House opposite The Mansion and before that, at the Swan Chambers in the High Street. In the new building, now Wesley House, an annexe was provided for the town library which in 1928 had been in Leatherhead Central School.

In spite of being described 'a gem of Georgian architecture',[2] the Manor House, on the present theatre site, was demolished. It was the home of Herbert K. Reeves, truly a town benefactor who moved to The Mansion in 1923. He sold that to the Surrey County Council in 1950 and donated 21 acres of his land in Fetcham Grove to the Council who, with further land from Major Howard, eventually built the Leisure Centre on the site. Mr Reeves, who died in 1959, gave Sweech House and other buildings on Gravel Hill to the Countryside Protection Society and Sweech House was fully restored in 1950. Land and money for the church hall in Church Road was donated by him and the hall's Reeves Room commemorates his generosity.

H. K. Reeves and his wife who last lived in The Mansion before moving to Somerset. H. K. Reeves was very much a town benefactor donating land and buildings including Sweech House and the parish hall.

[1] James Fowler and David Ellis, Mary Hurn.
[2] Frank Benger.

North Street in 1939 when, according to the billboards, the 'Quins hugged and kissed the Queen who received a loyal welcome in Ontario'; the Capitol Cinema, Epsom, was showing Bing Crosby in 'Paris Honeymoon' with 'Luck of the Navy' while the Picture House, Leatherhead, was screening 'Condemned Women' and the 'Amazing Dr Clittermouse'!

Even more indefensible than the destruction of the Manor House was that of the Swan Hotel which closed in September 1936 and, despite protests, was sold for development. The Council had been equally indifferent to the pulling down of the old King's Head Inn in 1929 and had not demurred when Emlyn House together with the Old Bull Hotel were demolished. But in spite of its ruthless attitude to old buildings, the Council was true to Surrey County Council's policy of maintaining open green spaces, in particular Chuter Ede had persuaded SCC to acquire Norbury Estate on Fetcham Downs. In 1932, LUDC protested at Wimbledon Borough Council's purchase of Randalls Park grounds from John Henderson for use as a cemetery and took their case unsuccessfully to the House of Lords. With the Greater London reshuffle in 1951, the cemetery came under the Borough of Merton and in 1961 a crematorium serving LUDC was added. In 1983 the Great Southern Group took over its administration. The chapel was mindlessly destroyed by arsonists in 1986 and rebuilt in 1987.

In 1936 the Leatherhead Gas Company was taken over by the Wandsworth Gas Company who provided high pressure mains gas so that by April 1938 gas-making ceased in the town. In 1949 the industry was nationalised and North Sea gas was connected in 1971. The Gas Company's offices were on Bull Hill. In North Street, the Congregational church had been sold in 1934 to the Guildford and District Industrial Cooperative Society. By 1930 the old building, next door to the slaughterhouse had become very dilapidated and rats ran over the back pews during evening service so it was decided to build a new church, Christ Church in Epsom Road, now the United Reformed Church.[1]

One of the Council's principal worries in the thirties was the same as in the twenties – traffic congestion. This became worse as the years passed and in June 1933 the *London Evening Standard* claimed that at weekends, Church Street had 'one of the worst bottlenecks round London'. Two months later the Council complained that traffic in the High Street, due to lack of parking, was causing loss of trade. Automatic traffic lights had recently been installed at Swan Corner, since on Sundays 850 cars an hour passed through. The traffic was eased appreciably by the completion of the Leatherhead by-pass in August, and two years later Belisha beacons were installed at school crossing places for pedestrians. Named after the then Minister of Transport

[1] Duncan Smith.

Hore-Belisha, these beacons were yellow globes supported by black and white posts. In February 1939, a one-way traffic experiment was introduced but abandoned after only a few months.

Few realised early in 1939 that by the autumn the country would be at war. Yet as early as October 1937, air raid precautions (ARP) had started with an appeal for 800 volunteers to act as ARP wardens. By February 1938, these wardens visited most homes to demonstrate how to wear the government-issue gas masks. Both the Red Cross and the Women's Voluntary Service (WVS) joined the Civil Defence, and it was not surprising that the town's arrangements were said to be the best in Surrey. The Chief Warden was I. J. O'Hea, founder of the Colt Group which later in 1968 was the centre of the 'I'm backing Britain' campaign. Jack O'Hea, a keen amateur cine-photographer, made many realistic training films to assist the local ARP.[1]

Leatherhead in the Second World War (1939–1945)

When war broke out in September 1939, a small National Defence Committee was set up in the town. With R. Sutherland as chairman, Messrs Murrells and Cressall appointed a fuel controller, transport officer and six male ambulance drivers. They purchased and requisitioned cars and lorries and designated the bus garage as a temporary decontamination centre and mortuary.[2]

It was some months before anyone was put to the test; Leatherhead's first concern being to welcome and find homes for the child evacuees from Streatham and Dulwich for whom play centres were set up. Troops from the Royal Corps of Signals were later billeted in the town.

A Food Office was set up in the Institute; ration books were issued to all, at the same time the hoarding of food was forbidden by law. There was also a Fuel Office at the Institute successfully controlling the amount of coal and petrol used.

Leatherhead suffered losses early in October 1939. Four local men died (two of whom were cousins) when HMS *Royal Oak* was torpedoed in the comparative safety of Scapa Flow. There followed seven months of the so-called 'Phoney War' when there was little war activity during the winter and spring of 1939/1940. Nevertheless, a state of readiness was maintained by frequent exercises. The Fire Service was nationalised in 1941 and the National Fire Station was set up in The

[1] Alan O'Hea.
[2] Joan MacAlpine.

Crescent, supplemented by the local Fire Station. With three or four appliances, some firemen joined the nightly convoys to London to help beat the fires of the Blitz. As incendiary bombs were considered a greater threat than high explosives, firemen ensured that house lofts were cleared and that there were firewatching groups in each of the town's offices, factories and streets. Stirrup pumps were issued.[1] Emergency medical services were at the Blind School which had now been taken over by King's College Hospital. A Home Guard unit (first called Local Defence Volunteers) was formed.

Churchill, who had in his lean years often written for Beaverbrook, appointed him Minister of Aircraft Production in May 1940 and Lord Privy Seal in 1943. It was in the former role he made an indispensable contribution to victory in the Second World War.[2] His appeal for light metal and aluminium in pans and saucepans for aeroplanes was a nonsense, yet in contributing them, as a journalist he knew people felt they were helping to win the war.[3] In 1942, Cherkley itself was bombed and set on fire. Then Lord Beaverbrook moved for a time to Wellbottom Cottage in his estate grounds. This later became the home of his doctor Alan Everett who had practised in Leatherhead for over 50 years.

There were concerts and films at the new Crescent Cinema to keep the spirits high. In August 1940 another cinema (St George's, formerly the Picture House) opened in Victoria Hall. There were dances at the New Bull Hotel and the composer, Dr Ralph Vaughan Williams gave talks, the last being at a concert with the Surrey String Players conducted by Kathleen Riddick.

A month later, the realities of war returned to the town with the arrival in June 1940 of 78 sick and wounded men from the British Expeditionary Force. They were taken to the Blind School Hospital, having had a 'miraculous deliverance from the Germans at Dunkirk'.[4] Many more casualties came and were cared for in Leatherhead's new Cottage Hospital in Poplar Road. Opened in May 1940, it replaced the Queen Victoria Memorial Hospital in Epsom Road, now Victoria House. That had been proudly supported by the community it served so well, but after the president, Sir Alfred Bucknill became a patient and discovered for himself the hazard of being carried on a stretcher up an ill-designed staircase from the operating theatre, the need for expansion was acknowledged. Charles Leach, advised by Dr Von

The Crescent Cinema built on the site of the Manor House and which is now the Thorndike Theatre.

[1] Joan MacAlpine.
[2] Michael Foot.
[3] Malcolm Muggeridge.
[4] P.M. June 1940.

245

Leatherhead Hospital which replaced the original Cottage Hospital at Victoria House in 1940 and became an NHS showpiece.

Bergen, acquired the present site from Mrs Still's Windfield estate and donated it to the town. Whether by foresight or good fortune or both, building materials were delivered by 1939 and so escaped the wartime clamp down on new buildings. A modern building with eminent staff, the hospital had an enormous reputation and after the war was treated by the Ministry of Health as an NHS showpiece. After 1948 it ceased to operate on a voluntary basis but was held in such pride and affection that a strong League of Friends grew up, devoted to retaining its caring individuality as well as warding off threats of closure. Since 1960 the League has worked and donated over £200,000 towards hospital equipment and amenities.[1]

Both the hospitals were soon needed when during late 1940 and early 1941, Leatherhead suffered many enemy bomb attacks. The first was soon after midnight on 27 August 1940 when 20 high explosive bombs were dropped on the Ashtead/Leatherhead borders near the Common. Several houses were damaged but there was, miraculously, only one casualty. Three days later, about 60 high explosive bombs fell in a line from Yarm Court to Crampshaw Lane, Ashtead in a daylight raid in which five people were killed. In September, the month of the Battle of Britain, there were three raids. The Leatherhead Golf club-house received a direct hit on the 6th; two cyclists luckily survived bombs exploding only 30 yards from them on the 10th and on the 30th, a land mine fell in a garden in Gaywood Road, Ashtead, killing four and injuring others.

People were now being evacuated from London in large numbers, and on 19 September 1000 arrived to be billeted in Leatherhead. October was just as bad as September for bomb alerts, nine falling on the 19th in a line from Southey Hall, Great Bookham to the Leatherhead by-pass, damaging shops, offices and houses. On 26 October two bombs fell on oil storage tanks at the waterworks and burning oil crept through the drains to the River Mole, taking nearly 24 hours to put out. With such bombing there was obviously a pressing need for more ARP volunteers; a recruiting drive produced 49 more wardens, 30 ambulance drivers and 276 firewatchers.[2]

Early in 1941 the first incendiary bombs were dropped, possibly jettisoned by retreating German planes being chased away from London. Hundreds fell from Hawks Hill to Ashtead, lighting up the surrounding hills; Fetcham Downs was likened one night to a huge

[1] Dr R. G. Gilbert and Colin Thomas.
[2] LUDC Report 1940.

candlelit Christmas tree. Some properties were burnt down, but due to the vigilance of the firewatchers, most fires were immediately and successfully extinguished. On 19 March 1941 two landmines fell, killing one, injuring 27 and causing considerable damage. One fell on St Andrew's Convent School injuring five nuns and destroying many of its buildings. The blast caused the collapse of St John's School gymnasium at least half a mile away.

After that, there was a long period from 1942 to the end of 1943 when no bombs fell on the town. By now public air raid shelters had been completed and were capable of holding 1012 people.[1] Previously the caves under the Swan Brewery site, once used as a store for barrels, had provided shelter from the air raids.[2] The Post Office issued helpful leaflets like *After the Raid*, *What to do about Gas* and *Beating the Invader*. To supplement the rations, a British Restaurant serving good cheap meals was opened at the rear of the Council offices by BBC personality Freddy Grisewood in June 1941. It was Surrey's first British Restaurant and by the end of the month it was serving 300 meals a day. Another first was a scheme to salvage war-damaged goods to be used as stock for the rapid reopening of bombed shops. Savings became very much part of the war effort and there were two large Savings campaigns; one in May when the Lord Chancellor, Lord Simon, came to speak, and another in October. During Warship Week, there was a Nelson flag day, a concert at the Crescent Cinema with songs by Isobel Baillie, Anne Ziegler and Webster Booth, and a sketch, *Nelson at Leatherhead*, by our own Frank Benger. The destroyer HMS *Scout* was adopted by the town and a plaque commemorating this, once displayed on the ship, now hangs with its wartime story inside Wesley House together with a plaque from 'Salute the Soldier' Savings campaign. An oil painting of HMS *Scout* hung with it has mysteriously vanished.

Canadian forces had been stationed in the town since 1940 and the YMCA set up a Red Triangle Services club for them in North Street. It was during 1941 that a new road, Young Street bridging the River Mole was built by the Canadians on the outskirts of the town. The new road was to by-pass the town's streets which were obviously too narrow for tanks and other armoured vehicles brought to them for repair. It is presumed that Young Street was named after the Canadian commanding officer or possibly, with nostalgia, after Toronto's Yonge Street, itself over 300 miles long. The Canadian Air Force units were

[1] LUDC Report.
[2] John Lewarne.

247

stationed at Tyrrells Wood while others were at The Mansion, Vale Lodge and Thorncroft Manor.[1] To commemorate their stay at Thorncroft they planted two maples, their national tree, close to the north side of the house.[2]

Except for a few minor hit-and-run raids, the town was relatively free of bomb attacks during 1942 and 1943 and the government ordered a cut in ARP staff. At its peak period there had been almost 800 ARP personnel, mostly part-time volunteers, in the town.[3] Despite these cuts, a County Rescue Training School was set up in Leatherhead to train first-aid parties, decontamination squads and wardens. By 1944, this was considered 'the best in the British Isles'.[4]

Early in 1942, the RAF moved into Victoria House in Epsom Road and made it a recruiting office. Once more a grand Savings fair was held, this time in St John's School in July when a Whitley bomber gun turret was on display lent by Archibald Frazer-Nash. Captain Frazer-Nash was a remarkable man whose contribution to the war effort was immense. His gun turrets were produced by Nash and Thompson, a subsidiary of Parnell Aircraft during the war. Made at Tolworth, Surrey, Swindon and Bristol, they were fitted to most British bombers as well as to some armoured vehicles, flying boats and torpedo boats. One turret, from a Wellington bomber ditched in Loch Ness, was rescued as recently as 1986 to be lovingly restored by the present Frazer-Nash Group in their Randalls Road headquarters. It is destined for the Brooklands Museum.[5]

1942 ended brightly with world-famous pianists Pouishinoff and Mark Hambourg performing at the Crescent Cinema, while in November the church bells rang out to mark a turning point in the war, the victory of El Alamein. They rang again at Christmas although this might well have been against wartime regulations.

The gallant defence of Stalingrad by their Russian allies caught the public's imagination. Late in 1943 the King presented Stalingrad, now victorious, with a gold and silver sword fashioned by RAF Corporal Leslie Durbin whose wife, artist Phyllis Ginger was the grand-daughter of James Ginger, the gardener at the Swan Hotel. December 1943 was a date to remember for the chairman of LUDC, Alan Walmsley, when his son, the commander of HMS *Saumarez* was involved with three other destroyers in the dramatic sinking of the German battleship *Scharnhorst*.

[1] Soc. Precs. LN, 21.
[2] Thorncroft Manor Guide.
[3] UDC Report.
[4] Sir E. J. Hodsell, CB.
[5] Dennis Griffin.

In the summer of 1944 the quasi-peacetime for Leatherhead sadly ended with the dropping of V1s, flying bombs known as doodle-bugs. These were pilotless high-explosive craft launched from the French coast which landed indiscriminately when their fuel expired. Sixteen fell on the area, the most serious at Chaffers Mead and Thorncroft Manor. Two hundred houses and 32 shops were badly damaged and the church clock stopped. Three doodle-bugs landed 100 yards from Ronsons in Oaklawn Road, another on Bookham Common and two in Newton Wood, Ashtead. The last bomb in the district, a V2 supersonic rocket, fell close to City of London Freemen's School in February 1945. The windows of 50 houses were broken but there was only one casualty.

In all, 591 high explosive bombs and over 4000 incendiaries fell on the Leatherhead area. Nearly 3000 houses had been damaged and there had been 800 air raid alert warnings. There were 112 casualties, 11 fatal (including three ARP workers). After the war, the ARP services commemorated their dead comrades by presenting the LUDC with a coat of arms which includes the first and only symbol of civil defence in heraldry, chain of portcullis surrounding the fire. A tablet at Wesley House records all this.[1]

Peace came and many of the restrictions were lifted – the nightly black-out ended and there was light in the streets. No longer was the wail of the air raid sirens (operated in working hours by the staff of Barclays Bank) heard with fear and VE-Day 'Victory in Europe' on 11 May 1945 was celebrated as Leatherhead always celebrates. There was a victory parade through beflagged streets, a bonfire at Swan Corner and open-air dancing. The church was floodlit and this time its bells rang a lawful Victory Peal as a thanksgiving service was held in Elm Bank Gardens. All the joy was repeated on VJ-Day 'Victory in Japan' in September, the focal point being the clock tower; a huge bonfire was lit at the top of Bull Hill for roasting a pig and there was dancing and singing and parties for the children.

Six children out of the 41 evacuees still living in the area, the Billeting Officer reported, could not go home because their homes had been bombed and some because their parents could not be traced.[2] While this was being dealt with, the National Defence Committee sold its vehicles, disposed of stores and disbanded – its work successfully accomplished.

[1] Mole Valley District Council.
[2] Joan MacAlpine.

From war to peace (1945–1950)

Between VE- and VJ-Day there had been a General Election which brought Labour to power under Clement Attlee. By 1946 most of the troops had left the area yet there were few signs of a return to peacetime life. Food parcels continued to come from Australia to supplement the town's rations which had not increased since the war.[1] There were still food and fuel control offices at the Institute. Leatherhead's fighting men were slowly coming home. Some took part in the great Victory Parade in London when 40 trainees from Queen Elizabeth's Training College had a privileged view from seats in the forecourt of Buckingham Palace.

The Prime Minister Clement Attlee and his wife came to Leatherhead in September 1946 to ceremoniously release the Stepping Stones over the Mole at Box Hill from being 'out of bounds', as they were in the war. And in the peace of the churchyard, the grave of a German airman W. Mennig Mann, shot down over Leatherhead in 1940 (and later re-interred in Germany) was faithfully tended by the parents of Pilot Officer Edward Arnold whose own grave lay nearby.[2]

The modern town (1946–1988)

This was slow to emerge. Nationally much was happening with the arrival of the National Health Service and National Assistance in July 1948 to launch the Welfare State of today. Locally, there was a great deal of new housing in the Cleeve Road, Kingston and Copthorne Roads area to replace bombed property and accommodate the many newcomers.

The town was changing and in 1946 a group decided to form the Leatherhead and District Local History Society with architect A. W. G. Lowther as its first chairman. One of the Society's aims was to research and produce a *History of Leatherhead*, which is at last achieved. The Society has flourished over the last 40 years and among its many publications, the annual *Proceedings* contains articles and reports by members on their researches. Two of the founder members, John Lewarne (now President) and Stephen Fortescue, still live in the area.

In 1951, although the war was now six years away, the rationing of food and clothing still continued and practically everything was in short supply. Few were yet able to enjoy what was then considered the luxury of foreign travel because of strict currency regulations.

[1] *Kelly Directory*, 1945.
[2] George Dench.

Dedication of the town's coat-of-arms. Leatherhead was the first town to include in its coat-of-arms, obtained in 1946, the symbol of Civil Defence – a flame encircled by a portcullis chain. The shield itself represents the town. The river and its valley is symbolised by blue and silver waves with green wedges while the swan rising above a wreath of oak leaves also refers to the river and the Swan Inn. In the lower shield the stag's head and book refers to the association of the City Freemen's School (the sword in the swan's wing being a city arms) with other schools in the town.

The cedar tree outside the Council offices (see p. 242) is felled in 1966.

However, better times seemed to be on their way as London staged the Festival of Britain on the South Bank of the Thames. Here, there was a new spirit of confidence in the future for post-war Britain and Leatherhead mirrored this with its own Festival staged that summer.

But with the winter, there was a time of mourning ahead. First there was the loss of two landmarks, the great 3-ton cedar tree outside Wesley House in 1966 and the clock tower. Originally built to house the town's fire engine in 1859 at a cost of £129 4s. 2½d., the clock was added to the tower in 1860. Latterly, it became a public lavatory and was demolished in 1952 at a cost of £77.[1]

In February 1952 the church bells muffled their peals and all council officials wore black ties on the day of the King's funeral. Now his daughter Princess Elizabeth was Queen.

Leatherhead with its long history of celebrations, excelled itself on 6 June 1953, the Queen's Coronation Day, with a parade followed by five hours of entertainment given by no less than 22 local organisations at the football ground. The following day, Sunday, there was yet another procession 2000 strong, to attend an open-air Service of Thanksgiving at Fetcham Grove.

The Operatic Society staged another appropriate production of *Merrie England* (this time inside at the Crescent Cinema) with professional singers Anne Ziegler and Webster Booth in the lead.

And so the new reign began and for all a new way of life when food rationing, the last of the wartime restrictions, was removed nearly 10 years after the Second World War ended.

Church and parish

In both world wars and in the peacetime years that followed, the churches in Leatherhead still played an important role in the life of the community. Though the parish's administrative role, so central for many centuries, was largely taken over by the LUDC in the 1920s, the Parochial Church Council also set up in the 1920s, continued. Pastoral care has increased with the growth of the town and the Church seeks ways to improve the lot of the old, poor, sick and disabled. Support is given to youth clubs like the Cygnet, the Samaritans and the night hostel for the homeless as well as to international charities, deprived city areas and missions overseas. There is a thriving and active 'Friends of the Parish' organisation.

Leatherhead's schools

At the turn of the century, the four Church of England schools described on pp. 179–181 still existed. These were the boys' school in Highlands Road, the girls' in Poplar Road, All Saints' and Gravel Hill infants' schools. The boys' and girls' schools were replaced by a new council school in Kingston Road in 1912. In January 1913 the new upper mixed council school opened in what is now Woodville School together with a new infants' school, and the girls' school in Poplar Road became a Church of England junior school.

As a result of increased population in the town, particularly in Kingston Road area, the schools were reorganised in 1926. The council infants' school closed and All Saints' and Poplar Road schools then took both infants and juniors. This temporarily resolved the problem of overcrowded classrooms but by the 1930s, the problem had returned. It was not resolved until 1953 when the juniors from All Saints' moved into the Kingston Road school which became Leatherhead County Primary junior school and All Saints' reverted to being an infants' school. At the same time, part of the senior school, known by then as the Leatherhead County Secondary moved into new premises in Dilston Road but it was to be more than twenty years before the whole school was united under the same roof. In 1964 the school was named Therfield when the Headmaster, Mr Claytor, found that it stood on land presented by King John in 1205 to Brian de Therfield.

In 1976 the schools were once again reorganised. All Saints' and Poplar Road schools became Church of England First schools and the junior school in Kingston Road became Woodville Middle school. In 1978, All Saints', just a century after its opening in the old ex-engine shed, moved into a new building across the common in Aperdele Road. In 1986, Poplar Road school moved into a new building in Forty Foot Road and was renamed St. Mary's Church of England First school, after the parish church.

Meanwhile two more State schools had opened; West Hill in 1963 for children with moderate learning difficulties and Woodlands in 1973 for children with severe learning difficulties.

It was not until 1935 that there was a Roman Catholic school in Leatherhead started by five nuns from the Order of St Andrew. Opened at 'Hillfield' off Grange Road, the school nearly came to an

[1] Minute Book Fire Brigade.

Entrance to St John's School.

untimely end in March 1941 when a land mine fell on the building but no one was killed. The senior school was eventually rehoused in 'The Knoll' in Epsom Road and the junior school went into 'The Grange' in Grange Road. In 1952 the foundations for a new senior school were laid on the hockey pitch site at 'Hillfield' and the whole building was completed in four months.

In 1971 St Andrew's became a co-educational comprehensive school and was considerably extended. The junior school closed in 1975 and the children transferred to the newly built St Peter's First and Middle school.

Only St John's and Downsend remain of the independent schools from the previous century. Their earlier history has been described (see p. 182) but in 1913 St John's was nearly destroyed by fire which completely gutted the main building despite the efforts of five fire brigades. Luckily there were no casualties but the library and all its books were lost. The damage estimated at about £20,000, was repaired by 1914 and the new buildings were opened.

The period between the two world wars was a time of considerable modernisation and expansion.

After the Second World War, a long and happy association began between the school and Field Marshal Viscount Montgomery who was chairman of the school council until 1966. 'Monty', himself a parson's son, always took a keen interest in the school which had been founded for sons of clergymen.

A new chapel was dedicated in 1963 and there has been further specialist blocks built recently.

Downsend, severely affected by shortage of teachers during the First World War, was acquired in 1918 by A. H. Linford with only one pupil. Numbers quickly built up and in 1921 Mr Linford was joined by his son and together they ran the school until the Second World War when A. H. Linford retired.

In 1929 a senior school was built which 40 years later, was converted into a dining room and theatre when a new senior school was built. Boarding was discontinued in 1968. Mr Christopher Linford joined his father as co-Principal in 1966 and remained as Principal when his father retired in 1977. So the school has been run by three generations of Linfords for over 70 years.

Of the schools in Leatherhead during this century which no

longer exist, one of the more celebrated was a girls' boarding school in what is now Queen Elizabeth's Training College. It was Leatherhead Court School founded by Miss Martha Wood-Tullis in 1904 and one of her ex-pupils, Winifred O'Shaughnessy de Wolfe Hudnut, married Rudolph Valentino. Music must have played a prominent part in the curriculum because when the school closed in 1934, the contents sold included 14 pianos and many other musical instruments.

The Misses Mary and Blanche Hewlins ran three private schools in Leatherhead over a period of 33 years. The first was Oxford House School at 4 Lower Terrace, Bridge Street for boys and girls from five to seven and girls up to the age of 11. In 1907 it was closed and the Miss Hewlins moved to Woodcote in The Crescent where they set up a school for young ladies which lasted for about three years. In 1915 they moved back to Bridge Street where they established the Dudley House School for boys and girls from five to seven which was always known as 'Miss Hewlins' School'. Even as late as 1932 pupils still learned to write on slates with slate pencils and when their hands were too cold in winter to hold their pencils properly, they were sent outside to warm up by running round the garden.

Other private schools which no longer exist include a preparatory school for boys and girls at Naburn in The Crescent, a kindergarten at Wesley Hall in Church Road, Redcot Preparatory School in St John's Avenue and more recently, St Christopher's boarding school for girls at Thorncroft Manor. This was founded in Great Missenden by Miss Muriel Ely and came to Thorncroft in 1962. Miss Ely died quite unexpectedly in 1969 and the school closed the following year.

The Lindens, like Downsend, opened with only one pupil in 1918 as a kindergarten and preparatory school in 'Little Lindens', Linden Pit Path. In 1935 it moved to Park Rise and Miss Josephine Ingram, its founder, retired to be succeeded by Miss Frances Marsden who was in charge for 44 years. By 1965 there were over 200 pupils and on Miss Marsden's retirement in 1971, the school was taken over by Downsend School and renamed Downsend Lodge. Another school, Ryebrook, was also incorporated into Downsend Lodge when its founder retired in 1979. This was also a kindergarten and preparatory school started by Miss Winifred Owen in Church Road. The building is now demolished but the cul-de-sac where it stood has been named Owen Place after the school's founder. The Rowans in Epsom Road, opened in 1949 by Miss

The Royal School for the Blind which has been in Leatherhead for the whole of this century.

Haybittle and Miss Schofield, also had only one pupil but within four years there were 137. In 1960 it was taken over by Clark's College. In September 1987 this school became another Downsend Lodge.

The Leatherhead School of Music and the Leatherhead Secretarial School came to be linked by a curious twist of fate. The School of Music was opened in 1926 by the Misses Elsie and Mabel Fuller in Devon House, at the corner of Church and Poplar Roads. Elsie Fuller died in 1944 but Mabel ran the school until 1962 when Sheila Hind became the new Principal until her retirement in 1978. Devon House was sold and it seemed as if the School of Music might be forced to close. However, Mrs N. C. Woolff, Principal of the Leatherhead Secretarial School, had in 1952 moved from Ashtead to 28 Bridge Street, part of a terrace of Georgian houses. She extended her successful school in 1978 by acquiring nos. 30 and 32 Bridge Street and so was able to offer a home to the School of Music which now shares the premises with the Secretarial School.

The Royal School for the Blind
By the mid-thirties the school had become a place of residential workshops rather than a school. With the Second World War, it was temporarily closed and the building requisitioned by King's College Hospital. After the war, part of the building was handed back but it was not until the 1950s, when the Chelsea Pensioners housed there finally left, that it was once more a School for the Blind. Improvements were made but little was done to change the style of a large institution in an antiquated building, now outmoded in concept. Some 20 years later, it did change and communal rooms were built and single and double bedrooms replaced the former partitioned dormitories. The result was a total transformation. Now the whole emphasis has shifted from that of an institution segregated from the local community to a place where residents are encouraged to cater for their own needs and participate as much as possible in the life and activities of the town. The provision of flats has enabled some of the residents to marry, the first wedding taking place in 1982.

The Princess of Wales opened the extensions in November 1982 when the main hall was named after Miss H. M. Timmins, the oldest resident who joined the school in 1910 and until recently was its chapel's organist.[1]

[1] Linda Heath, *Of Good Report* (LDLHS, 1987).

The town and its industries

By 1961, the population of Leatherhead was over 9000 and employment was mainly in its local industries. One of the largest employers was Ronsons with 2000–3000 including outworkers. Ronsons, founded in America by Lewis Aronson I in 1898, originally made church ornaments. In 1918 it began manufacturing cigarette lighters, and the rights to sell and service the lighters in the UK were acquired. The agency, with premises in London's Caledonian Road was heavily bombed in the Second World War. As a result, Ronsons moved to Leatherhead and bought Dorincourt where their war work was making among other things, bomb fuses. These were manufactured on government-subsidised machinery which after the war was modified to make lighters. Five million lighters were produced before Dorincourt was sold in 1953 to Queen Elizabeth's Training College and Ronsons moved to its custom-built factory in Randalls Road. Here the firm diversified and was also very successful in the developing of butane and battery lighters. However the Japanese, Ronsons' best customers, produced their own lighters, not only inexpensive to buy but incorporating a competitive piezo mechanism. The order to market these lighters came to all Ronson subsidiaries from the US parent corporation who had long been in difficulties. These intensified worldwide especially in the service field. Desperate attempts by Ronson UK to solve the corporation's financial problems only resulted in the liquidation of Ronson UK and in 1981, the sale and subsequent demolition of the Leatherhead factory.

At the east end of the town, bordering on Ashtead, Goblin BVC, makers of vacuum cleaners, washing machines and clocks employed 1000 workers. The founder, Hubert Cecil Booth was also the inventor of the first vacuum cleaner. In 1904, he produced the world's first portable vacuum cleaner which only needed two operators, one to pump the bellows and the other to operate the cleaning tool. In 1921, his company produced the first electric upright bag model and a few years later, the cylindrical model, the whole range coming under the trade name of 'Goblin'. In 1938 Goblin BVC moved to a complex in Ermyn Way and during the Second World War made munitions which included mine-sinkers, shell fuses and camouflage netting.

Post-war, Hoover became a major competitor and so dominated the market that vacuum cleaning became known as 'hoovering'.

Herbert Booth, the inventor of the world's first vacuum cleaner. Booth began his career by designing battleships and later the Great Wheels at Blackpool, Paris and Vienna. He patented his cleaner in 1901. Bright red, it had a 5 hp piston engine with a team to operate it. Having cleaned the carpet for the coronation of Edward VII in Westminster Abbey, he sold two machines to Buckingham Palace and received the Royal Warrant of Appointment to His Majesty. He moved his factory from Fulham to Ermyn Way where he established the Goblin Works.

Nevertheless, Goblin had diversified and itself contributed to the generic vocabulary with Goblin 'Teasmade'.

H. C. Booth died in 1955 and in spite of expanding in 1959 to manufacture miniature electric motors (some used in Concorde), Goblin slowly had to run down its organisation. It finally closed in 1984 and the valuable site on which it stood was eventually taken over by Esso.[1]

Esso hope to make it their UK headquarters by 1990 and house 1000 employees in an attractively designed complex in a landscaped 22-acre setting.[2]

Also based in Leatherhead is ERA technology, an independent self-supporting research and development organisation. It provides confidential service in electronic and electrical engineering and material sciences for governments and industry on contract. Established in 1920 as a cooperative research association for the British electrical industry, ERA is now one of the largest independent research organisations in the UK.

With a staff of 380, half of whom are scientists and engineers, ERA's activities extend from the design of microwave antennae for satellite communications to the investigation of solid-state devices in power engineering and include such diverse topics as the fundamental aspects of dielectric materials, plasma etching, engineering metallurgy and the application of microprocessors for automation and control.

In 1984 the Duke of Edinburgh toured its research laboratories and in May 1987 the new office and laboratory complex was officially opened by the Duke and Duchess of York.[3]

In 1958, the Press drew attention to the work in Randalls Road of the British Food Manufacturing Industries Research Association when they were examining canned and other foods recovered from Shackleton's 1908 Antarctic Expedition and Captain Scott's 1910 Cape Evans camp site. As a result of the publicity, the public produced their own canned treasures for laboratory inspection. A 58-year-old Christmas pudding issued during the Boer War was found to be quite edible although an 1849 tin of roast mutton had undergone some deterioration. The opening of these hand-made and hand-soldered cans, early examples of canning technology, was filmed and specimens of the food sealed into glass ampoules. It is believed the empty cans are now at the Science Museum.[4]

[1] P. J. Vincent.
[2] John Sylvester.
[3] ERA report (Joanna Haddon).
[4] *Chemistry and Industry 1958* and Peter R. Smith.

Neil and Spencer, the dry-cleaning machine manufacturing company, have still a small office here although their works is now in Horsham. Many new software industries and companies have moved into Mole business parks and there is space for many more as office blocks replace houses and shops all over the town.

Far away from the world of high technology is the wrought iron forge and works of Richard Quinnell in the Oxshott road. It is a family business founded in 1937 and Richard Quinnell himself has been a prime mover in the revival of the blacksmith's art. His work and that of fellow metalsmiths exhibiting in his Fire and Iron Gallery demonstrates the potential of the art in steel, brass, bronze, stainless steel and aluminium. There are examples of Richard Quinnell's work to be seen in Oxford (the Swan gates of St Hugh's College); in Guildford (the Tunsgate Edward and Eleanor sundial designed by Ann Garland who in the 1950s lived in Vale Lodge) and in the Swan Centre itself (Isolink, inspired by Brunel, in forged steel and originally shown at the Victoria and Albert Museum).

Still in the arts, Surrey Sound, a professional recording studio established in 1975 in Kingston Road, is used regularly by top musicians and groups such as Paul McCartney, Cliff Richard, the Police and Godley and Creme.[1]

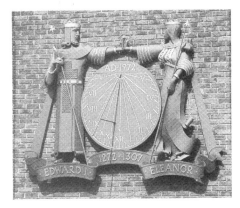

The Edward and Eleanor sundial in Tunsgate, Guildford. Designed by Ann Garland who once lived in Vale Lodge, it was executed by Richard Quinnell.

Social welfare

The post-war years in Leatherhead have seen not only the development of industry but a greater awareness of the needs of the sick, elderly and disabled. As the town has the highest percentage of over-65s in Surrey, the number of homes for those of advanced years has naturally grown steadily. There are many housing associations including Mount Green which for over 20 years has provided accommodation for the elderly, the wheelchair disabled, single parents and for young couples, starter homes.

The Surrey County Council formed a Social Services Department in 1971 which has welfare sub-offices in Leatherhead dealing with Home Care services, Meals on Wheels and Health Visiting. A Day Centre for the Elderly equipped from an appeal fund chaired by Lady Aitken was opened in the Swan Centre in 1982. The Samaritans have a house in Church Road where there is nearby a Night Hostel for homeless travellers founded by the Council of Churches.

[1] Mike Cobb.

Great Train Robbery

In August 1963 the world's largest cash haul at the time (over £2½ million in £1 and £5 notes) was taken from the Glasgow to London mail train. The thieves divided the money and hid much of it in the Home Counties. After £30,000 was discovered in a caravan on Box Hill and £101,000 was found by a Leatherhead resident in two holdalls in woods near Holmwood, local country walks had more of a purpose!

The Citizens' Advice Bureau, now in Wesley House, was started in 1965. Also in Wesley House is Leatherhead United Charities who apportion income from many established, and some ancient, charities to the needy. There is also a Red Cross and St John's Ambulance service founded in 1948.

Perhaps the most heartening of Leatherhead's social work has been the care for the disabled. With Queen Elizabeth's Training College, the School for the Blind and Remploy, there is also Victoria House which, before 1940, was the town's hospital and is now a home for the disabled enlarged greatly to house 25 people. Sport and recreation for the disabled provided by the Swans Club, which was founded by Mrs V. I. Hardman, MBE, in 1975, is enhanced by the Elizabeth Stuttard Memorial fund set up in 1983 to give holidays and other benefits to younger Swan Club members. Covering a wider field of charities, the Leatherhead Lions Club formed in 1973 sponsors an active programme of colourful fund-raising events which include the town's annual carnival.

The social stirrings of Leatherhead after the war were taking place at a time when Surrey County Council was pressing for the reconstruction of the town's road system. There had been talk of the need for a south orbital road for many years but all became subsumed in a major plan drawn up in April 1972 for the redevelopment of the town. This was the starting point of today's Leatherhead which took 10 years to come to fruition. Before that, the 80-year-old Leatherhead Urban District Council was incorporated into the newly constituted Mole Valley District Council which based itself in Dorking. It covers a widespread area bounded by Ashtead, Bookham, Abinger, Capel, Forest Green, Ockley, Leigh, Charlwood, Betchworth, Buckland and Mickleham.

The Thorndike Theatre

In 1960, the Crescent Cinema in Church Street was pulled down and the Thorndike Theatre built upon the site. As the 'Leatherhead Theatre', it was originally housed in the old Victoria Hall which in spite of having a tiny stage, pigeons in its corrugated roof and rats in the basement, was taken over by the Under Thirty Group of professional young actors in 1950. With Jordan Lawrence as artistic director, it succeeded where two previous companies failed. Managed by Hazel Vincent Wallace, Leatherhead Theatre became one of the five top regional theatres and built up a reputation for exciting drama. With true pioneering spirit, a training scheme for theatre management was established and a policy of service to the young and old in the community evolved through garden parties, balls and coffee mornings. The serving of food in the theatre itself helped to make it a real social centre.

As its audiences grew larger, there was an obvious need to rehouse the company. Dame Sybil Thorndike agreed to give her name to a new theatre to be built on the site of the Crescent Cinema. In the 1960s, the Arts Council together with LUDC was able to assist in launching an appeal which raised in two years a remarkable £420,000 towards the building.

Designed by Roderick Ham, the Thorndike won him many awards including one for its amenities for the disabled. The theatre was opened in 1969 by Princess Margaret with Lord Snowdon whose portrait of Dame Sybil hangs on the mezzanine floor. The company itself was glad to move, not least because of the tragedy in the old Leatherhead Theatre when the Green Room manager Major Byrne was murdered in 1968 by a deranged young man later found unfit to plead.

Over the years, the Thorndike has become a real arts centre with exhibitions, films and concerts. Its studio theatre in the Casson Room, developed by Joan MacAlpine, presents minority drama and is the base for many county youth activities. In spite of the inevitable budget problems, the theatre and the town are proud that so many well-known actors and actresses have made their career debut at the Thorndike. Several productions have transferred to the West End, including *Stepping Out* and *The Matchgirls*. Dame Sybil herself made many appearances in her own theatre, the last not long before her death. Today Roger Clissold is the theatre's artistic director.[1]

The Flood in 1968

Heavy rain fell on 14 September followed by a non-stop deluge on 15 September when 4·26 inches fell in six hours and the town's drains were overwhelmed. The River Mole rose and by late on 15 September became a torrent and burst its banks swamping the surrounding countryside and flooding the Bus Garage and the Fire Station. With Fetcham virtually cut off, the bridge was closed and the occupants of a bus stranded on it, spent the night on its upper deck. Traffic built up

The Thorndike Theatre contract is signed by Chairman Greville Poke watched by Michael Marriott and Dame Sybil Thorndike (seated), Hazel Vincent Wallace and Joan MacAlpine.

[1] Hazel Vincent Wallace.

pical scenes in Leatherhead on Monday when flood water from the Mole had reached its peak.

NOW WE COUNT TI
COST OF FLOODIN

Homes ruined, roads blocked

FLOODS which engulfed the district at the beginning of this week were the living memory. Leatherhead Council have estimated that about 1,072 million of water poured through the town during the worst of the flood, engulfing h disrupting traffic in two days of disaster.

As the water receded this week, leaving a trail of waterlogged homes, abandoned cars, potholed roads and disconnected telephones, the full extent of the damage was becoming apparent.

Leatherhead Advertiser banner picture of the floods in 1968 when the River Mole broke its banks and changed course.

Travellers have rested near this bridge site for centuries. Recently trenches have been dug up Young Street to deter caravans attempting to extend the permanent gipsy site established by the Mole Vale District Council by the bridge in 1984.

The drought of 1976 when the River Mole at Young Street was reduced to a trickle.

and many cars were abandoned as deep swirling water effectively blocked the way in and out of town. It was estimated that over 1000 million gallons of water poured through Leatherhead in those two days, engulfing 200 houses, some flooded to a depth of 5 ft.

An emergency rest centre run by the WVS at The Red House (on the site of Belmont Lodge) provided food for 250 people and shelter for 60. Nine hundred telephones were out of order and for some houses, there was no electricity. Both Leatherhead and Guildford Pumping Stations were out of action so there was little drinking water. However, LUDC set about hiring and borrowing drying equipment and with the Fire Brigade and many volunteers, helped to pump and dry out the damaged properties. The sun came out on 17 September and the waters slowly subsided.

In 1969, the Fire Brigade moved from the old Fire Station they had used since 1926 to new premises in Cobham Road large enough to house their newest appliances.[1] With 29 full-time firemen, they cover a 26 square mile area.

Changing weather

After the overflowing of the River Mole in 1968, it is difficult to visualise it reduced to a trickle as it was in the drought of 1976. It was the hottest summer of this century, only rivalled by the summer of 1826 in the previous century. Temperatures were high for months and the year ended equally memorably with a white Christmas.

Another record in extremes was reached in the winter of 1963 when the mean temperature all over England was −30°C with nine consecutive days below freezing in the month of January. The Thames above Kingston froze so that it was possible to walk across the river.[2]

Leisure and sport

The Leisure Centre which had been under discussion since 1961 when the LUDC planned to replace the popular swimming pool at West Wing, was eventually opened in 1975. As a sports complex, it offers a bewildering variety of facilities and is widely used by young and old alike. Its swimming club competed for the first time in an international meeting in Holland in 1986.

In 1984, a Water Park was added. Built in collaboration with Ashtead Rotary Club, the Manpower Services Commission and local

[1] Chief Fire Officer Wadey.
[2] National Meteorological Library, Bracknell.

companies, it provides two lakes on which to learn sailing, boating, sail boarding, water skiing and canoeing.

Cricket

The Leatherhead Cricket Club moved to its present home in Fetcham Grove in the 1930s. It was founded in 1850 and its pitch was then the Kingston Road Recreation Ground. Then its membership was dominated by shopkeepers so that games were played on Wednesdays and Sundays. After its move to the ground it now shares with the Hockey Club founded in 1985, there were games on Saturdays and Sundays. In 1970, the club was involved in forming the Surrey Cricketers' League and its first two elevens compete in this. On 14 June 1985, the club was host to the Lord's Taverners in a special celebrity match played in perfect weather. The club chairman, Brian Aspinall, is Secretary to the National Cricket Association at Lords.[1]

Football

Until 1920, Leatherhead Rose was the only representative side playing here and it was proud of its record dating back to the 19th century. Then a rival team, Leatherhead Juniors later called United, was formed. The Rose club ground had been in Kingston Road but in 1933 it moved to Barnett Wood Lane while the United played in Forty-Foot Road recreation ground. After the war, in June 1946 both clubs amalgamated and with H. K. Reeves as its first President formed the Leatherhead Football Club, as it still is today. They were for four years the champions of what was then the Surrey County Senior League, a feat never before attained. In 1958 they were selected to the prestigious Corinthian League becoming champions five years later and so gained promotion to Division 1 of the Athenian League and to its Premier Division the following year. In 1963 floodlighting was installed for evening matches.

In 1969, they achieved what no other team had done before; they won the Surrey County FA Senior Challenge Cup, the Senior Shield and the Intermediate Cup. Their success continued after election to the Isthmian League as finalists in both Surrey and London Senior Cups and semi-finalist in the FA Amateur Cup in 1971 and 1974.

The Tanners, as the team is often called, made national headlines when they reached the 4th round of the FA Cup in 1975. With 1st

Gina Campbell, daughter of Donald Campbell, with her powerboat *Bluebird* in the background. In 1984, she became the fastest woman on water reaching a speed of 122·85 mph.

[1] Leatherhead Cricket Club report.

Division opposition in Leicester City, they played away from home to 24,000 spectators and millions more watched on television as they were two goals up at half-time but ultimately lost gloriously at 3–2. They reached the final of the FA Challenge Trophy in 1978 but lost to Altrincham 3–1.[1]

Golf

There are two main golf clubs in Leatherhead. The Tyrrells Wood Club was founded in 1924 and the MP, Sir Rowland Blades later Lord Ebbisham, was its first Captain. The club celebrated its Diamond Jubilee in 1984. Leatherhead's other golf club on Leatherhead Common was founded earlier in 1906. Before the Second World War its professional was Alfred Perry who became British Open Champion in 1935. Phil Runciman was its Captain for over 10 years and President for three years before his death in 1953. Bobby Locke, the South African professional played at the club in 1955. With the building of the M25, the clubhouse had to be demolished but has now been replaced.

The Leisure Centre caters for **Tennis** as it does for **Squash**, **Badminton**, **Table Tennis** and **Gymnastics**. Early in the century there was a tennis club at Thorncroft and today the Leatherhead Tennis Club has courts at Cannon Grove, Fetcham.

The **Bowling Club** formed in 1920 plays on a Cumberland turf green in Forty-Foot Road and has a ladies section. The **Angling Club** grew out of the Bus Garage Angling Club in 1946. It now has over 1500 members, 400 of whom are juniors. The club has acccess to the Mole, the Isle of Wight Pond on Bookham Common and the Rookery Pond in Ashtead Park. They fish mainly for dace, chub, roach, bream and perch. With a team of 12, they regularly enter the National Angling Championship and in 1986, fishing on the River Trent in Nottingham, they came second in the Second Division.

There is another angling club, the Sunmead, founded in 1953.[2]

In this century, there has always been **Riding Stables** in the area and recently, there is **Riding for the Disabled** in Bookham.

Pigeon fanciers have a **Homing Society** based at the British Legion Headquarters in Upper Fairfield Road.

Clubs and organisations

In 1976 at a meeting convened by the Leatherhead Society, there was

[1] J. W. Hewlins.
[2] R. Boychuk.

266

LEATHERHEAD FOOTBALL CLUB

SURREY DAILY ADVERTISER PIC

WEMBLEY SOUVENIR 1978

Souvenir of The Tanners football team who made national headlines when they reached the Final of the FA Challenge Trophy in 1978 but lost 3–1 to Altrincham at Wembley.

The Swan Centre today.

public support for the restoration of the community facilities of the Institute, in particular for the restoration of the main hall which had been out of use for over 30 years. With professional advice and many volunteers from the Leatherhead Community Association and others, the work was completed and the hall opened on 18 July 1987. Named the Abraham Dixon Hall after the Institute's founder, it was made a family occasion with two of his descendants, Michael and James Dixon, being present at the ceremony.

The Institute is now the base for 18 affiliated clubs which happily is how the founder envisaged it in 1893.

Another long-established club, the Working Men's Social Club in Upper Fairfield Road, celebrated its 75th anniversary in 1986. In its early days, it was associated with the Liberal Association but took its present name in 1922.

The Leatherhead Unionist (now Conservative) Club nearby in Linden Road dates from 1922.

The Swan Centre

Preparations for the building of the Swan Centre began in 1979 with the demolition of the 'Prince of Wales' public house in Lower Fairfield Road and some of the houses in Middle Road which lay in the path of the future Leret Way. In conjunction with this, a one-way traffic system was introduced round Station Road, Randalls Road and Bull Hill in March 1981. It was then possible to close the High Street to through traffic. Church Street was also closed as far as The Crescent and full pedestrianisation of the inner town was introduced.

The official opening of the Swan Centre by Councillor Rex Thorn was on 4 November 1982 and for the first time Leatherhead shoppers had a partially covered arcade with an integral car park. This backs on to the one-way system and has the effect of shielding, some say fortifying, the town from the prying eyes of visitors. A controversial clock tower was built at the entrance which intrudes on the vista down ancient Bridge Street.

The whole development, the most drastic transformation since the town was laid out in the 12th century, epitomises the neo-traditional architecture of the 1980s. The very names appeal to the past: Leret Way (after the Domesday form of Leatherhead) and Swan Centre (after the inn regrettably demolished in the 1930s). The Swan Centre

The Great Storm of 1987 felled thousands of trees locally. This one destroyed a car near Epsom Road.

design is post-modernist and vernacular, with steep roofs, timber parapets and deliberate echoes of traditional Surrey building in its brickwork and tile-hanging.[1]

When the Swan Centre was completed the M25 motorway was well advanced and the route from Wisley to Reigate and on, through Leatherhead (Junction 9), was opened on 6 October 1985.

The wind of change

There is no doubt that the great storm that swept through southern England in the small hours of 16 October 1987 was not as severe as the Great Storm of 1703 which blew off Leatherhead's church spire. That storm killed over 8000 people, while in 1987 there were thankfully relatively few casualties. Unfortunately, the same cannot be said about the 15 million lost trees; locally thousands blocked roads, disrupted telephone, gas and electricity services and damaged buildings.

Mole Valley District Council led by its Chief Executive Tony Huggins dealt very successfully with this major emergency. Eight pumping stations were out of action and with the River Mole rising, an amber alert was sent out (later to become red on 20 October when eight inches of rain was recorded for the month).

The sound of traffic silenced by impassable roads was replaced with the shriek of chainsaws as essential highways and driveways were cleared.[2] Local names like Givons Grove, Beech Avenue and Tyrrells Wood overnight lost some of their significance while the mammoth task of repairing the damage, inspecting trees and clearing wrecked woodland took many months – in some cases, years.

Immediate plans for replanting began with £10,000 contribution from the Mole Valley District Council but the long-term impact of the tragic uprooting of so many mature oak, beech, yew and lime trees has changed forever the face of the local landscape.

And so it is with the townscape of Leatherhead, like a woodland felled and replanted, and as yet not comfortable enough in its new format to be anything but a town at the crossroads.

[1] John Blair.
[2] *Surrey Mirror.*

An engraving of Leatherhead parish church by Allen *c.* 1850.

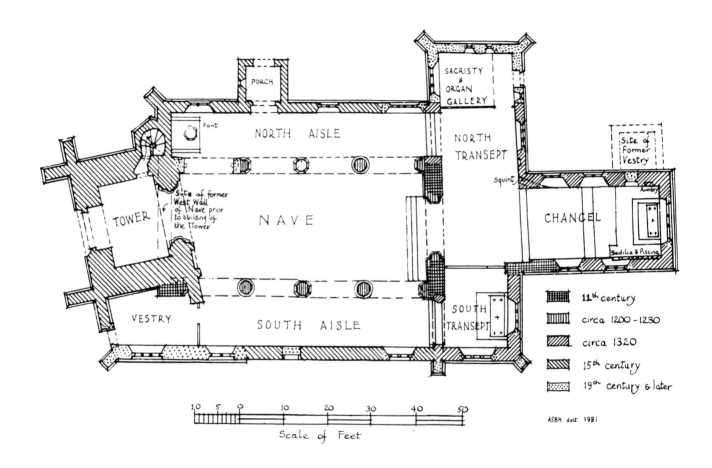

PORCH

SACRISTY & ORGAN GALLERY

Font

NORTH AISLE

NORTH TRANSEPT

Site of Former Vestry

Squint

Aumbry

Site of former West Wall of Nave prior to building of the Tower

TOWER

NAVE

CHANCEL

Sedilia & Piscina

VESTRY

SOUTH AISLE

SOUTH TRANSEPT

Legend:
- 11th century
- circa 1200 - 1230
- circa 1320
- 15th century
- 19th century & later

ASBH delt 1981

1   5   0   10   20   30   40   50
Scale of Feet

Ground plan showing the development of the church by Antony Hill (taken from the church guide).

272

The Parish Church of St Mary & St Nicholas

LEATHERHEAD'S parish church is built in a prominent position overlooking the valley of the Mole on the southern edge of the town. Its fine flint-faced tower is an impressive sight on the approach from Givons Grove and when seen from across the Mole near Thorncroft Manor. After dark, floodlighting strikingly picks out the details of its structure. The flag, which is flown on special occasions is that of St George with the diocesan arms. A sloping lawn edged with flowers and trees makes up the lovely garden beneath the tower close to the vicarage. Sadly, an avenue of limes was destroyed in the 1987 storm. From the churchyard gate nearby, the main fabric of the church behind the tower can be seen and also part of the large churchyard with its dark yews and winding paths. Here there are many Portland stone chest-tombs and humbler monuments which include 19th-century timber foot-posts, the last representatives of what seems to have been a long tradition.

Despite many restorations, the church of today is substantially what it was 500 years ago and some parts date from the late 11th or early 12th century. But for reasons described on p. 29, it appears that this was not Leatherhead's first church. The mid-Saxon 'old minster', recorded in Domesday Book in the last stages of its decline, seems to have stood somewhere near Patsom Green in the north-west of the parish. This much older and more important church was evidently abandoned in response to the settlement shifts of the 10th and 11th centuries. The new church built by the lords of Thorncroft manor, was

The fullest account of the history of the church is by G. H. Smith in *Proc. LDLHS* for 1963–70.

W. J. Blair, 'Churchyard monuments in the Leatherhead area', *Proc. LDLHS*, **iii** (9), 1975, pp. 313–15, and **iv** (2), 1977, pp. 19–24.

273

sited in order to suit the convenience of themselves and their tenants.

The manorial church of Thorncroft

The continuous history of Leatherhead parish church can be traced from the 1090s, when the royal steward Eudo Dapifer gave it to Colchester Abbey.[1] Since Eudo was the son-in-law of Richard Fitz Gilbert, lord of Thorncroft manor in 1086, it seems almost certain that it had been founded as a private church to serve the manorial household and tenants of Thorncroft. This explains the position of the church on the south edge of the town, not far from Thorncroft manor house. The abbots of Colchester retained patronage of the church until Edward I forced them to surrender it to the Crown in 1286.

Although no Anglo-Saxon or Norman architectural details remain visible, the church probably incorporates the shell of a building from this date.[2] The 13th-century nave arcades seem to have been pierced through the walls of an earlier aisleless nave. It is hard to explain the space between the chancel arch and the chancel proper except on the hypothesis that it once contained a crossing or central tower, removed to allow a clear space in the crossing area when the chancel was rebuilt in the 14th century. The early church can best be reconstructed as a 'three-part' plan: nave, axial tower and chancel. This is typical of larger late 11th-century manorial churches, and was exactly paralleled at Bletchingley, another Domesday manor of Richard fitz Gilbert. So whether or not a pre-Conquest church had stood on the site, the earliest fabric now remaining was probably built by the first Norman lord of Thorncroft between c. 1070 and c. 1090.

The nave and transepts

During the 12th century, churches which had begun as 'private' and 'manorial' became in the full sense 'parochial': the centre of a parish community with a wider range of activities and increasingly elaborate rituals. Thus the simple two- and three-cell churches built between c. 950 and c. 1150 were enlarged by the rebuilding of chancels and the addition of aisles, transepts and western towers. Leatherhead parish church illustrates all these developments.

Whereas the patrons maintained the chancel, the nave was the property and responsibility of the parishioners. Leatherhead's increasing prosperity, its local economic importance and perhaps the

[1] W. J. Blair, 'Origins of Leatherhead parish church', *Proc. LDLHS*, **3** (10).
[2] Ibid.

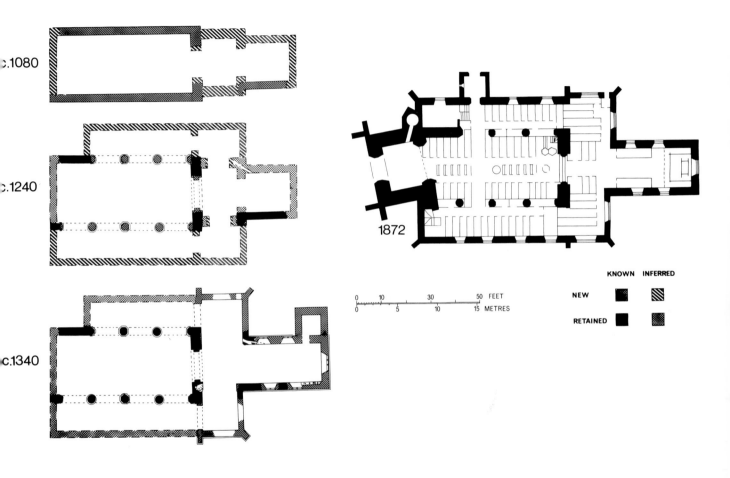

c.1080

c.1240

c.1340

1872

0 10 30 50 FEET
0 5 10 15 METRES

	KNOWN	INFERRED
NEW		
RETAINED		

Four stages in the development of the church. The 1872 plan shows pew arrangements before the 1873 restoration; traced directly from the original in the parish chest.

Leatherhead Church, Surrey.

1 May 1858.

Fragments of early 14th-century Flemish brass found in the churchyard and now mounted on the chancel wall.

creation of the new town are reflected in the addition of aisles during *c.* 1200–1230. The arches were built in a simple Early English style, the supporting columns alternately round and octagonal. The easternmost capital on the north side is sumptuously carved with 'stiff-leaf' foliage. The south arcade is four bays long but the north had only three, the fourth bay not being added until 1891. The levels of the bases rise slightly from west to east, reflecting an earlier slope of the floor. The aisles gave more room for processions and enabled additional altars to be placed at their east ends. The chancel arch is also 13th century, with small scallop-shells as stops to the mouldings. Only one furnishing of this period survives: the small chest with its scrolled wrought-iron straps.[1]

A standard feature of later medieval liturgical elaboration was the provision of a rood-loft over the chancel arch, to enable lights to be lit in front of the great rood or crucifix which dominated the nave. Door openings on either side of the chancel arch would have led to staircases giving access to the loft; remains of the stair on the south side were discovered during the 1891 restoration,[2] and the upper doorways are still visible in silhouette. The fine rood-screen survived late enough to appear in early 19th-century watercolours.

It is uncertain whether the Norman church had transepts. Both are now essentially of the 14th and 15th centuries, but masonry visible externally in the east wall of the south transept suggests an earlier, possibly 12th-century stage. The squint in the north transept evidently pre-dates the rebuilding of the chancel in the 14th century, for its sight-line has been changed to give a view to the new altar further east. It is possible (although there is no clear evidence for this) that the transepts housed chapels for the manorial families.

The chancel

During the first half of the 14th century the chancel was lavishly rebuilt with fine tracery windows in the 'curvilinear' style. It was almost certainly built in the 1340s by Leeds Priory in Kent which was given Leatherhead church by Edward III in 1341. The canons of Leeds appropriated the living shortly afterwards, and held it until the Dissolution.[3] It was probably at this time that the dedication of the church, previously to St Mary, was expanded to SS. Mary and Nicholas, the joint patrons of Leeds Priory.

[1] P. M. Johnston, 'Two chests', *SAC*, **xxviii**, 1915.

[2] *Leatherhead Observer*, 1 August 1891.

[3] *Proc. LDLHS*, **iii** (2), 1968, pp. 72–4.

The piscina for washing altar vessels, and the three sedilia for the priests officiating at Mass, are original features; there was a small window in the back of the middle seat.

This chancel, like many others, deflects slightly from the line of the nave, probably because it was re-orientated when the ground plan was laid out.

On the outside of the north wall of the chancel are the blocked silhouettes of a doorway and a square opening. Excavations have shown that these opened from the chancel into a room 8 ft square. This may have been an anchorite's cell or a sacristy, contemporary with the 14th-century chancel and demolished at the time of the Reformation.[1] During the excavations two fragments were found of a brass fillet inscription including the name 'Margaret', evidently from an early 14th-century monumental Flemish brass.[2] These are now mounted on the chancel wall.

The end of the middle ages

The west tower was built in about 1500, with a tall spire rising above it. Perhaps to leave room for processions around the church, the tower is conspicuously out of line with the main axis of the church, causing its east wall to encroach on the nave. The tall tower arch and the west window are impressive features in the Perpendicular style. On the north side of the tower is an internal gallery; graffiti on its floor suggest that it may have been used as a schoolroom in the 17th and 18th centuries.

At about the same time the aisles were widened to the level of the transepts, with large Perpendicular windows to provide more light, and the north porch was built. A blocked doorway in the south aisle probably dates from this widening.

The octagonal font is also late 15th century, as is the small monumental brass of a man and wife with six children raised against the west wall of the north aisle.[3]

It was the practice to use the church not only for worship but also for morality plays, parish feasts and other local functions. As the medieval population was mainly illiterate, the Gospel and the lives of the saints were taught visually by means of paintings covering the church walls.

Until the 15th century the congregation stood at services.

[1] P. M. Johnston, 'An anchorite's cell at Leatherhead church', *SAC*, **xx**, 1907, pp. 223–8.
[2] *Proc. LDLHS*, **iii** (7), 1973, pp. 186–7.
[3] M. Stephenson, *Monumental Brasses in Surrey* (1970), p. 329.
[4] *Proc. LDLHS*, **iii** (4), 1970, pp. 118–19.

The church during the Reformation and the religious changes of the 17th century

After the break with Rome in the 1530s and the dissolution of Leeds Priory, Henry VIII handed over the patronage of Leatherhead church in 1541 to the Dean and Chapter of Rochester, and it is still held by them. By this time the church had developed very largely to its present form, and its exterior survived all the many upheavals of religious change and conflict in the 16th and 17th centuries. The interior, however, must have suffered severely when the Protestant governments of Edward VI and Elizabeth ordered the removal of 'superstitious' images, vestments and monuments from all parish churches. A communion table replaced the 16th-century altar-slab, though Leatherhead somehow managed to preserve this and it is now kept behind the present altar. The rood was taken away from the chancel arch, but the screen survived. Any paintings on the walls would have been whitewashed over and replaced by texts such as the Creed, the Lord's Prayer and the Ten Commandments.

A survey was made of the church's goods in 1549, and four years later all not needed for use were ordered to be seized.[4] The first of these inventories shows the possessions of the church before the Reformation.

There were two gilt chalices with patens; three copes, one blue velvet, another white damask and the third green and yellow; six vestments; and three corporals in cloth-of-gold, white damask and red silk. There were nine altar-cloths, two curtains for the altar end, and a further two curtains of blue silk. The list also includes five towels; two surplices; a cloth for the lectern; a cloth painted with Christ's Passion for the Easter sepulchre; and a black cloth for the hearse. There were two Mass books (one manuscript, with silver clasps, the other printed); an antiphoner; two manuals; and a gradual. Two sacring bells, two hand bells and four bells in the tower are listed, as well as two big brass candlesticks and six small; four pewter cruets; a copper cross with a staff and two cross cloths; a Lenten veil; a brass chrismatory and censer; two holy water pots of brass and one of lead; and lastly, two cloths to cover the font.

By 1553, all that remained in the church was one chalice, a red figured-velvet vestment for the communion table and three bells in the tower.

Late medieval screens which were once in the parish church from a watercolour by Hassell.

279

Scratch dial on the north splay of the west window of the north porch is a medieval form of sundial. A hole for a pointer or style has been drilled into a stone or into a joint between two stones from which radiate several scratched lines sometimes surrounded by a circle. The style is placed in the hole and the sun casts a moving shadow so that the dial marks the passage of time. The style must point due south for the noon line to be vertical all the year round but as no style survives, we can only speculate. Medieval man had little need to know the exact time since his life and work revolved round the hours of daylight. If he was paid, it was by the day rather than the hour. However the priest needed to know the third, the sixth and the ninth hour (measured from daybreak) in order to commence certain church services. For practical purposes these were halfway through the morning, noon and halfway through the afternoon – DEREK RENN.

[1] *Cal. S.P.D.* (1687–89), p. 243.

Prominent members of the congregation

In Elizabeth's reign these included Edmund Tylney, Master of the Revels to the Queen, and Robert Gardiner, Sergeant of the Royal Wine Cellar. The helmet borne at Gardiner's funeral in November 1571 was later fixed to the east wall of the south aisle above a brass inscription by Thomas Churchyard, the Court Poet to Queen Elizabeth I. With the spelling modernised, this reads:

> Here friendly Robert Gardiner lies, well born of right good
> race,
> Who served in court with credit still, in worthy realm and
> place.
> Chief Serjeant of the Cellar long, where he did duty show,
> With regard to all degrees, as far as power might go,
> He passed his youth in such good frame, he came to aged
> years;
> And thereby purchased honest name, as by report appears.
> A friend, where any cause he found, and courteous to all;
> Of merry mood and pleasant speech, however hap did fall.
> Four children for to furnish forth the table round he had
> With sober wife, most matron like, to make a man full glad,
> Prepared to die long ere his day, which argues great good
> mind.
> We leave him where he looked to be; our Lord receive his
> spirit,
> With peace and rest in Abram's breast, where we at length
> may meet.

On the chancel floor are ledger stones to Richard Dalton, a distinguished 17th-century resident who was like Gardiner, Sergeant of the Royal Wine Cellar and was also a friend of Samuel Pepys; and to Lowde Cordell, a Page of the Royal Bedchamber, who died in 1685. It was at about this time that the Vicar of Leatherhead, Robert Hanbury (1679–1689), was made Chaplain to King James II.[1]

Church services

The church services in Tudor and Stuart times paid more attention than previously to readings from the Bible and to sermons or homilies. A Book of Homilies presented by Alexander Akehurst, dating from

1683 was preserved in the church but was unfortunately stolen in 1974. There were also fewer processions than in pre-Reformation days. During the Civil War and Interregnum no feast-days were allowed, and between 1653 and 1660 even marriage services in church were forbidden (see p. 108). This was all to change at the Restoration, with the return of 'Anglican' traditions. Also dating from the 17th century is the large chest, decorated with patterns made of brass studs and known as the Slyfield chest.

Vestry improvements to the church (1700–1800)

During the 18th century, the Vestry members of the parish were active in seeking ways to improve the church fabric and its amenities. They authorised general repairs to the church in 1701/1720 and this work probably included the construction of a low, elliptical arch within the chancel arch. About this time the Royal Arms, commandment boards and paintings of Moses and Aaron were placed over the chancel arch.[1] The spire was blown down in the great storm of November 1703 and not rebuilt. In 1746, the Vestry arranged for the building of a gallery across the middle aisle adjoining the belfry,[2] and 10 years later they supported the construction of a dormer window over the north aisle,[3] opposite the one built much earlier. About this time they also installed a three-decker pulpit, probably complete with sounding board.[4] The tower was covered with stucco in 1775 because of its poor condition, and near the end of the century its west door was widened to allow room for the parish fire-engine to be kept there. The choir probably sang at services from a gallery in the tower, and in 1792 the Vestry put money aside for the purchase of a base viol 'for the use of the said parish choire'.[5]

Shortly after Queen Anne's death in 1714, Dr Shortridge, Rector of Fetcham, left an endowment to the Vicar of Leatherhead and other neighbouring clergy, in return for which they were required to preach a sermon every year on 31 January, the anniversary of Charles I's execution in 1649. This sermon is still given.

Monuments proliferated in this century. The Dalton family, so well known in the 17th century, were commemorated in the 18th century also. Admiral Sir James Wishart, a lessee of the Rectory (Vale Lodge), has a monument as does Lt.-Gen. Humphrey Gore who owned The Mansion. On the east wall of the porch there is a monu-

[1] *Proc. LDLHS*, **iii** (3), 1969, p. 95.
[2] Vestry Minutes, 10 August 1746.
[3] Ibid., 14 March 1756.
[4] Ibid., 25 October 1761.
[5] Ibid., 1 April 1792.

ment to Mrs Diana Turner, granddaughter of the Earl of Salisbury, who died in 1736. She was a friend of the Dacres who lived in Church House and requested that she should be buried in the porch where, since she was an invalid, her sedan chair used to be placed during the services. On the wall of the south aisle is a tablet commemorating the accidental death in 1806 of Miss Harriet May Cholmondeley, while accompanying the Princess of Wales (later Queen Caroline), when their carriage overturned in Leatherhead.[1]

The Rev. James Dallaway's alterations (1820–1826, and later)

The Rev. James Dallaway, the distinguished antiquary, who was Vicar of Leatherhead between 1804 and 1834, made a number of changes to the east end of the chancel in 1820–1826, placing the altar here once again and installing new communion rails. He also renovated the south transept, put new windows in the north and south aisles, and in 1830 arranged for the purchase of an organ which was placed in a gallery at the west end of the church. In 1843, after Dallaway's death, it was replaced by a larger instrument built by Snetzler, the original keyboard for which is still preserved. About this time, the top tier of the 18th-century pulpit and its sounding board had been removed, as were the Royal Arms and the paintings of Moses and Aaron. Dallaway's work, now largely destroyed, had a simple elegance lacking in the Victorian fittings which replaced it.

Restorations and innovations: 1873, 1874 and 1891

It was in the 19th century that the greatest changes to the inside of the church took place, not all of them perhaps for the best. The first large restoration was in 1873 directed by Arthur Blomfield. One of the major undertakings was the extension of the north transept to form a vestry for the clergy, with a heating area below and a new organ loft above. The organ was then moved here from the tower. Heating pipes were installed in the nave, and as part of this work, the nave floor which sloped upwards from west to east, was levelled. Blomfield also removed the old box pews and replaced them with the present oak ones. The next year the chancel was strengthened, a new roof built, and the window at the back of the sedilia was probably blocked. A new altar and reredos in the Gothic style was presented at this time in memory of the Rev. B. Chapman (Vicar 1836–1871), and a stone pulpit

Watercolour by Hassell of 18th-century pulpit once in the parish church.

[1] E. W. Bayley, *History of Surrey* (1850), IV, p. 440.

The nave looking east before the 1873 restoration. Original photograph is in the church chest.

Lych gate erected in memory of Harriet Millett in 1885, with a much-loved verger, Mr Crockford, *c.* 1916, in the foreground.

was given. The brass eagle lectern was donated to the church in 1888.

A further large restoration was carried out in 1891, again under Blomfield's supervision. The aisles and transepts were re-roofed, the south aisle was extended to make room for a choir vestry, and alterations were made to the chancel arch. All the galleries were removed, and the arch at the west end of the north arcade was inserted. The old porch was re-opened after the entrance made 20 years before had been filled in and a window put in its place. The font was moved from near the chancel steps to its present position; a fine chandelier, dating from 1763, now hangs over it.[1] The mosaic paving and the marble steps to the chancel given to the church at this time, and paintings of the Annunciation were placed over the chancel arch in the former upper doorways of the rood-loft.

The tower was restored in 1894, and choir-stalls were provided in 1889. During the 19th century three chalices and four patens were added to the church's communion plate which also includes the very fine 1661 cup presented by the Rev. James Dallaway.[2] The churchyard gate close to the north porch, was erected in 1885.

The Parish Magazine was first published in 1880 and still thrives today.

The church today

There has been no large-scale restoration work in the church during this century, though its appearance inside has been altered by the darkening of the roof of the nave and aisles in 1963, and the colour-washing of the columns and arches to give more light and bring out the architectural details. The 19th century stone pulpit was replaced by the present plain oak one in 1962. The south transept screen was put in place in 1928 and the aisle walls around the font were panelled in 1937. In the early part of this century most of the windows were filled with stained glass as memorials. The window near the font contains scraps of medieval glass collected by the Rev. James Dallaway and re-assembled in memory of the Rev. Gerard Coleridge (1926–1944). The east window is a memorial to Canon Utterton, Vicar from 1876 to 1907. The novelist Anthony Hope was buried in the churchyard in 1933.

Recent changes and additions include the making of a curtain in 1981 by the ladies of the parish to cover the west door. This features

[1] W. Hooper, 'Brass chandeliers in Surrey churches', *SAC*, **xlvii**, 1941, p. 41.
[2] T. S. Cooper, 'The church plate of Surrey', *SAC*, **xi**, 1893, 102–4.

local dignitaries and town buildings. Some hassocks for the pews were also made. Books of Remembrance are kept under the tower arch and in the north transept. There is a Garden of Remembrance in the churchyard. A new organ was installed in 1984.

The bells of the church made a special celebratory peal on the Jubilee of the Elizabeth II's accession in 1977. Of the 10 bells, four are dated 1816, five 1877 and the tenth, 1924. In 1694, according to the Vestry Minutes, the bellringers were paid 1s. 5d. for ringing but 1s. 6d. when they rang a knell for Queen Mary who died at the age of 33 from smallpox.

In 1986, the 900th anniversary of Leatherhead parish church was celebrated in prayer, music, flowers, crafts and exhibitions. A new banner designed by Anthony Hill was commissioned. Today, as in the past, the church is still active in the community and has the assistance of Capt. Gardner of the Church Army working in North Leatherhead. While cooperating ecumenically with other churches, the long tradition of worship and care for the people continues.

Incumbents

c. 1100–1286 Rectors appointed by Colchester Abbey
(Names of rectors not known c. 1100–1259)

1259 Simon
1279 Fulk Lovel

1286–1341 Rectors appointed by the King

1286 Hugh de Candal or Kendal
1289 Henry de Durham
1303 Alexander de Convers
1324 Robert de Hoton
1330 Stephen le Blount
1340 Thomas de Crosse

1341–1541 Rector appointed by Leeds Priory 1345 John Olaver

1341–1541 Vicars appointed by Leeds Priory

1346 William de Harple
1349 Thomas Plomer. Instituted January, died March 1349
1349 Reginald Goderynton. Instituted March, died April, 1349
(The last two were presumably plague deaths.)

1349   Thomas de Halghton

1375   Henry Warthull

1377   John Alleyn

1378   George de Aperdele

1381   Thomas de Great Ocle

1387   Henry Derby. During his period as vicar, on 17 June 1395, William of Wykeham, Bishop of Winchester, commissioned John, Bishop of Glasgow, to re-consecrate Leatherhead church after it had been polluted by the shedding of blood.

1401   Roger Long

1402   John Rothewelle. Resigned in 1402.

1402   John Herde

1408   John Galeys

1414   Thomas Clerk

(Names of vicars not known between 1415 and 1456)

      John Myssendene. Died 1451.

1451   John Burtley

1468   Thomas Trott

1471   Otho Michel

1476   John Cothowe (or Curteys)

1489   John Westby

1491   John May

1506   Thomas Abel

1507   Thomas Clyfford

1510   Robert Russell

Vicars appointed by the Dean and Chapter of Rochester (1541 to the present day)

1557   William Walkeden. Resigned in 1561.

1561   Simon Tysse

1571   John Vaughan

1590   Richard Levytt (or Levitt). Deprived by Parliament, 1646; he was 90 years old at the time.

1646/7   Thomas Mell. Appointed by Parliament. Subscribed to the Act of Uniformity, 1662.

1671   John Frank

1679   Robert Hanbury. Chaplain to King James II.

1689 Robert Johnson. Held the living for 63 years.

1752 Robert Laxton

1767 Samuel Markham. Largely an absentee.

1797 Richard Harvey

1804 James Dallaway. Distinguished antiquary and author. Wrote a short history of Leatherhead to accompany his wife's drawings of the town.

1834 James Barker

1836 Benjamin Chapman. Founder of Leatherhead's first National School in 1838. Reredos erected in his memory.

1871 Thomas Thompson Griffith. Vicar for only five years. Built the Vicarage still standing in Vicarage Lane.

1876 Frank Ernest Utterton. Built All Saints' Church and founded the Parish Magazine in 1880. Stained glass of east window in his memory.

1907 Edward Jackson Nash. Served only three years. Remembered for his fine bass singing voice.

1910 Thomas Frederick Hobson. Formerly headmaster of King's College, Rochester, and an Oxford athletic Double Blue. He formed the first Parish Church Council in 1920 and set up the town's District Visitor service.

1926 Gerard Hartley Buchanan Coleridge. Descendant of the poet. Made the south transcept into a Lady Chapel and re-instituted the annual preaching of the King Charles sermon. Built All Saints' parish hall.

1944 Frank Arundel Page. Formed the 'Friends of the Parish Church' and in 1945 introduced Midnight Mass at Christmas. President for 13 years of the Countryside Protection Society who planted a tree in his memory by the parish hall which he himself had opened in 1948.

1959 Kenneth Vernon James Ball. Opened the redesigned parish church hall in 1963 and worked ecumenically in the town and through the Council of Churches until he retired.

1971 Alexander Dorner Morris. Works with his curate, Keith Hodges, to unify his large parish and to continue the ecumenical work of his predecessor. Arranged and celebrated the 900th anniversary of the church and in 1987 was made an honorary canon of Guildford diocese.

One of the stations of the cross by Eric Gill in the Catholic Church of Our Lady and St Peter, Garlands Road.

Parish records

Parish Registers exist from 1656, but there are also a few entries of baptisms in 1623, 1626, 1647 and 1649, copied into the 1656 book. No other registers survive, though they had been ordered to be kept since 1538.

The Vestry Minute Books are complete from 1694, 12 volumes in all. There are also three books of Overseers of the Poor accounts, 1749–1765, 1773–1790 and 1790–1810; a Report of an Assessment Committee, 1819; and a Bell Ringers' Book, 1808–1877. The Churchwardens' Accounts for 1695–1738, excepting 1701–1703 and 1710, are bound up with the first of the Minute Books. Most of the other Churchwardens' Accounts are lost.

ALL SAINTS' CHURCH

This church was built in Kingston Road towards the end of the 19th century to serve the rapidly growing population in the north of the parish. It was designed by Arthur Blomfield to seat 300 people, at a cost of £1610. It was consecrated by the Bishop of Winchester on 23 February 1889. Recently extensive repairs were found to be necessary, and in 1981 the church was converted into a dual-purpose centre, the chancel becoming a small chapel seating 50 people, separated by a folding screen from the nave which is used as a church hall. The new All Saints' Church Centre which includes housing for the elderly, was re-dedicated by the Bishop of Dorking on 28 March 1982.

CATHOLIC CHURCH OF OUR LADY AND ST PETER

This church was built in Garlands Road in 1922–1923 by E. Goldie, and endowed by Sir Edward Hulton, the publisher. Stained-glass windows were put in about 10 years later. The Stations of the Cross in Caen stone were designed by Eric Gill, the eminent sculptor. Previously, part of a house, 'Editha' in Linden Gardens, served as a chapel for eight years. The first parish priest was Fr. Pitts.

CONGREGATIONAL CHURCH (UNITED REFORMED CHURCH)

The first Congregational Church in Leatherhead was a barn in the centre of the town, formerly used by strolling players, which was opened as a place of worship in 1816. The church became fully active in 1829, and a larger building was soon found to be necessary. A piece of land near the crossroads at the town centre was secured and by 1844 a new church had been built, capable of seating 250 people. This remained in use for just over 90 years when it was replaced by the present building in Epsom Road. Christ Church was dedicated on 1 May 1935, and in October 1972 it became known as the United Reformed Church.

METHODIST CHURCH

The first 11 Methodists met in 1860 in rooms in Bridge Street. In 1885 Stephen Mould helped to establish meetings by hiring Victoria Hall with Dr Frederick Cumming from Cobham as missioner. In 1887 an iron building was erected on a site purchased in Church Road and the present church was built in 1893, the school buildings being added in 1905.

The church seats 300 and was erected as a memorial to John Wesley to commemorate his visit to Leatherhead at the end of his life.

MOUNT ZION CHAPEL (STRICT BAPTIST)

This is situated in Church Road, close to the Methodist church. It was built in 1869.

EVANGELICAL CHURCH (CHRISTIAN BRETHREN)

This is in Kingscroft Road, near Kingston Road roundabout.

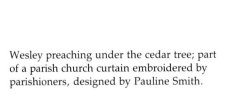

Wesley preaching under the cedar tree; part of a parish church curtain embroidered by parishioners, designed by Pauline Smith.

Randalls Park House, the home of Nathanial Bland who built it in the early 19th century after demolishing an earlier house of the same name.

Buildings Past & Present

THE EARLIEST surviving Elizabethan and Stuart buildings in the town are a small number of timber-framed houses, modest in size and character (see p. 58). As stone and wood were in ample supply, the earlier medieval houses were box-framed in construction with closely spaced heavy timbers transmitting the weight of the roof to the ground. When wood became dearer due to the demands of the ship-builders, the later houses had lighter timbers, spaced further apart and infilled with wattle and daub or with brickwork in various patterns. They were weatherproofed with clay tiles, slates, overlapping boards or plaster.

In the mid-16th century, a radical change in house design took place. Houses once single storied, were built on two storeys throughout and chimneys replaced the open hearths so enabling halls to be floored over in wood to make upper chambers which were reached by ladders. The town's remaining 17th-century buildings were mostly simple two- or three-cell ordinary village houses, but it is known that during this period there were at least half a dozen fairly large and important houses. These have either wholly disappeared like RANDALLS PARK and CHURCH HOUSE, or have been replaced by other buildings like VALE LODGE, built on the site of the former RECTORY. The present MANSION is on the site of a Tudor and Stuart 'Mansion' while THORNCROFT has been rebuilt and modified many times over the centuries.

'Cradlers', 33–35 High Street which was a greengrocer's shop before its recent restoration.

The following chapter describes some of those buildings recorded in and around Leatherhead which no longer exist, and others which fortunately can still be seen today.

The High Street

The street's alignment and width remains much as it was at the beginning of the century. However the buildings themselves have greatly changed; disfigured by shopfronts, their interiors have been altered with little regard paid to historic features.

CRADLER'S HOUSE (Nos. 33–35) is the oldest surviving building in the town. It is a 14th-century open-hall building which has recently been restored (see p. 64).

Nos. 37, 39 and 41 date from the late 17th and early 18th centuries and No. 41 has a fine panelled room on the first floor. Nos. 53 and 55 are basically 16th-century buildings with cement rendering above the shop fronts, no doubt covering timber-framing.

The DUKE'S HEAD, despite its 19th-century appearance, has a 17th-century structure. It was known as the DUKE OF CUMBERLAND in the 18th century and Courts and occasional Vestry meetings were held there. In 1798 Thomas Kershaw was innkeeper and in 1851 it was described as 'a commercial inn and posting house' with John Lawrence as innkeeper. John Young of Dorking owned it in 1892. Behind its rendered façade with parapet and bay windows, there is a timber-framed building with a tiled roof. Part of the external wall of the cellar was dry stone walling and its floor was part brick-paved and part soil. The cellars are now undergoing extensive rebuilding. At one time the property extended back to Fairfield Road and included an orchard, kitchen garden and stable buildings, with a farrier working nearby. The town band used to play in the forecourt early this century.

The PRINCE OF WALES public house, built in 1906 on the site of the Old Black Hut or House, was demolished in 1974 when the new town centre was built.

The KING'S HEAD inn was situated on the east side in King's Head Alley, just off the High Street. In 1719 it was owned by Edward Toye who also owned the Swan Hotel. The original inn was destroyed by fire in 1794 and after rebuilding, it had several owners, the Skilton family holding it for over 20 years in the mid-19th century. The old inn, described as 'one of the beauties of the town',[1] was replaced by a

'Prince of Wales' public house which was demolished for the making of the Swan Centre.

[1] F. B. Benger.

modern public house in 1930 on a site opposite the original. The new 'King's Head' building was eventually converted into shops in 1961.

Nos. 8 and 10 are listed as built in 'regency brick' before 1885 when they were said to be a 'school for young ladies' and subsequently Shinners drapery store from 1885 to 1935.

The LETHERHEAD INSTITUTE at the top end of the High Street was built and endowed by Abraham Dixon of Cherkley Court in 1892. On the subscription of 2*d*. a week, it provided educational, social and recreational activities for all members of the community. In 1987 the Leatherhead Community Association with the help of local volunteers, refurbished the hall on the first floor and named it after its founder.

The SWAN HOTEL stood at the junction of North Street and the High Street and was the centre of the town for over 300 years until its demolition in 1936. The first reference to its existence was in 1637 when it passed from Thomas Godman to the Barefoot family and it was mentioned by John Evelyn in his diary in 1667. It is said that a Chancery court came there in 1705 to deal with the disputed inheritance of the wife of the landlord Edward Toye. An even earlier 17th-century proprietor, Edward Shales, had the right to mint his own tokens which passed for currency at the time. By 1791 many stage coaches called there and changed horses on regular routes from London to Dorking, Horsham, Guildford and Brighton until well into the 19th century. The marlpit behind the hotel was not dug out for marl after the 17th century and became part of the gardens which stretched back as far as Fairfield Road. Prize Jersey and Alderney cows were bred and kept in separate stalls in the cow yard and taken daily in slow procession to pasture near Thorncroft and Downside. By the 1850s the hotel was the property of William Moore and later his daughter Emily. Under the Moores, the 'Swan' became a top-class hotel with 'quiet comfort, good food and drink' and suites of apartments were available for guests. Banquets, receptions and dances were held there and the busy yard was always full of landaus, broughams and coaches. Well-known visitors included Jenny Lind, the singer; Ellen Terry, the actress and the young Princess of Teck, a relative of Queen Mary. The swan mounted on the porch was saved when the hotel was demolished. For many years it has graced a Fetcham garden and it is hoped it will soon be nesting in the Museum. Behind the site of the Swan Hotel in a

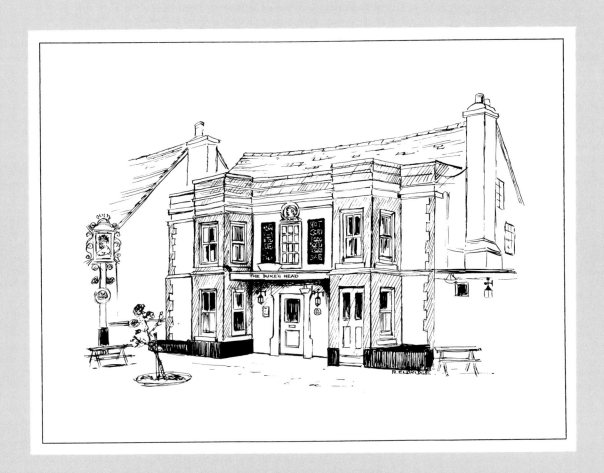

The 'Duke's Head', High Street.

Terracotta flowers from the Swan Brewery 1889 now incorporated into No. 31 High Street.

private car park, there is a tablet set in the wall which reads: 'Near this spot poor Jack, a pony owned by Joseph Hemsley of the inn, was shot on 30th April 1833 in the 42nd year of his life'.

The SWAN BREWERY was established by George Moore in 1859. In 1874 a steam brewery was built next to the 'Swan', where the entrance to the new shopping precinct is today. The brewery was built on the tower principle containing a ground floor mill and engine room with a malt store above and a mash room with a capacity for 4000 gallons on top. There was also a tun room for racking beer, a stillion room for storing 500 barrels and cellars which were in concrete and extended under the 'Swan' yard and stables. By 1904 with F. Hue Williams as its chairman, the brewery was the most important commercial enterprise in the town with about 150 dependants. Best malt hops from Kent and Worcester produced pale ale and stout and porter which was served at 19 brewery public houses in the district. In 1921 it was sold to Mellish and Neale of Reigate and subsequently closed down. Two terracotta panels of flowers removed from the brewery (later Barclays Bank) when the building was demolished, have been incorporated into the wall of No. 31, a 1986 building.

Epsom Road

Just beyond the High Street in Epsom Road, there were once two large properties, LINDEN HOUSE on the left and WINDFIELD HOUSE on the right. The sites are now occupied by flats and maisonettes that bear their names. The BARN behind Linden Court dates from about 1600.

ST JOHN'S SCHOOL was built in 1872 (see pp. 182 and 254) and the UNITED REFORMED CHURCH (Christ Church) in 1935 (see p. 288). VICTORIA HOUSE, opposite, is a home for the disabled and was built originally in 1905 as the town's hospital (see p. 220).

Bull Hill

WESLEY HOUSE was erected in 1935 on the site of Kingston House and became the offices of the Leatherhead Urban District Council. Two Spanish field pieces, elaborately decorated brass four-pounders captured at Santo Domingo, are in the entrance hall. They were presented to the town by H. K. Reeves of The Mansion in 1940. The building remained the headquarters of LUDC together with their offices in the Red House, now demolished. When they became part of the Mole

Rear view of the Swan Hotel *c.* 1910.

The Cottage on Bull Hill restored by the Countryside Protection Society.

Valley District Council, they moved their offices to Dorking in 1983.

KINGSTON HOUSE, the original site of Wesley House, was mainly a Queen Anne structure and was the home of the Rev. Belson where Wesley preached his last homily in 1791. It became the home of Emily Moore, the proprietor of the Swan Hotel who died at Kingston House in 1930.

THE RED HOUSE, formerly BELMONT LODGE, was originally the home of George Fish Richardson and was part of a large estate he sold in 1873 (see p. 161). In 1915 it was taken over as a Red Cross hospital and after 700 wounded soldiers had been treated there, it closed in 1919. Described as a 'charming old Georgian mansion standing in 10 acres', it became a residential hotel in 1921 and was purchased in 1949 as additional offices and a Day Centre for the LUDC. It was sold in 1985 for redevelopment as a commercial property, now also named Belmont Lodge.

THE COTTAGE is a 17th-century timber-framed labourer's cottage restored by the Countryside Protection Society.

At the junction of Bull Hill with Station Road was the OLD BULL INN, earlier called the BLACK BULL. The first known innkeeper was Thomas Williamson in 1798 and the inn became a port of call for carters taking lime from Dorking to Kingston. It is recorded that the Stag Hunt met there in 1852. At the Station Road side of the inn, a large room hung with portraits of Derby winners was much used for meetings and entertainments. The forecourt of the OLD BULL became a meeting place for the town and developed into a mini-Speakers' Corner where Suffragettes, and later Liberal and Conservative supporters, expounded their theories using a lorry as a platform (see pp. 222–223). The inn was demolished in 1925 and the Gas showrooms built in its place (now also demolished).

North Street

The NEW BULL HOTEL was owned by Friary Brewery who transferred their licence from the OLD BULL. The central section of the building was once ELM HOUSE, previously the home of Charles Howell, Dr Hearden, S. Nathan, Henry Courage and Mrs Weston, among others.

On the west side of North Street was the LION BREWERY referred to in Thomas Cooper's will of 1799. It was a freehold dwelling with malt house and brewery, seven store cellars, cooperage, three stables

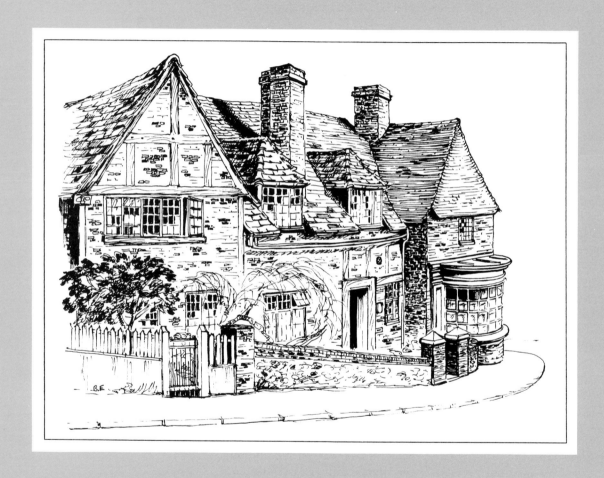

Sweech House, Gravel Hill.

and a millhouse, outbuildings, a large garden and eight tenements, yard and paddock. Thomas Cooper was also proprietor of the 'Rising Sun', Fetcham where he began his successful trade 'brewing six-penny beer made from fine spring water'.[1]

Old photographs of Leatherhead show a clock tower at the junction of Gravel Hill and North Street. Built in 1860 to house the town's fire engine, the clock itself was given to the town by the old Congregational Church, once in North Street, because it could not afford to pay the tax imposed on public clocks.[2] Near this site, a STOCKS HOUSE stood in the middle of North Street and appears on a 1629 map and 1782/1793 town plan by Gwilt. From an old drawing, stocks can be seen outside so it was probably used to house offenders. A new building (1983) close to the site, has been given its name.

It is thought that on an island site next to the Stocks House was the MARKET HOUSE, part of the Leatherhead market place. Elias Allen's survey of 1629 shows a large building on the site and John Aubrey writing in his diary in 1673 records it being in the town in 1623. It may well account for the strange alignment of the old crossroads. By 1782, it had disappeared and was not shown on the Gwilt map.

Gravel Hill

SWEECH HOUSE (Nos. 2, 4 and 6) is probably the most eye-catching building in Leatherhead. It is an amalgam of three 16th-century buildings (though part of No. 2 may be 15th century) and all are timber-framed. The south range seems to represent a complete small house with smoke-blackening in the roof suggesting it was once an open hall house. This too was aligned to the street and may well have been part of the first architectural urbanising of Leatherhead. Then Gravel Hill was known as 'The Borough' and tenements were recorded there as early as 1300. It was due to H. K. Reeves and to the initiative of the Countryside Protection Society that Sweech House has survived.[3]

Nos. 8–10, a pair of cottages in warm red brick with slate roofs, date from about 1845, having windows with glazing bars and are part of the Sweech House curtilage. Between Nos. 8–10 and 12–14 there is a side lane with a terrace of six flint early 19th-century buildings known as 'Flint Cottages'.

No. 12–14 is a mid-19th-century brick-faced with stucco building which unfortunately obscures the side elevation of No. 16–18. Dated

[1] W. J. Blair, 'The old Rising Sun, Fetcham', *Proc. LDLHS*, **4** (5), 1981.

[2] R. D. Pearson, 1972.

[3] J. Harvey, 'Sweech House', *Proc. LDLHS*, **3** (5), 1971, pp. 146–53.

1799 on the Gravel Hill frontage, the date possibly indicates the time of its renovation since the building is earlier. It is built of knapped flints with brick quoins and has a tiled roof. Brick steps with original iron-work balusters lead up to the entrance.

No. 20 is an early 19th-century cottage in warm red brick which has no window glazing bars and its roof has been retiled with concrete tiles.

JUBILEE COTTAGES next to Sweech House were built to mark Queen Victoria's Diamond Jubilee in 1897.

Kingston Road

Below Fairfield Road and continuing down Bull Hill, there was BRAD-MERE POND on Kingston Road which was infilled at the beginning of the century. No. 24 Bradmere Cottage is the last reminder of the name in the area.

Nos. 109 and 111 are a pair of weather-boarded houses dating from about 1800 with a plain tiled roof and a central chimney stack.

Just at the railway bridge to the right is the old Leatherhead station ENGINE SHED, abandoned in 1867. It is now (1988) part of an engineering firm and about to be dismantled. Between 1877 and 1899, it served as an infants' school until All Saints Infants' school replaced it.

The RAILWAY ARMS is on Kingston Road at the Plough round-about. It dates from 1851 when it was described as a 'beer house with 2 cottages'. Purchased by Hodgson Kingston Brewery in 1891, it was rebuilt shortly afterwards and only one of the cottages survived. It is rather unusual in that it is a three-storied building with a steeply pitched roof (with a flat roofed addition). A path behind once led from the inn to Leatherhead's first railway station until 1867 when it was replaced by two stations adjacent to each other nearer the town.

Its near neighbour, the PLOUGH, was run by two carpenters in 1841 but by 1861 it had a publican, John Walker, whose family owned it until 1892. It was at one time owned by the Swan Brewery. The building is Edwardian with three gables, half timbered above face brickwork with a tiled roof. A mural in one of the bars was executed after the Second World War by a French artist.

Further along Kingston Road, the ROYAL OAK was probably built on the site of an old coaching inn which had stables, an orchard and a garden. Records show that in 1826 it was occupied by Thomas Gadd, followed by Edward Mills in 1839. In 1851 it was run by John Constable who farmed 90 acres and was still the owner in 1870. The present building is rendered and in Georgian style.

Bridge Street (North side)

No. 2 was built in 1928 and is timber-framed in neo-Tudor style but the timbers are genuinely constructional.

No. 6 is a timber-framed 17th-century building with rough-cast front.

No. 8–10 is an early 19th-century building stuccoed with a slate roof. There is an earlier building at the rear, partly used as a bakery.

No. 12–16 is a mid-19th-century building.

No. 18–20 is an early 19th-century building in stock brick with a slate roof.

No. 22 is a red-brick 19th-century building with a slate roof and somewhat continental windows.

The former coachbuilders Venthams and Sons occupied the premises between Nos. 22 and 24. It was basically a much altered early 19th-century building and was demolished in 1986. An early hand-operated petrol pump from its garden is now in the garden of the Museum at Hampton Cottage, Church Street. The new property is appropriately called THE COACH HOUSE.

No. 24 was an early 19th-century building stuccoed over lath and plaster. It was restored in 1986 in the original style. The relatively long and raised front garden gives some idea of how Bridge Street looked in the previous century.

No. 26 is an early 19th-century house of red brick with a slate roof. Its ground floor has been marred by many alterations and an extension to its eastern side.

Nos. 28–34 is a terrace of early 19th-century houses of stock brick with slate roofs. With the exception of No. 34, the original ironwork around the raised front gardens remains.

The RUNNING HORSE near the bridge over the River Mole is the finest of Leatherhead's few remaining open-hall houses. Built on glebeland, it is unlikely that it was built as an inn. Its two-bay cross-wing jettied over the street has an impressive upper chamber with an open truss matching the hall. It has all the appearance of a high-quality private house *c.* 1450–1550. Records show that in 1414 John Cradler

The crossroads at
North Street and
Bridge Street. Top,
showing Wilde's
teashop and bakery,
which had brick ovens
on the right, and
Hewlins the chemist
and the old saddler's
shop on the left *c.*
1912–14. Below, the
bakery was replaced
with a mock Tudor
building in 1928.

was granted the lease of a tenement on adjoining land but with an abuttal to the 'Running Horse'. It is best known as the supposed dwelling of ale-wife Elinour Rumming who was immortalised in the comic poem *The Tunning of Elinour Rumming* by John Skelton, Henry VIII's poet laureate. Skelton who himself enjoyed fishing in the Mole, described her grotesque appearance and the riotous scenes in her tavern giving a gutsy account of peasant life at its lowest. Although there is no firm evidence of her living at the inn or even that it was an ale-house in her time, in 1525 Elinour was fined 2*d.* at Pachenesham Magna for selling ale at excessive prices. Early tenants were William Fish in 1682, Fetherstone Hall in 1712 and William Hale in 1730. After that there were many owners and in 1889, George Moore of the 'Swan' bought it at auction. During the mid-19th century, another inn called the NEW RUNNING HORSE was built on the opposite side of Bridge Street but within 10 years it was just a 'beer and lodging house'.

LEATHERHEAD BRIDGE over the Mole is probably with the parish church, the oldest building in the town. It is mentioned in a 1286 deed, and 50 years earlier, Simon de Ponte held land nearby. In 1362 John Plomere of Rochford was licensed to collect alms for the repair of the bridge which over the centuries was frequently necessary. In the 18th century, it was barred off and reserved for those paying towards its upkeep so that most travellers used the ford alongside it.[1] Later it became the responsibility of the county and it was rebuilt as it is today by George Gwilt in 1782 (see p. 132). The bridge piers are very much older and under at least nine of its 14 small arches, arch stones of a medieval bridge can be traced.[2]

Bridge Street (south side)

No. 5 is a fine early 19th-century stuccoed building with a slate roof. Although the windows have lost their glazing bars, the original shop front remains but the Doric columns are a 20th-century addition.

No. 7–9 was a saddlers and harness-makers from the 17th century until 1905, run by the Ragge and Lloyd families (see p. 151). The building was demolished by the Civil Defence in an exercise in 1939.

No. 15–17 is a timber-framed building which may date in part from the 16th century.

No. 33 is a charming early 19th-century stuccoed building with a slate roof and 'gothick' windows.

[1] D. F. Renn, 'The date of the first Leatherhead bridge', *Proc. LDLHS,* **3** (5), 1971, p. 153.
[2] D. F. Renn, 'The old bridge at Leatherhead', *Proc. LDLHS,* **3** (6), 1972, pp. 165–7.

Bridge Street showing the 'Running Horse'.

No. 35 is a red-brick building with a slate roof and dates from about 1840. It is unfortunate that the high shop front on its eastern side obscures the façade above it.

No. 37 is an 18th-century flint and brick building whose front has been rendered.

No. 39–41 is a late 17th-century timber-framed structure, with a jettied front.

No. 43 is an early 19th-century stock brick building with a slate roof. It is marred by the wooden facing to the ground floor on the street frontage.

No. 45–51 is a mid-19th-century terrace.

THE TANNERY, originally run by Bartholomew Chitty in 1826, was situated with its mill near the river at the lower part of Minchin Close (see p. 151). In 1901 part of the mill was in use as a swimming bath. The mill was demolished when Minchin Close was built.

Church Street

This is a street of contrasts since from the crossroads up to The Crescent, modern façades have in the last 50 years replaced most of the old buildings.

No. 3 dates from about 1600, but the shop front obscures much of its old timber-framed structure which is only visible at its southern end.

THE MANOR HOUSE described by James Dallaway as a 'handsome brick building by George Ballard dated about 1720', was demolished in 1936. It became the site of the Crescent Cinema and later the Thorndike Theatre which was completed in 1969. A number of adjacent shops were added at this time. A new building, No. 19, is now called Manor House and is part of the site of the home and surgery of Dr Granger (1922). In 1920, one of the last occupants of THE MANOR HOUSE was H. K. Reeves who later moved to The Mansion.

THE MANSION is possibly on the site of a main house of a sub-manor belonging to Kilburn nunnery, held in the 14th century of Pachenesham manor. 'Minchen' or 'Minchun' is the Middle English word for 'nun' and perhaps 'Mansion' is a corruption of that word. With the dissolution of Leeds Priory by Henry VIII, the property was granted to the Stydolf family of Mickleham and Pachenesham and it was leased by one of Henry's yeoman falconers, Robert Cheseman.

'Waytes', 24/26 Church Street taken in 1956 just before its demolition.

Later it was occupied by Edmund Tylney, Master of the Revels to Queen Elizabeth; the Earl of Nottingham, Lord Lieutenant of Surrey until his death in 1642 and Sir Thomas Bludworth, Lord Mayor of London at the time of the Great Fire in 1666.

The house was rebuilt in 1739 by Alexander Akehurst in warm Flemish brick, well proportioned and evenly fenestrated with nine two-windowed bays.[1] It was probably remodelled by William Wade, one time Master of Ceremonies at Brighton and Bath who died in 1810. The present house has a tiled roof and flint remains of the earlier house are visible on the southern side (Vicarage Lane). The eastern (Church Street) façade has window dressings and stone quoins dated about 1810. There is a seven-bay centre with the end bays brought slightly forward. When it was sold to Herbert Reeves in 1922 it had 10 acres of grounds and a boathouse.

In 1949, LUDC agreed with SCC to compulsorily purchase the building for use as a library, health clinic and more recently, as a youth employment and careers centre.

No. 24–26 was a comparatively small house known as WAYTES, one-time copyhold of Thorncroft Manor and judging by its great fireplace, chimney stack and visible timber-framing, it was a 16th-century structure. In owner James Roberts' will of 1842, he set up a charity to benefit the poor of Leatherhead which is still administered. James Roberts was an engineer who paid two guineas a year towards the upkeep of the town's fire engine. Most of the houses north of Hampton Cottage, including Waytes were demolished for a new shopping complex after the Second World War.

No. 29 dates from 1880 and is a building of some quality with its Church Street frontage rendered and formalised to match its neighbour, No. 31.

SURREY HOUSE, No. 31, has a frontage dated about 1850 although the rear of the house has earlier features. It was used as a school for a short time under George Alcock who later moved the school to Cameron House. He retired in 1900 and died in 1921. It was purchased by the LUDC in 1922 for council offices, having formerly been the headquarters of the Liberal Club. It was sold again in 1932.

CAMERON HOUSE, No. 33, is an early 18th-century structure with both later and earlier additions. It has a saddle-back roof with a higher extension of a later date. It was still a boys' preparatory school in 1907.

[1] F. B. Benger, 'Pen sketches of old houses', *Proc. LDLHS*, **1 (7)**, 1953, pp. 7–12. Nairn and Pevsner, *Buildings of England (Surrey)*, (1971), p. 341.

When the house was sold in 1919, Herbert Reeves of The Manor House objected to 1½ acres of its grounds being converted into a garage. In 1986 'the garage' became a printing firm.

JOSIANS, No. 35, is a 17th-century brick building with a tiled roof. There is an entrance to a yard on the northern side through an old brick wall.

MANSION COTTAGES are 16th-century cottages at the rear of No. 35, timber-framed and nogged with brick. No. 1 is part of a three-bay 17th-century house. Other cottages in Mansion Alley were built by making use of the small frontage and infilling the strips.[1] No. 2 had no bathroom up to 1982 and residents reached the house by walking to the end of the row and round the backs of the gardens. The central chimney stack is late 17th century. Nos. 3 and 4 are later extensions.

LONG COTTAGE No. 37, dates from about 1700 with its eastern end in brick and the upper part is clap-boarded.

No. 39 is probably an early 18th-century rendered brick building with a slate roof. The original pitch of the roof at the rear has been modified for later additions to the building.

WATERLOO COTTAGES are situated between Nos. 39 and 41 and are a modest group of late 19th-century warm red-brick terraced houses.

No. 49 and No. 51 are a pair of small white-painted villas dated 1840, each with a ground floor verandah.

No. 53 attractively blends a 16th and 17th-century house with a charming late 17th or early 18th-century brick façade. It has a projecting central bay with sailing courses at first floor and parapet level and there are pilasters at each end.[2]

No. 55 is a small late medieval timber-framed building of two bays, now a garage situated on the corner of Church Street and Church Road. It may be the remains of a small single-range house which included a 'cockloft'. However, this could also be interpreted as the cross-wing from a larger house of which the open-hall range has been demolished. If this is correct, three of the four medieval houses in Leatherhead so far identified are more lavish than those in surrounding villages, reflecting the greater wealth of the farming and trading community in late medieval Leatherhead.[3]

HAMPTON COTTAGE, No. 64, is a labourer's cottage erected on glebe (church) land sometime between 1642 and 1682. It is timber-

[1] Joan Harding, Domestic Buildings Research Group and *Proc. LDLHS,* **3** (6), 1972, p. 167.
[2] F. B. Benger, *What to Look at in Leatherhead* (LDLHS, 1975).
[3] W. J. Blair, '55 Church Street', *Proc. LDLHS,* **4** (4), 1980, p. 103.

53 Church Street.

Timber framing revealed when plaster was stripped from Devonshire Cottage in 1980.

framed of elm, some re-used and prefabricated as were all timber-framed houses in the town. Some of the original wattle and daub infilling of walls can still be seen. In a terrier of 1682, the cottage was referred to as the home of the widow of William Fering, a falconer, working possibly for the lord of the manor, either at Thorncroft or Pachenesham. Since it was church property, most of the tenants worked for the Rectory (now Vale Lodge). In 1872 Margaret Ottaway, a widow of a 'brewer of the Swan Pit Brewhouse' owned it, together with Devonshire Cottage (No. 66). She left it in 1822 to her niece Caroline Fisher who married Albion Ockenden of Littlehampton. It seems that is how the cottage got its name. In 1946 it was sold and in 1960 became the property of Mr and Mrs Hollis, Mrs Hollis being Hilda Barnard, the daughter of a Swan Hotel coachman. She was a dress-maker and lived and worked in the cottage. The Leatherhead and District Local History Society set up the Leatherhead Museum and Heritage Centre Trust to purchase the property in 1976. They carefully restored it and it is now the Leatherhead Museum.[1]

DEVONSHIRE COTTAGE, No. 66, is a more ambitious building than its immediate neighbour Hampton Cottage. It probably dates from the late 16th century when it was owned by Richard Rogers of The Rectory, but by 1708 it belonged to The Mansion. The building follows the extended hall range and jettied cross-wing form although the roof is post-medieval. During plaster stripping in 1979 some of the external framing has been revealed. There was a family connection with Hampton Cottage since Margaret Ottaway died there in 1886 and the Ockendens who had 10 children, moved next door when they grew older, leaving the larger house to the younger members of their family.

No. 84 was built in 1880 and was formerly the lodge and coach house for The Vicarage.

THE OLD VICARAGE, No. 80, is on the site of an earlier building which overhung the lane by the side of The Mansion that runs down to the river.[2] Something of its character can be glimpsed from an account of repairs in 1669 which refers to a hall, a kitchen, cellar and malt-house.[3] It had been extended by the Rev. Laxton in 1756 but by 1806 it was considered 'very ancient and dilapidated' by the Rev. James Dallaway. He himself made additions to it. Designed by William Butterfield, the present building was erected in the early 1870s by the

[1] Mary Rice-Oxley, *The Story of Hampton Cottage, Leatherhead* (LDLHS, 1986).

[2] W. J. Blair, *The Early Town of Leatherhead* (LDLHS, 1980), pp. 6 and 11.

[3] Court of Arches, Lambeth Palace Library B/12/6.

Hampton Cottage (Leatherhead Museum) and Devonshire Cottage.

Rev. Thomas Griffith. It is brick rendered with brick quoins and dressings and has a tiled roof. It is now divided into separate establishments and the new Vicarage is in St Mary's Road.

No. 86 is an early 20th-century house which blends well with No. 84 and has a pleasant forecourt.

No. 88 is a large three-storied building dating from the late 19th century. With its general appearance suggesting a strong French influence, it is something of a curiosity.

Church Road

Opposite the church, there is a terrace of three cottages Nos. 30, 32 and 34 in stock brick adjacent to two new blocks of flats, STENNING COURT (named after a one-time churchwarden, Claude Stenning) and SKEET HOUSE (named after Edward Skeet, a 17th-century town resident and benefactor). The PARISH HALL was completed in June 1963.

THE WHITE HOUSE, NO. 18, is an early 18th-century building of white clapboard set on a small island site. There is a Sussex hip gable at one end, unusual in this area, and a clapboard extension added during the first half of the 19th century. It was known in Victorian times as 'Jenden's Corner' since it was owned and run as a grocer's shop by the Jenden family. It has recently been refurbished as offices.

Most of the west side of Church Road is taken up with the 1869 MOUNT ZION CHAPEL and the METHODIST CHURCH (see p. 289).

At the junction of Church Road and Poplar Road is DEVON HOUSE, once the Leatherhead School of Music. This area was clearly one of Victorian housing expansion with THE LILACS, No. 27, HOLLY COTTAGE, No. 15–17 and No. 21 whose plaque dates it late 19th century.

MAGAZINE PLACE, thought to have been so named when ammunition was stored there at the time of the Seven Years' War, and BYRON PLACE, named after Admiral Byron of Linden House, both lead off Church Road. In the attractive and narrow CHURCH WALK, No. 1 was once the JUG HOUSE, so called when ale-making was very much a cottage industry and beer was sold there. The former Leatherhead almshouse was also in Church Walk.

Highlands Road

Much of this area was open fields before 1865 when it began to be

The White House, Church Road.

Highlands Farm.

developed for housing. In 1838, No. 3 was the boys' school and later the girls' school (see p. 181).

One of the first houses built in St Nicholas Hill in 1911 was FAIR WINDS, the home of Abraham Dixon's daughter, Letitia.

THE ROYAL SCHOOL FOR THE BLIND transferred from Southwark where it was founded in 1799. The foundation stone was laid in 1901 by Queen Victoria's daughter, Princess Christian of Schleswig Holstein, and the school was opened in 1902 (see pp. 220 and 256).

YARM COURT, once FLINT HOUSE, stood at the western end of what is now FIRTREE ROAD. Being one of the highest points in the town, it was often the centre of bonfire and firework celebrations at the beginning of this century. Auctioned in 1910, when it became the property of Walter J. Smith, it was described as 'a prepossessing house on a hillcrest with entrance lodge, 14 bedrooms and dressing rooms, lounge halls, billiard and reception rooms'. There was stabling for five, a cottage for the coachman and 21 acres of 'winter and pleasure gardens'. In 1935 the whole was developed as a housing estate. The lodge still stands.

HIGHLANDS FARM on the western side of Headley Road, is set in what used to be the open fields of the parish. Once the property of Lord Cunliffe, the house was built in the late 1800s although the tarred weather-boarded barns are 17th century and there is an 18th-century well house. The farmhouse is a neat three bay brick box with two weather-boarded bay windows on the ground floor. There is also a granary on staddle-stones[1] and a fine wrought-iron weathervane.

Gimcrack Hill

THE PRIORY has the elements of an earlier house, the LINK HOUSE. This house was so-called because of the obligation the resident had for keeping a torch or lynk lit before the altar in the parish church. It is known that Edward Hudson lived there in the 1740s. The present building dates from 1830 and was built by William Cotton, FSA. There are many modern buildings within its courtyard and part of the estate is now converted into flats. In 1937 it became LAWRENCE WEAVER HOUSE, a health and education centre set up as a memorial to Sir Lawrence and Lady Kathleen Weaver, founders of the Ashtead Potters. It was opened by George Lansbury, the Labour MP, and despite a host of good intentions it failed to prosper and closed down in 1939.

[1] Nairn and Pevsner, *Buildings of England (Surrey)*, (1971), p. 341.

Prior's Ford 1966 showing Donald Campbell's proposed *Bluebird* on the right with *Bluebird 7* and his own 'E'-type Jaguar.

There is nearby an 18th-century brick building now called LAWRENCE WEAVER HOUSE.

CAMPBELL COURT is a modern block of flats built on the site of an early 20th century house called PRIOR'S FORD. During the last years of his life, it was the home of Donald Campbell, CBE. Beating his father Sir Malcolm Campbell's records of the 1930s, Donald Campbell in 1964 aiso became the fastest man on land (403·1 mph) and on water (298 mph). He was killed on Coniston Water in January 1967 when his craft *Bluebird* disintegrated while achieving a speed of over 300 mph. His daughter Gina lives locally and continues the family tradition. In 1984 she gained the ladies' world water-speed record of 122·85 mph off-shore powerboat racing in yet another *Bluebird*. She presented the wheel of her father's *Bluebird* car to the Museum in 1985.

CHURCH HOUSE, shown on the Elias Allen map of 1629, lay between the church and The Rectory and was long occupied by the Godman and Dacres families (see pp. 83–84). According to the 1664 Hearth Tax Returns, it had 13 hearths and so was probably a large timber-framed Tudor building.

ELM BANK HOUSE and estate was owned for many years by the Rickard family (see p. 159) and was described as a 'mid-Georgian residence with 21½ acres of land'. It was demolished in 1924 when the whole was sold for development and became the St Mary's Road estate.

ELM BANK COTTAGES are CLOVELLY, No. 33, and HOPE COTTAGE, No. 35, date from 1869 and 1872 respectively. They adjoin the footpath leading from Worple Road across St Mary's Road to Downs Lane with their entrances once being in Worple Road. They have retained their long front gardens but have been greatly altered by modernisation.

ELM BANK GARDENS preserves the name of the house and the 17th-century fine warm red-brick wall may have enclosed the grounds of CHURCH HOUSE.

Dorking Road

BRIDGE COTTAGE, No. 77, was formerly the lodge to Thorncroft Manor although in its present position it stands almost as a lodge to Leatherhead itself. It was designed by Col. Drinkwater-Bethune who lived at Thorncroft from 1836 until his death in 1844. The façade of the` lodge with its half Doric columns is almost like a little temple. It has recently been restored.[1]

The wall from below Campbell Court to the foot of Gimcrack Hill may have been constructed in 1750 when the Turnpike Trust widened the road to Dorking to make room for stage coaches on regular routes.

THORNCROFT has had a house on the site of one of Leatherhead's two feudal manors since Domesday. It is known that rebuilding in 1497 was undertaken by the then owner, the Warden of Merton College, Oxford, who was also Dean of Rochester. (Merton College remained the 'owners' until 1904.) This appears to have been a major operation, using timber from many areas. Among many improvements, a chimney was constructed and Nicholas Rumming, no doubt a relative of Elinour, was employed as one of the workmen. In 1545 Robert Gardiner, Sergeant of the Wine Cellar to Queen Elizabeth I, lived there and it is known that the cellars were extensive. A century later, Richard Dalton, Sergeant of the Wine Cellar to Charles II, lived at Thorncroft. The last Dalton, William, was killed in a duel in 1751.

The present house was designed by Sir Robert Taylor and completed in 1776 and it possibly incorporates in its cellars the remains of the earlier manor house. This had been demolished by Henry Crabb Boulton when he acquired the lease and commissioned the present house which his nephew extended when he inherited it. The present building is stucco-covered, with a slate roof, five two-bay windows and except for a heavy porch and a flight of entrance steps, the front is plain. The present owners have added an imaginative glass extension reflecting the trees and surrounding countryside.[2]

Downs Lane, nearly opposite the entrance to Thorncroft, leads to two large houses, Vale Lodge and Downside. VALE LODGE is on the site of THE RECTORY, sometimes called the PARSONAGE HOUSE. It was not the priest's residence but let to a lay tenant. In Domesday, it was a 40-acre estate of glebeland with river meadows opposite over the Dorking road. When the Rogers family lived there in Tudor and Stuart times, it was the largest and most successful farm in the area (see p. 79). It was described in 1649 as 'a fair dwelling house consisting of a hall, parlour wainscotted, two butteries, a cellar and a kitchen, 2 other necessary low rooms, 5 chambers and 2 garretts, 4 barns, a stable and a granary and a podder house [derived from 'poddy' a dialect word for a hand-fed calf] with a garden and an orchard adjoining of 2 acres'.[3]

[1] Joan Harding, Domestic Buildings Research Group.
[2] F. B. Benger, 'Thorncroft Manor', *Proc. LDLHS*, **1**, 1952, p. 21. Booklet published by Howard Humphries and Sons.
[3] A. R. Bax, 'Parliamentary survey of church lands', *SAC*, **XVII**, 1902, p. 106.

Letherhead

J. Hassell 1822

CHURCH HOUSE

Thorncroft Manor House.

Bridge Cottage, the entrance to Thorncroft and to Leatherhead.

VALE LODGE was apparently rebuilt in brick about 1780 and is stuccoed with a slate roof, partly mansard. The house tenancy was held by John Whiteford and Thomas Dickens until 1840 when it became the home of the Budd and Leach families until this century. The house is now divided and is separately occupied.

GATE LODGE, formerly the lodge to The Rectory, is a flint and brick white rectangular building erected in the early 19th century.

BATTLEBOROUGH and STABLE LODGE were formerly the stables of Vale Lodge.

DOWNSIDE beyond Vale Lodge, was owned by the Tate family who lived there from about 1888. It was built for William Lee in 1860 but Alfred Tate improved and emphasised its Italianate aspect. As an exhibitor at major rose shows, he had an extensive rose garden set among terraces and ponds.[1] In 1919 it was bought by the publisher Sir Edward Hulton and in 1934 it was sold again to Major E. Howard. The house is now divided and there are new houses built in its grounds.

GIVONS GROVE was once a farm, part of the manor of Thorncroft. Once it was known as Gibbons Farm, perhaps because a yeoman farmer called Charles Gibbons tilled it. He is mentioned in the parish registers of 1686 as is another Gibbon, Henry, who died in 1734. It maybe because the meadows of Thorncroft so near the Mole were often flooded that a new building was built near the farm. It was described in the *Universal British Directory* of 1791 as 'a beautiful house and garden, the property of Henry Boulton [who leased Thorncroft] and occupied by Sir William Altum'. The Boulton family sold the estate of 238 acres in 1859 to Duncan Fletcher who sold it to Thomas Grissell of Norbury Park in 1865. The house was let with 40 acres to Russell Sturgis of the bankers Baring Brothers and it remained with that family until 1919 when it was sold to Humphrey Verdon Roe, the aircraft manufacturer and his wife Dr Marie Stopes (see p. 156). It was sold again in 1927 as a 'large house with 21 principal and secondary bedrooms and dressing rooms, reception rooms, park, cottages, home farm' and so on, all in 130 acres. It was purchased by a syndicate who planned to build houses in half-acre to three-acre plots and demolish the wings of the mansion, so making it a smaller more attractive residence.[2]

GIVONS GROVE FARMHOUSE is part 16th century. It has a clock tower and a parapet and the beamed interior has an oak staircase.

[1] Alastair Forsyth, *Yesterday's Gardens* (RCHM/HMSO, 1983).

[2] S. E. D. Fortescue, 'Givons Grove', *Proc. LDLHS*, **4** (7), 1983, pp. 188–90.

Leatherhead By-pass

CHERKLEY COURT, earlier known as Cherkley Yews, was built in the early 1870s by Abraham Dixon and it stood in 313 acres. In 1893 it was struck by lightning and only the walls survived the subsequent fire. It was rebuilt by Dixon to the original design and he lived there until his death in 1907.[1] It was bought by Sir Max Aitken, later Lord Beaverbrook who furnished it with the help of Mrs Rudyard Kipling, the original books for the library being provided by Bonar Law.[2]

TYRRELLS WOOD (now Tyrrells Wood Golf Club) once stood in 250 acres and the house was built by Roger Cunliffe. It is a substantial red-brick structure and has massive chimney stacks above its gabled roofs. It was bought by Henry Keswick, MP, in 1913, and sold again as a residence and sporting estate in 1922. In 1925 some of the land was sold for housing development.

BOCKETTS FARM gets its name from one of the fields (La Bochard) which comprised the demesne acres of Leatherhead about 1300. At that time the farm and the land between the Mole and the present Dorking road had been part of Little Pachenesham but the carving out of this farm from the manorial demesne of Thorncroft is recorded in a deed of *c.* 1170 (see p. 35). The six-bay barn is built of machine-cut timbers and set on toadstool staddles. There is a Georgian granary which must have been the grain store for the threshing barn. It is a three-bay low barn with open semi-aisles to keep the rats away from the grain.[3]

BARNETT WOOD FARMHOUSE is an almost undisturbed 17th to 18th-century farmhouse. It is timber-framed with a steeply pitched old tiled saddleback roof. There is a large brick chimney breast on the south-west side. Gable ends are tile hung.[4]

Randalls Road

BROOK WILLOW FARM, though externally uninteresting, was found in 1977 to contain substantial remains of an unusual timber-framed late 14th century house. It seems to have consisted of a square open hall with a parlour or service bay partitioned off beneath a cragloft, the central truss being open at the first-floor level between the cragloft and the hall. Fragments remain of a cusped four-light window over the jetty at the eastern end.

PATSOM HOUSE, PATSOM FARM and PATSOM COTTAGE are

[1] G. Hayward, 'Cherkley Court', *Proc. LDLHS*, **4** (3), 1979, p. 73.
[2] A. P. J. Taylor, *Beaverbrook* (1974), p. 108.
[3] Joan Harding, Domestic Buildings Research Group.
[4] Joan Harding, Domestic Buildings Research Group.

17th-century buildings grouped around the junction of Randalls Road, Oaklawn Road and Woodlands Road. They are all half timber and brick and some have been enlarged.

RANDALLS PARK in the manor of Little Pachenesham was originally the home of the Sands family, most influential during Tudor and Stuart times (see p. 77). The family came to Leatherhead from Shere after 1529 and married into a farming family who held land of the Stydolfs which subsequently Sands bought. In his will of 1598, Robert Sands shows the inheritance was a 'homely reality' and not mere paper ownership. 'Sheep, cows, casks, ploughs, cheeses etc' were referred to as well as '10 acres of wheat now sown'. His grand-daughter married into another well-known Leatherhead family, the Skeets. When their fortunes declined at the end of the 17th century, a deed of mortgage gives the only contemporary description of the house: 'The great house and gardens, the little house adjoining it, the wash house, the brew house and 2 rooms over it used as a granary, a pigeon house, a duck house and stables and a great thatched barn . . . the cart house and a place for fatting hogs with a cisterne in the same court . . . the garden courtyard, a piece of land to plant beans in between the garden and the orchard . . . the saw-pitt yard . . . and bare field, the rookery lane leading from the highway to the great house . . .'[1] A later house on the site was demolished by Nathanial Bland in the early 19th century who built another on a different site in the park. This was bought by Robert Henderson in 1856. One of his daughters, Agnes Mary, became the first wife of Walter, Lord Cunliffe of Headley Court. In 1932 his son, John Henderson, sold the estate to Wimbledon Corporation. Two fields of the Common Meadow to which the town had won the right in 1849 were saved by LUDC. The last Randalls Park House was demolished just before the Second World War when the crematorium was built.

WOODLANDS PARK at the beginning of this century was a 500-acre estate extending from the river to Oxshott and included land between Woodlands Road and Oaklawn Road. Originally a 1000-acre estate, it was owned in 1802 by the Smith family. The house now called the Woodlands Park Hotel, was bought in 1885 by F. C. Bryant of the matchmakers, Bryant and May. In 1900 it belonged to J. W. Benson, the Bond Street jeweller, and it was acquired by E. L. Ralli just before the First World War. He and his family lived there until 1929 when the

[1] F. Bastian, 'Sands of Randalls', *Proc. LDLHS,* **2** (3), 1959, p. 77.

14th-century Brook Willow Cottage rebuilt mainly with original timbers but with modern brick coursing.

Rowhurst, Oxshott Road.

estate was broken up. In the 1930s the house was a hotel, and then in 1939 an old people's home, and in 1975 a residential education centre. LEATHERHEAD COURT, now part of Queen Elizabeth's Training College, is difficult to date although the clock tower is inscribed '1897'. The weathervane over the tower in the shape of a fox possibly confirms that a pack of local hounds were kennelled there and that the house may have been designed as a hunting lodge for meets, hunt balls and other occasions. Such a role was short-lived since in 1904 it was leased to Martha Wood-Tullis and described in 1932 as 'a high class school for young ladies'. The school closed in 1933 and the property was acquired by the Training College.[1]

Oxshott Road
ROWHURST was once a farm and brickyard and the house is a two-bay timber-framed wing of a mid-16th-century building. It has an end smoke bay added in the early 17th century. It is said that it was once a hunting lodge for Hampton Court Palace and in 1762 it was owned, with 40 acres, by Robert Ragge. It is now an iron-working forge with a gallery to exhibit blacksmiths' art. The house is the home of the Quinnell family.[2]

Decay and renewal
By 1960, the attractive little town that Leatherhead had only recently been was in a sorry state. The Swan Hotel had disappeared, other old buildings were decaying and new ones lacked distinction. In 1962, Nairn and Pevsner were blunt enough: 'Perhaps Leatherhead is the most pitiful of Surrey small towns, because the old pattern here was smaller and humbler than most and hence was pushed aside more easily. Apart from the church, no building is worth a visit and the townscape has gone along with the old buildings.'

The town was not merely unattractive but inconvenient too. Few felt that it was one in which conservation made much sense. In a clean sweep, little would be lost and much gained.

But a clean sweep was not made; and despite many damning judgements, Leatherhead reflects in miniature the changing attitudes of the 1970s to conservation and the built environment. Notwithstanding its decay, or perhaps because of it, the town has escaped the greater evil of comprehensive 1960s development. Gradually a wider

[1] Joan Holman and Marion Herridge, Domestic Buildings Research Group, 1986.
[2] Joan Harding, Domestic Buildings Research Group.

public came to realise that potentially attractive buildings still lurked behind drab façades and ugly shop-fronts, and that demolition was not the only remedy. The reaction away from modernism and functionalism came very late for Leatherhead – but not too late.

Before its environment could be improved or its trade prosper, Leatherhead needed a relief road to take through traffic from its crowded streets.

In 1971 plans were submitted for a relief road system and conservation areas were designated in November 1974 and the road approved by the county in August 1975. The way was clear for the planning of a shopping precinct and in April 1976 a public inquiry was held to decide between three schemes. One was submitted by the Leatherhead Society, another by Woldcrest and another by the Council. This last scheme, eventually reworked by Building Design Partnership of Guildford, was finally realised and work proceeded in earnest.

The relief road was complete in the summer of 1981 and in December the Swan Centre was officially opened. Architecturally it is bound to become dated, yet as a contribution to the environment it should stand up well beside its equally dated 1960s counterparts in the town.

Traffic was now excluded from the town's main streets and a rehabilitation scheme was launched which was over-hasty and brought problems of its own. Traders moved into the Swan Centre leaving the High Street shops empty while numerous building works made the street scene yet more derelict. Complaints about the pedestrianisation grew and traders protested they were being ruined in a 'ghost town'. In response to pressure, Bridge Street and North Street were re-opened, leaving the High Street and Church Street as permanent pedestrian areas.

Much of the High Street has been rebuilt piecemeal and has not yet settled down as a thriving street but its oldest remaining house No. 33/35 is now fully restored, traders are returning and a street market is establishing itself at the weekends. Around the outskirts of the town, commerce and industry attracted by the proximity of the M25, are moving into new or refurbished business parks and offices.

With its new centre, the town has completed its most drastic transformation since the 12th century when it was first laid out. By laying new foundations on the old, Leatherhead looks forward to a future worthy of one of Surrey's oldest historic centres.

What would the girl on page 146 think of this view on Bull Hill today? Yet, just five minutes' walk away on page 334 there is reassurance for her in a timeless Leatherhead scene.

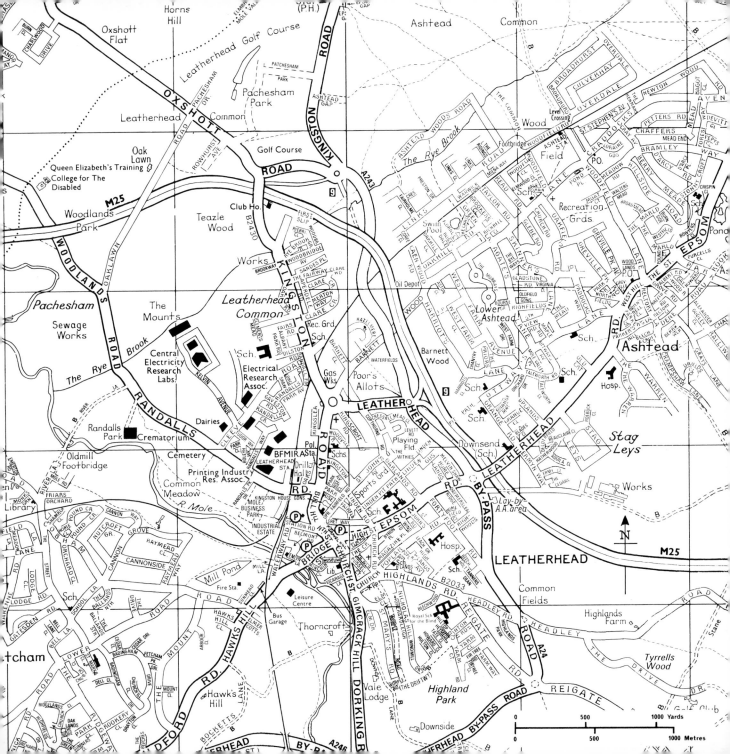

THE RIVER MOLE runs its silvery course
  Below the old bridge by the Running Horse
With whispers in woodland and flints among fern
And many a mystery in a watery turn.
There lost in its deeps, the past pauses maybe
For the hand that can search and the eye that can see.

                                        E.V.

334

Epilogue

PRIOR to the explosion of transport facilities, families lived in the same area from one generation to another. After the First World War, many large estates were sold as building sites to be occupied by newcomers. This process continued with renewed vigour after the Second World War. Those who came to the area after the First War and had houses built in plots of 2 acres or more, have now in turn divided their land further as building plots. These new houses were rarely occupied by natives of Leatherhead.

The Leatherhead and District Local History Society was formed in 1946 to record and preserve as much as possible of old Leatherhead before it was lost in the mists of time.

I hope this book will encourage a knowledge of the history of Leatherhead so that by wise and enlightened development, the town at the crossroads may continue to be a jewel in Surrey's countryside and a desirable place in which to live.

John Lewarne

PRESIDENT, LEATHERHEAD AND DISTRICT LOCAL HISTORY SOCIETY

Glossary

ANCHORITE   Hermit or recluse

BARROW   Grave mound

BEADLE   Manorial official responsible for enforcing discipline

BONDMAN   See VILLEIN

BRUERA   Woodland and scrub

BURGESS   Townsman holding municipal rights

BURH   Small Anglo-Saxon fortification

BYRE   Cow house

CENSER   Vessel used for incense

CHANCEL   Part of church containing the altar reserved for the clergy

CHANTRY   Endowment for a priest to pray for the souls of the founder, his family and friends, often in a special chapel within the parish church

COPE   Processional cloak

COPYHOLD   Former villein holding, held from the late middle ages onwards by a transcript ('copy') of the relevant court roll entry

CORPORAL   Cloth on which the sacred bread was placed during Mass

CUCKING STOOL   Stool fixed on a swivelling plank by a pond, for ducking scolds and other offenders

CURTILAGE   Area attached to dwelling house as part of its enclosure

DEMESNE   Land under the direct control and management of its lord, rather than in the hands of tenants

DISTRAIN   To seize goods of a tenant for non-payment of rent

ENCLOSURE   Land (either arable or pasture) held as one unit and fenced around (in contrast to common field land)

FARMER   Used in the middle ages not in the modern sense but for the lessee of a manorial demesne

FLINTS   Hard stones, flaked or chipped by prehistoric man to form tools

FOLK MOOT	Meeting of the local community in the Anglo-Saxon period
GLEBE	Land belonging to a parish church for the support of its priest
HAYWARD	Manorial official responsible for maintaining fences and impounding stray animals
HERIOT	Forfeit of the 'best beast' to the lord of the manor on change of tenancy; often replaced by payment of money
HIDE	Normal unit of land measurement from the 7th to 10th centuries. Notionally the amount of land needed to support one free peasant family; later formalised as 120 acres
INTERREGNUM	Period between the execution of Charles I in 1640 and the accession of Charles II in 1660
IRON PYRITES	Yellow iron sulphide minerals
LEDGER STONES	Flat grave stones
LESSEE	Tenant holding land by lease on a fixed rent
LUCERNE	Plant grown for use as fodder
LYNCHETS	Ridges formed by prehistoric ploughing on slope
MARLPIT	Chalkpit or source of lime to fertilise the land
MANORIAL COURTS	Courts of the lord of the manor concerned mainly with land transactions and minor offences
MESSUAGE	Dwelling plot comprising garden and croft
NAVE	Body of church
OLIGARCHIES	States controlled by a small group
ORDINANCE	Government decree
PARCELS	Pieces of land
PATEN	Shallow dish for eucharistic bread
PILLORY	Wooden framework with holes for head and hands of offender exposed to public ridicule
PINFOLD	Manorial pound for straying animals
PISCINA	Stone basin near altar for use in rinsing sacred vessels
POTSHERDS	Broken pieces of earthenware

RECUSANTS	Those who refuse to obey the State's authority or attend Church of England services
REEVE	Manorial official usually a villein responsible for the day-to-day running of the manor
REREDOS	Ornamental screen covering wall at the back of the altar
RESTORATION	Return of Charles II in 1660 after the Commonwealth period
ROOD SCREEN	Screen separating nave from the choir
SEDILIA	Stone chair in wall of chancel for use of priests
SENESCHAL	Steward, often responsible for managing several manors of one lord
SPCK	Society for the Promotion of Christian Knowledge
STATER	Ancient Greek coin
STRATA	Layers of any deposited substance
SWALLOW HOLE	Sink hole
TENEMENT	Holding of land often including a house and croft
TERRIER	Survey of land holdings
THEGN	Anglo-Saxon nobleman or gentleman
TRANSEPT	Transverse part of cruciform church
TUMULI	Grave mounds
VILL	Rural community, probably with a main settlement and elements
VILLEIN	Tenant holding land by servile tenure, normally labour service
VIRGATE	Customary unit of peasant land holding, normally of a standard size (13 or 26 acres in Leatherhead)
YEOMAN	Independent member of a class below gentry of small freeholding farmers. Alternatively, a lesser official in a royal or noble household

Abbreviations

BL	British Library
Cal. H.L.	Calendar, House of Lords
CJ	House of Commons Journal
Cal. SPD	Calendar, State Papers Domestic
EMS	John Blair, *Landholding, Church Settlement* in *Early Medieval Surrey* (Surrey Archaeological Society Research Volume, forthcoming)
1235 Eyre	*The 1235 Surrey Eyre*, ed. C. A. F. Meekings, i–ii (Surrey Record Society xxxi–xxxii, 1979–83)
HMC	Historical Manuscripts Commission
HMSO	Her Majesty's Stationery Office
LJ	House of Lords Journal
LDLHS	Leatherhead and District Local History Society
LUDC	Leatherhead Urban District Council
MDLD	W. J. Blair, 'Medieval Deeds of the Leatherhead District'; parts I–VIII, *PLDLHS*, **iv** (2), 1978–**iv** (10), 1986: cited by document number
MM	Merton College, Oxford, muniments
PM	Parish Magazine
P.R.O.	Public Record Office
SAC	Surrey Archaeological Collections
S.R.O.	Surrey Record Office
VCH	Victoria County History

Illustrations

Index

Acknowledgments

The editor would like to thank:

Mr and Mrs A. S. Anderson

Mr and Mrs Claude Blair

British Library

Bryant and May

Mr and Mrs Browning

David Bruce

Carolyn Brunton

Joan Burnett

Mr and Mrs Cairns

Gina Campbell

Jean Coombes

Natalie Cormack

Ernest Crossland

George Dench

Peter Edwards

Mr Ekins

Alan Everett

Mabel Fuller

Geoffrey Gollin

The Misses Granger

Greater London Record Office

Guildford Muniment Room

Hampshire Record Office

Margaret Harris

Mrs Hawkins

Margaret Hayden

Mr Holland

Bernard Hooker

F. B. Humphrey

Mr and Mrs Thomas Jenden

William Jenden

Miss Jupp

Ruth Koch

Lambeth Palace Library

Leatherhead Advertiser staff

Leatherhead Library staff

John Lewarne

Mr and Mrs Thomas Lewis

Tom Locke

London University Library

Dorothy Lutman

Joan MacAlpine

Phyllis Mansell

Merton College, Oxford

Mr and Mrs Edward Mizen

Mrs More-Molyneux

Greta Morley

Elizabeth Nowson

Sheila Pankhurst

George Philip and Son

Bert Powell

Public Record Office

Arthur Rapley

The Misses Read

Rona Roach

Mr Rogers

John Sankey

Henry Sawyer

Kate Sayers

Charles Simmonds

L. A. Smith

Mrs Stazicker

Liam Sumption

Surrey Archaeological Society

Surrey Record Office

Surrey Wildlife Trust

Audrey Sykes

P. Townsend Smith

Eric Trunkfield

Edwina Louise Vardey

Giles Vardey

Lucinda Vardey

Melissa Vardey

P. J. Vincent

Chief Fire Officer Wadey

Hazel Vincent Wallace

Cliff Webb, West Surrey Family History
  Society

Jeffrey Wheatley

Arthur Weller

Eric Wilde